Integrating Technology in the Classroom

Tools to Meet the Needs of Every Student

Boni Hamilton

International Society for Technology in Education
EUGENE, OREGON • ARLINGTON, VIRGINIA

Integrating Technology in the Classroom
Tools to Meet the Needs of Every Student
Boni Hamilton

Editor: *Paul Wurster*
Associate Editor: *Emily Reed*
Production Editor: *Lynda Gansel*
Copy Editor: *Kathy Hamman*
Indexer: *Wendy Allex*
Book Design and Production: *Kim McGovern*

First Edition
ISBN: 978-1-56484-345-6 (paperback)
ISBN: 978-1-56484-490-3 (e-book)

Printed in the United States of America

ISTE® is a registered trademark of the International Society for Technology in Education.

About ISTE

The International Society for Technology in Education (ISTE) is the premier nonprofit organization serving educators and education leaders committed to empowering connected learners in a connected world. ISTE serves more than 100,000 education stakeholders throughout the world.

ISTE's innovative offerings include the ISTE Conference & Expo, one of the biggest, most comprehensive ed tech events in the world—as well as the widely adopted ISTE Standards for learning, teaching and leading in the digital age and a robust suite of professional learning resources, including webinars, online courses, consulting services for schools and districts, books, and peer-reviewed journals and publications. Visit iste.org to learn more.

Related ISTE Titles

Digital Storytelling: Guide for Educators
Midge Frazel

Interactive Whiteboards in the Elementary Classroom
Tony DeMonte

Making Connections with Blogging: Authentic Learning for Today's Classroom
Lisa Parisi and Brian Crosby

Serious Comix: Engaging Students with Digital Storyboards
Eydie Wilson

Teaching Literacy in the Digital Age: Inspiration for All Levels and Literacies
Mark Gura

Web 2.0 How-To for Educators, 2nd ed. Revised and Expanded
Gwen Solomon and Lynne Schrum

To see all books available from ISTE, please visit iste.org/resources.

About the Author

Boni Hamilton has been writing and teaching for more than 25 years. She has taught all ages, from preschoolers to adults, and in a variety of contexts, from regular K–12 classrooms and undergraduate courses to special education, gifted/talented, and ESL classrooms. Boni began using computers in 1975 when her husband, John, bought a TRS-80 with his first student loan. Her initiation into using technology with students and teachers came about through volunteering in elementary schools. She served as the Assistant Director for Instructional Technology for Littleton Public Schools in Littleton, Colorado. More recently, Boni earned an EdD in Educational Studies from the University of Northern Colorado and is currently a PhD student in Education and Human Development at the University of Colorado Denver in Urban Ecologies. She is working on a major government-funded grant project to build online professional development modules to help practicing teachers work effectively with multilingual learners. Boni and John have two adult children, Nick and Jamie.

Acknowledgments

My humblest thanks to the nineteen Voices of Experience friends, some of whom I know only through email, whose experiences demonstrate the myriad ways teachers can use technology to engage students in learning. I am forever grateful for your generosity.

Deep appreciation also to my writing group—Mary Bartek, Diane Marty, Jean Reidy, and Judith Snyder—whose candid feedback and unstinting encouragement guided me back to my "real people" voice.

Dedication

This book is a tribute to my husband and best friend John, who inspires, mentors, encourages, and abets me in computer-related investigations; my mother and adult offspring, Nick and Jamie, who didn't complain when I spent every day of Christmas break pounding out this text; and teachers and students whose accomplishments so often exceeded what I thought was possible.

Contributors

Nancye Blair
Technology and gifted specialist
The Schools of McKeel Academy
Lakeland, Florida

Sally Brown
Associate professor of literacy
Georgia Southern University
Statesboro, Georgia

Jennifer Bond
Third grade teacher
Glengary Elementary
Commerce Township, Michigan

Kathy Cassidy
First grade teacher
Westmount School
Moose Jaw, Saskatchewan, Canada

Lauren Brannan
Former technology support teacher
J. E. Turner Elementary School
Wilmer, Alabama

Tracy Coskie
Associate professor
Western Washington University
Bellingham, Washington

Sheri Edwards
Teacher and technology director
Nespelem School
Nespelem, Washington

Michelle Hornof
Fifth grade teacher
Alderwood Elementary School
Bellingham, Washington

Tracey Flores
Third and fourth grade English
language development teacher
Landmark School
Glendale, Arizona

Ayana Jackson
Kindergarten teacher
Garrison Elementary
Washington, District of Columbia

Laura Herring Dariola
Second grade teacher
Sheridan School
Washington, District of Columbia

Linda Jones
Fourth grade teacher
Lois Lenski Elementary School
Centennial, Colorado

Chris Moore
Fifth grade teacher
East Elementary School
Littleton, Colorado

Jean Reidy
Children's author and two-time
winner of the Colorado Book Award
Greenwood Village, Colorado

Candy Shively
Director of K–12 initiatives, retired
The Source for Learning
Reston, Virginia

Marie Tribur
Fifth grade gifted and talented cluster
teacher
Clayton Elementary School
Englewood, Colorado

Nicolette Vander Velde
Fifth grade teacher
East Elementary School
Littleton, Colorado

Diane E. Vyhnalek
First grade teacher, retired
Lois Lenski Elementary School
Centennial, Colorado

Trecie Warner
Third grade teacher
Lois Lenski Elementary School
Centennial, Colorado

Contents

Contents

CHAPTER 11
Leveraging Technology for Multilingual Learners **199**

CHAPTER 12
Web 2.0 Tools **207**

CHAPTER 13
Advanced Multimedia **229**

CHAPTER 14
Teacher Resources **243**

CHAPTER 1

Paths Toward Integration

NO MATTER WHERE you are in your journey to include technology as an instructional tool in your classroom, this book will help you identify next steps along the path to integration. Bear in mind that you are seeking *your path*. Your classroom reflects the individual you are—the skills, experiences, beliefs, and knowledge that make you distinctive. Your teaching style, your approaches to curriculum, and your relationships with students reflect your individuality. All of these factors influence the technology you decide to use in instruction.

Only you know the *right* path for you and your students. You will select the most effective technologies to advance your students' academic growth. The path you choose will enhance your distinctiveness as an educator. What this book provides is access to ideas for technology tools and projects, so that you can choose the ones that fit your students' needs and your teaching style.

To illustrate how approaches to technology integration differ, this book includes the voices of teachers who share how they have used technology successfully. Many of these same teachers provide links to their websites or email addresses to encourage other teachers to interact with them. Additionally, you can find live links for each chapter's resources on my wiki (http://bonihamilton.wikispaces. com/home). Because we have experienced how exciting and powerful these tools can be, I've written this how-to book so you can select the ones that best fit your and your students' needs.

As you read, keep track of ideas that capture your imagination. Choose the path that fits your own style and comfort level. You might decide to ask a fellow teacher to brainstorm ways both of you could incorporate appealing ideas into your classes. If you are cautious about using new forms of technology, you could first share an idea with a small group of students. Many students are proud of their tech skills and some would willingly experiment with a new tool or idea during lunch or after school. Then they can help you manage the technology when you introduce it to the class. You might also consider recruiting tech-savvy parent helpers or high school students to mentor you and your students in the use of technology tools. No matter what path you follow for increasing technology integration into your classroom, creating the map, selecting the tools, and setting the pace must all be distinctly your own.

Organization for This Book

Any chapter may be your entry point into using additional technology with students. Search for a chapter that presents a technology tool familiar to you. As you see how to expand the uses of a familiar tool, you will become comfortable with other technologies that will save you time and spark your students' interests.

Within each chapter, I present ideas along a continuum of increasing difficulty. The information under each subheading starts with simple explanations and proceeds to those that are more complex (i.e., ideas are arranged by increasing levels of difficulty). Many of the ideas I share use examples from primary or intermediate grades, where most of my teaching has taken place. However, *almost all technology tools can be used at any grade level through secondary school and college.* Does that surprise you?

Consider the digital camera. Would you limit its use to a particular grade level? Of course not. As a technology tool for demonstrating learning, the digital camera spans all ages and content areas.

Perhaps in the past you've been asked to implement technology without sufficient training or experience to feel confident. Lay that fear aside. This book is organized to empower you to choose technology tools that feel comfortable and manageable to you.

After all, you are the content expert for the subjects you teach. The tools are simply efficient and motivating vehicles for engaging your students in learning.

Naturally, from grades K–12, content levels of projects increase in sophistication and complexity. For instance, the act of drawing on a computer screen works as a novice entry point into using technology for students at any grade level. However, what students learn to draw should increase in complexity. Primary students can draw and label simple pictures, while intermediate students draw systems (such as the water cycle), political cartoons, vocabulary illustrations, or other projects that require higher-level thinking. Secondary students may draw more complex systems or create innovative art projects. The rule of thumb is to think first of the content students need to master and then decide which tools will best help them absorb and demonstrate what they know.

You can access all the website links within this book at http://bonihamilton. wikispaces.com/home. Each wiki page contains the links and supplemental materials for a chapter. Supplemental materials include research support for the chapter and, when appropriate, updated information on tools or sample projects.

By the time this book is published, some of its examples may be supplanted by newer material. Though the tech world changes rapidly, its essential ideas are relatively timeless. Once you have learned how to use tech tools effectively in your classroom, you will readily adapt to changes and be just as excited as your techie friends when upgrades and new applications (apps) for your favorite programs come along!

Foundational Premises

The following eight premises create the backbone for this book.

Premise 1: Classroom technology use has two modes: Instructional (teacher use) and Demonstration (student use).

Teachers make choices about how they implement the use of technology in their classrooms. Teachers may incorporate technology into the instruction they deliver during whole class or small group interactions. This *instructional* use includes showing video clips, using visuals via a document camera, demonstrating a website, modeling use of a digital recorder or e-reader, directing a Skype session, and playing podcasts. As suggestions for instructional use in this book are fairly easy to implement, only Chapter 4, "Instructional Use of Technology," discusses potential ways to use technologies in instruction.

In the *demonstration* mode, students demonstrate what they know and can do. Many teachers think that planning for students to take the lead in using technology and then guiding them seems more difficult than conducting instruction themselves. Student demonstration uses can include creating projects, conducting research, solving problems in all content areas, accessing interactive websites, interacting with people around the globe, building a web presence, and producing videos. In demonstration uses, students actively control the digital tools while teachers guide them. Typically, when students manage the tools, teachers may feel as if their classrooms are on the verge of being out of control. A slightly hectic, somewhat noisy atmosphere is a natural positive sign that students are no longer sitting silently, depending completely on the teacher. Instead, they are excited about what they are learning and eager to show the teacher and each other their progress.

Premise 2: When students use technology, they talk.

Many excellent teachers feel most comfortable when their classrooms are quiet, when only one person speaks at a time. If you have hesitated to use tech tools because of this, that's perfectly understandable. I used to feel the same way. However, please do not let this preference prevent you from trying out various technologies that may well pique students' interest in your course's content and motivate even the students who appear least engaged. Students tend to talk when they use technology, but they do not need to scream or use obnoxious language. Most often, they are speaking enthusiastically, sharing good news about locating a key source or a great website.

You will be able to hear the difference between productive talking and off-task behavior. When students use tech tools, they talk—and if their work is engaging, their talk is productive. Students want to talk to you and their peers about the tasks they are doing, the problems they encounter, and the discoveries they make. In fact, one student's discovery of a tool, a solution, or a factoid can become useful knowledge for the whole class in only minutes. Rather than squelching conversations, teachers should design students' tech tasks to encourage discussions about what they are learning. This approach allows students to practice the life skill of teamwork, while making deeper connections with each other than a teacher alone could instigate. I used to prefer a quiet classroom until I heard the productive buzz of students using technology. Now a quiet classroom makes me nervous; if no one is excited enough about an idea to pass it along, how can I be sure anyone is learning?

Premise 3: Students learn when they actively participate.

Who really learns when teachers do all the planning, lecturing, and explaining? The teachers themselves—not necessarily their students. All this hard work cements the content knowledge into the teachers' brains forever, but unfortunately, not into their students'. Students learn when they participate in learning—by exploring ideas, connecting the ideas to what they already understand, and creating ways to share their knowledge with others. Professional staff developers approach the concept of student participation in different ways, but they advocate for the same outcome: make learning active. Problem-based learning, essential questions, inquiry lessons, discovery, scientific method, and virtual manipulatives ... all of these learning methods give students the responsibility for actively pursuing knowledge. In turn, students internalize the understandings they have acquired (that is, cementing the knowledge and skills into their own brains) because they have experienced various satisfying processes of gaining knowledge. Tech tools are designed to make participative learning easier to initiate and differentiate.

Premise 4: Teachers must teach responsible, ethical, and safe use of technology tools.

This premise is not negotiable. All students need to learn responsible, ethical, and safe management of technology. As a society, we cannot count on parents or social institutions or others to teach students these skills. Nor will a one-time reading of rules suffice. Teaching responsible, ethical, and safe use of technology must happen every year in every classroom.

Responsible: Maintaining personal privacy, honoring others' rights and privacy, treating others kindly, avoiding traps set by malicious or ambitious third parties on webpages, and handling technology equipment with care.

Ethical: Honoring copyrights, respecting other students' files and passwords, and obeying school policies and procedures.

Safe: Asking adults for help when confronted with inappropriate content or behavior, participating only on sites that honor child safety laws, and evaluating online sources for authenticity.

Chapter 15 of this book addresses the basic concepts of responsible, ethical, and safe use ("COPPA, Internet Safety, and Copyright"). In addition, teachers need to seek more fully developed materials to support their instruction on these topics. An excellent resource, *How to Protect Kids' Privacy Online: A Guide for Teachers* (www.educationnewyork.com/files/teachersFTC.pdf), can be downloaded. Teachers also need to determine in advance the consequences of irresponsible, unethical, and/or unsafe behavior. They should guide discussions of the possible consequences of such behavior with students before any use of technology. Students will make mistakes, and each incident can be handled individually. However, students need to understand that if a person's intent was malicious, he or she must face serious consequences.

Premise 5: Students have a right to use technology in every classroom every year.

Sending students off to a computer lab for instruction while teachers remain in the classroom for instructional planning time (often called "specials") has falsely negated the sense of urgency for in-class use of technology. Computer labs, particularly when the teacher is not involved in the teaching or planning for lab time, must be considered as extra lessons, not essential instructional extensions of the classroom. Of course, in ideal conditions, teachers direct the content of computer lab time so that the activities become seamless extensions of what students learn in their classrooms. Then work can flow between the computer lab and the classroom. However, even when students have computer experiences in a lab weekly, teachers are responsible for planning additional time with technology within the classroom walls. The technology need not be limited to computers; as the following chapters demonstrate, students can use tools, such as cameras and MP3 players, to capture learning as well. Research has found that students comprehend content at more long-lasting levels when they learn with technology than when they have the same unit of instruction without technology. Students have the right to the best instructional practices.

Premise 6: Not all technology tools are created equally.

Too often, technologies with high coolness factors, such as interactive white-boards, student response systems, and video gaming systems, have limited effect on students' academic growth. Often, technologies that accommodate only one student at a time during a whole class experience replicate worksheets and slow the pace of learning. Or, tools may require teachers to spend more time preparing than students spend interacting. This is generally productive for neither the teacher nor students. Build your technology integration on simple tools that require students to do the work. Even in the choice of software, simpler is generally better than glitzy. These fancy, cool products, usually with high price tags, are not better than simpler ones.

Premise 7: Everything is easier with a partner.

Using tech tools in your classroom at first requires more than just a fearless spirit. Find someone—a colleague, parent, community member, high school student, or spouse—who is willing to support your first forays into student use of technology. Then pair your students. Have them ask one another for help before they tug on your sleeve. When you debrief them, you'll be surprised at the unexpected lessons they have learned from each other, and you'll enjoy learning along with them.

Premise 8: Teachers must be flexible about incorporating technology.

No one can predict the particular surprises that will arise during a technology project, but everyone knows something surprising will happen. Sometimes the glitches, such as internet outages, affect everyone. Other times, one or two students end up with screens that look far different from everyone else's. Consider these setbacks as useful opportunities to teach life skills: flexibility and problem solving. For instance, if you have arranged for a 1:1 setting and five laptops are not working, ask yourself whether it is absolutely essential that every student have a computer. This may be an excellent time to encourage students to work with part-ners at computers. What if a student accidentally turns off all the toolbars on his/her screen? Ask the student's partner to help. If the partner does not know what to do, use this as an opportunity for the class to learn from collaborative problem solving. Network outage? Start a writing lesson—those can be accomplished on any computer without going to the network. Even after fourteen years of working with students on computers, I constantly run into new challenges. What has changed is my attitude about setbacks. A setback in a technology-based lesson is the same as a setback in any other lesson. It just involves different tools. Professionals adapt lessons when setbacks happen.

Teachers often view technology glitches as reasons to stop planned lessons. Yet, when glitches happen in a lesson without technology, teachers rarely give up. No activity or computer experience is so vital to one day's learning that it cannot be adjusted or accomplished at another time. Modeling flexibility and problem solving will teach students at least as much as a seamless lesson will.

Identifying Your Teaching Beliefs

Deep in our souls, teachers hold inherent beliefs about how students learn. Unless urged to think about those beliefs, teachers may not consciously reflect on them. Yet, these beliefs underlie every decision we make about teaching: how we arrange our classrooms, what students accomplish, our choices of materials and methods, the content of our instruction, and our incorporation of tech tools for student use.

Being aware of your own beliefs about how students learn is critical because your beliefs influence your attitudes toward technology in the classroom. Analyzing your teaching theories can reveal where you should begin as you integrate digital tools with instruction. Below are brief explanations of two major theories, behaviorism and constructivism, and a description of blended theories, a middle ground between them. As you read, consider which theory or theories resonate with you. Behaviorism and constructivism are at opposite ends of a continuum of teachers' beliefs; most teachers blend various degrees of the approaches.

Behaviorism

Behaviorism is the scholarly term for this teaching theory. Teachers may be more familiar with terms like teacher-directed, teacher-centered, traditional, direct instruction, or transmission. Essentially, this theory suggests that teachers hold the knowledge and transmit that knowledge to students through what teachers reveal and explain in instruction (often lectures). Teachers who hold this theory believe that students learn best when they are given information in small blocks and have mastered each block of the material. Teachers reinforce students' correct responses (repetition of the information) and proceed to add more information—layer by layer—on students' basic mastery. For instance, at the elementary level, teacher-centered teachers begin instruction in reading with letter recognition and gradually build skills by adding sounds, combinations, words, and sentences. In math, the learning starts with the smallest units—numbers and shapes—and gradually increases in complexity. At any point, the teacher can assess students' knowledge, based on behavioral responses to a task, to determine whether or not to move on.

When a behaviorist teacher integrates technology into instruction, students work individually on projects, everyone is simultaneously instructed on skills through whole group presentations, and working together is discouraged. Final products look identical, except for content. Some students work sluggishly because they resist this regimented or cookie-cutter approach.

At the extreme, in classrooms where teachers maintain this belief, students sit individually in rows, materials tend to be paper-based, classroom talking involves the teacher more than the students, and student work is usually individually completed and identical in form. In other words, the teacher controls what happens and when it happens. Students learn solely from the teacher rather than from one another—even when they use computers.

A teacher who holds this educational belief may be dynamic, engaging, and high-achieving; invariably, the teacher will also be controlling. If the teacher has strong management skills, these classrooms tend to be orderly and quiet. Student learning is driven through what the teacher considers important.

Constructivism

As with behaviorism, constructivism is known by other terms: learner-centered, student-centered, transactional, or nontraditional. This theory suggests that students learn through active participation in acquiring knowledge, social interactions, and the connection of new information to what they already know. Although the teacher still must have knowledge of the content, his or her role is to structure experiences so that students internally build or construct understanding of concepts. Their constructions of knowledge will be shaped by the social inter-actions they have with other students and the teacher, so that eventually, students come to some common understandings based on what they have experienced.

This theory acknowledges that students' experiences outside of school give them funds of knowledge that differ from one another. Experiences in the classroom help students connect new information to the knowledge they already have acquired. For example, when I think of the fraction ¼, I relate it to money: four quarters make a whole dollar. When I tried to transmit my understanding of fractions to one student, he could not understand. He and I were frustrated until I finally understood that he had nothing in his experience that connected with my money example. His internal understanding of fractions connected to measuring with a tape measure. When he was allowed to use measurements to discuss fractions, he, as well as several other students who were struggling, understood the concept. Their social interactions, which included discussions with other students who had other funds of knowledge about fractions, allowed the class to develop common understandings about why fractions are important and how we use them in everyday life.

Constructivists teach reading through a whole language approach—using rich print resources, reading chorally with students, singing songs that incorporate reading skills—and spend less time on specific reading skills unless a child shows a deficit. In math, the teacher is likely to approach number sense or geometry by distributing manipulatives and asking students to talk about what they discover.

In constructivist classrooms, teams of students decide which digital tools would be most appropriate for the projects or learning they undertake. Final products vary widely, and often student groups seem almost competitive about their work. Students learn technology skills as they need them, and their learning is often self-motivated.

Student-centered classrooms tend to be more social, active, and messy. Not everyone learns the same material at the same time and in the same way. At the extreme, students work in groups most of the time and explore topics that they then teach to their peers. The rooms are noisy and may even feel chaotic. Students may uncover useful information that surprises the teacher, so he or she asks these students to present what they have learned to the rest of the class. At other times, students may construct misconceptions about the content; then the teacher and students discuss their explorations, and the teacher must redirect them.

A teacher with this core belief about how students learn may also be dynamic and engaging, but the engagement generally will come from student excitement about what they are learning. The teacher facilitates and guides the activities in the room but does not try to keep all students progressing at the same rate. If a teacher has poor classroom management skills or a poor understanding of the big ideas of a unit, the class may learn less. Generally, teaching with constructivist beliefs means that students take longer to get through units, but they learn content more deeply.

VOICES OF EXPERIENCE

Linda Jones, fourth grade teacher
Lois Lenski Elementary School, Centennial, Colorado

Teachers can employ numerous creative approaches for students to learn to work collaboratively on curriculum-based projects by using computers. Working in small groups imitates adult life and will generate energy for students to complete more challenging work. Diversity in abilities and interests is an asset for collaborative work because students behave more confidently in groups. As students work together, they engage in interactive learning and effectively teach each other a wide range of content, as well as new ways to analyze problems. Interactive group learning encourages students to offer their ideas to a few peers instead of speaking in front of the entire class. Students who are shy or have experienced failure in the past feel smarter and more empowered as they collaborate in small groups. By closely observing how students communicate and present their ideas in groups, teachers can differentiate instruction to benefit each individual. I have discovered that well-structured group work enhances achievement for all students.

As students work together on computers, they teach one another skills that I do not always know. They apply advanced formatting techniques to complete a project. They can bookmark a location or create a hyperlink; design slides for presentations; cut, copy, and paste pictures; and cite web locations. They are able to narrate movies using voice-overs, share stories, and write more creatively.

Blended Theories

Many teachers will recognize parts of behaviorist and constructivist theory in their teaching. Behaviorism and constructivism represent the extremes along a continuum of teachers' beliefs. Most teachers blend various degrees of these two approaches. Teachers who adopt a blended approach recognize that students have different levels of receptivity to particular content areas or units, as well as different learning preferences. The teacher provides a skeleton of basic skills for the whole class, which is a behaviorist method, and then releases most students to build on the skeleton skills, based on paired and shared work, which is constructivist. A small group of less independent students works closely with the teacher in a step-by-step manner. This small group still gets time to interact socially, build on their own funds of knowledge, and explore ideas actively, but the teacher monitors their work more closely.

At the primary level, a teacher with a blended approach exposes students to the rich texts and environmental print (i.e., the common logos for products and restaurants, street signs, and the symbols young children "read") of constructivist teaching. This teacher also works with students in guided reading to teach skills in small blocks of instruction, as a behaviorist teacher would. In math, all students use manipulatives. While some students try to solve problems in self-directed groups, other students receive the teacher's more focused, direct help to create accurate, meaningful solutions.

In blended classrooms, the teacher may design a project or product with a broad outline and free students to work within the outline to be creative. Some students may work in groups and others as pairs or on their own, according to their needs. The teacher sets boundaries while encouraging experimentation within the boundaries.

The classroom of a blended theorist teacher varies between focused, quiet work and active participation in discovery. Teaching based on blended theory is perhaps harder to plan for because students work in such different ways. The teacher may worry that some student groups need more teacher support than others do. Finding balance is not easy. In such situations, technology comes to the rescue. When teachers can use technology effectively to teach and then allow students to use technology to demonstrate what they know, areas of instructional unevenness tend to balance themselves. The child who needs extra experience with a reading skill may access a website for practice while the teacher checks in with a group working on a technology-based project. Students do not and will not finish all the material at the same time or even finish all the same material, but teachers keep the big ideas, what students must learn, in sight so that all students complete basic levels of comprehension and most achieve much higher levels.

VOICES OF EXPERIENCE

Trecie Warner, third grade teacher
Lois Lenski Elementary, Centennial, Colorado

Perspective. It changes with each lens you look through.

My career in educational technology began with teaching kids to keyboard because that is what technology teachers were supposed to do. "The quick brown fox jumped over the lazy dog. Type those words as quickly and accurately as you can. Fifth graders should be able to type 40 words per minute."

That first job was as a paraprofessional working with Chris, a new school librarian who also had to figure out the quickly changing world of educational technology. Chris was an experienced media specialist, but using Macs and productivity software with teachers and kids was in its infancy. I was by her side, helping to figure out how to use the machines to teach curriculum.

I saw connections between curriculum and research, how library materials and the internet could support classroom learning. Helping teachers to see these connections was difficult though. Teachers wanted to do their work the way they'd always done it. Technology felt like an add-on.

As we navigated ever-changing technology, including, in our case, switching from Mac to PC platforms, I saw that kids were powerful users of technology— creating, researching, problem solving. I thought technology had all the answers. But teachers had only started to see the advantages, and many simply did not get it at all.

Continued

Adoption was a slow process. While classroom teachers were slowly adopting and adapting to technology, I got my teaching license. As a professional, I worked in computer labs and libraries, where I could keep up with the cutting edge of technology. I urged teachers to connect technology and library uses with classroom content. I co-taught with them and modeled innovative uses of technologies. Keyboarding was no longer a learning objective; we were too busy creatively using technology for projects and collaborations.

Then I was moved to a third grade classroom due to budgetary cutbacks. My perspective has changed. Now, using technology is only one of a thousand new things I have to think about. How do I keep up with the cutting edge? How do I use technology to accomplish the learning goals my students need to meet? I find it hard to leverage what I know about how to use technology effectively to support learning when there are so many other demands on my students and me. I struggle to make the best use of the limited equipment I have in my classroom.

I know that using technology with my students is not about teaching them technology tools. It's about finding ways to extend their thinking and giving them the right tools to demonstrate what they know. I also know that I'm responsible for it all—the skills and the content! Sometimes the students and I have wonderful experiences with technology, and sometimes the document camera is the only technology I use.

Kids are still powerful users of technology. I see it not just one day a week for an hour but every day in the classroom.

Teacher Beliefs and Technology

What research shows about learning theory and computer use is that teachers in highly behaviorist environments find technology hard to implement. When students get technology in their hands, teachers lose some control over classroom learning. Computers and other technologies, such as cameras and digital recorders, do not just fascinate students; these tech tools change the learning environment. Most human beings do not accept changes in their lives quickly. For teachers, changes do not always fit into their plans. A preservice teacher, attempting to teach computer skills to preschoolers, was at first frustrated when the young children did not conform to her plan for how they would demonstrate their new skills. While using an online digital device, the students found editing tools that the teacher did not realize existed. With the tools, which they taught each other spontaneously, they turned a teacher-directed, technology-based, non-individualized activity into a project that expressed their interests and viewpoints. The final project revealed far more differentiation than the teacher had planned, and she realized the students' demonstrated creativity and collaboration. Students had, in the end, "owned" the technology tools and the end product.

With technology, students' roles in the classroom change. They become engaged as critical reviewers, technical support, and learning partners. One researcher found that students never read one another's writing notebooks without an invitation, but as soon as words went onto a screen, students felt entitled to review and comment on the work. The screen placed students' work into a public domain for critical review.

When students have technical problems, they are likely first to ask for help from their peers. This benefits the teacher and students: A problem can be solved without teacher input, and students practice a key life skill: problem solving.

As they use tech tools, students talk to one another more often. For the teacher who prefers a quiet classroom, the social realities of technology use require significant shifts in thinking. Talking while they use tech tools helps students acquire, evaluate, and cement new knowledge. Rather than resist the rise in chatter, teachers can leverage the need for talk by pairing students with different strengths so that they learn from one another.

No matter what learning theory you hold, when technology is added to a classroom, the learning environment changes. Teachers can change their approaches while the technology is in use, or they will experience frustration trying to impose boundaries on student use. When teachers understand their own learning philosophies, they can use that knowledge to guide decisions about how technology will fit into their classrooms. Teachers at the behaviorist end of the spectrum will be comfortable starting with interactive website explorations that can enrich the content learning or one-time, whole class experiences, such as Skype visits. Teachers closer to the constructivist end of the continuum may be ready to plunge into a project where teams of students research an aspect of the content and create a project to teach others.

VOICES OF EXPERIENCE

Marie Tribur, fifth grade gifted and talented cluster teacher
Clayton Elementary School, Englewood, Colorado
mtribur@gmail.com, www.mrstribur.com

Teaching has come a long way from when I started teaching 34 years ago. Students were all sitting in their assigned seats, at their perfectly aligned desks, facing the front of the room, pencil in hand, no engagement except listening, of course.

Today, if you were to walk in my classroom, you would see every student with their own laptop that is hardwired to the tables. Computers are always on and never put away. Kids are working together all over the room. Class gurus willingly go around trouble shooting, so everyone has a chance to complete their projects. When given projects, students may be partnered with someone who does not sit close to them, so kids are often working in Google Chat, sharing ideas with partners who sit across the room. Students working on the same Google document are given equal access, so they can both view and edit. When the document is complete, students send it to me for credit and approval.

Technology integration definitely allows for differentiation. Consideration is given to partners, depending on the subject area and strengths and weaknesses of the students. Science and social studies are integrated in reading and writing. All writing is done on laptops. Students are taught how to create folders and organize their projects or documents.

I use a program for spelling. Vocabulary (content) words are put into the spelling program at school or at home at my convenience. Part of their spelling program requires them to use their vocabulary words in a paragraph. Their paragraphs have to make sense and be connected to the subject area from which the words came. When their assignment is complete, I log into the program (at home if I want to), read their paragraphs, make comments, score them (1–5), or, in some cases, reject the assignment to be done over.

Math is easily integrated because our district bought a program that does an initial placement test to be sure each child is at the correct level. Thorough reports are available, and small groups can be created based on students' needs. Additionally, we have a great reading program that does the same thing. Most of the material is nonfiction. Kids learn about digital-age information that concerns them. They read about the importance of collaboration and how to solve problems. Technology takes all the guesswork out of proper placement for students. Through reports, you can find out reading strengths and weaknesses and actually create worksheets to put together small groups to work on specific skills.

Teachers today do not have to know everything. You can Google it! I talk about things in science today that I would never have talked about ten years ago. With technology, I can teach myself and feel fairly confident about the accuracy of what I am teaching.

Technology integration has given me the freedom of turning my students loose and becoming a facilitator. Technology integration allows all students to move at their own pace. Never again will kids in my class sit with pencil in hand in perfectly aligned rows of desks and not be engaged.

Understand that teaching theories are inherently different. Teachers are individuals whose varied experiences as teachers and learners have shaped their views about how students learn. The theories are not good or bad—just different. Reflecting on your personal beliefs will guide your choices of technology tools within your classes. Think about taking one small step outside your comfort level to see how it changes the dynamics of your classroom. Even if the change makes you slightly uncomfortable, pay attention to what happens to your students. If more of your students are engaged, participating actively, and thinking deeply, the change might be worth making permanently.

Technologies
to Support Bloom's Taxonomy

Benjamin Bloom's *Taxonomy of Educational Objectives* (1956, 2001 [rev. ed.]) can help teachers classify their objectives to determine the various challenges of students' learning. Students need experiences at all levels of the taxonomy. Here's how technology fits into the domains of Bloom's taxonomy.

The knowledge level or remembering. The lowest level of the taxonomy, remembering, refers to recalling, listing, describing, locating, recognizing, or naming. Many of these tasks involve memorization and show basic knowledge. In technology use, tasks at the remembering level might include conducting simple online searches, making an acrostic or bulleted list, writing facts, or listing main events.

The comprehension level or understanding. One step up from remembering comes understanding. At this level, students explain, compare, discuss, interpret, restate, summarize, sort, and infer. Technology tasks that demonstrate understanding include conducting an advanced Boolean search, drawing a picture of an event, making a flow chart of events in a story or history lesson, outlining or summarizing a text, sorting into a Venn diagram, journaling, or commenting on a blog.

The application level or applying. Tasks in the application level require students to apply what they understand to new situations. Applying refers to solving, using, illustrating, constructing, classifying, and examining. Students working at this level may be solving problems on a math site, taking or selecting pictures to illustrate a concept, editing written work, developing a plan, uploading documents to a wiki, interviewing with a digital recorder, making a pattern, building a presentation, or contacting an expert.

The analysis level or analyzing. With analysis, students begin to use critical thinking skills to understand concepts. Verbs that fit into the analysis level include compare/contrast, investigate, organize, plan, structure, link, and deconstruct. Students working at this level with technology tools may be writing an advertisement, creating a Venn diagram on a subject of study, researching a concept, building a concept map, developing a questionnaire, writing a blog, conducting a survey, or developing a spreadsheet.

The evaluation level or evaluating. In evaluation, students use higher-level thinking skills to appraise ideas or materials based on criteria. Students might decide, choose, justify, debate, recommend, rate, or prioritize at this level. In the past, when students conducted research in library books, the materials had already been vetted, so while the information might not be current, its source could be trusted. With online research, however, students must appraise the credibility of a source before using it. Other technology-based tasks also require evaluation skills, such as writing a persuasive argument, engaging in an online discussion group, narrowing a search to target results, or critiquing books on a book review site.

The synthesis level or creating. Synthesis, the highest level on Bloom's taxonomy, describes what happens when students use their knowledge to create or produce something new. When students engage in synthesis, they are active learners who make choices about how to demonstrate what they know. At this level, students create, compose, invent, predict, design, or propose. With technology, students might create a public service announcement video, compose and perform a musical composition, change a current song or poem with new rhythms or words, design a logo or book cover, collaborate on a discussion board or wiki, write and record a podcast, or propose an invention. At this level, what students produce generally has significance to them.

Learning domains lie along a continuum. To progress to the highest levels, students must have mastered the skills at the lower levels. Consider this when introducing technology use in the classroom. Students may need technology experiences at the knowledge level before they can progress to the more complex experiences. For instance, before independently creating a 2-minute video, students may need to participate in whole group experiences with video cameras to build independent skills. Teachers can use the concept of learning domains to consider how to scaffold students' experiences with technology for optimal success on each project.

To help you imagine how technology and Bloom's levels fit together, many ideas in the book will be tied to a Bloom's level.

CHAPTER 2

Digital-Age Teaching and the ISTE Standards for Students

EVERY GENERATION OF TEACHERS—and students—has faced the question about what students need to know and be able to do at the end of the K–12 educational system. Expressed simply, we want young people to mature into responsible adults who live satisfying lives because they have the skills to support themselves and the dispositions to treat others well. How these mature, responsible adults should develop is not simple to describe. An even more complicated problem for educators is how these ideal adults can be nurtured and encouraged because children start school with inherent abilities and unique traits. Individuals are shaped by their environments and experiences, so each person matures differently. Educators, even the very best ones, are only a few among many influences in students' lives.

The International Society for Technology in Education (ISTE) has crafted a description for a model digital-age citizen through the ISTE Standards for Students (ISTE Standards•S). Six general categories describe what students need to know and be able to do to be *digital citizens* in a changing world. The ISTE Standards•S complement state and national standards and describe the skills and dispositions we want all students to have, even when they are not using technology. However, digital-age students are now using digital tools and need to practice the skills and dispositions described in the ISTE Standards•S.

In order for students to gain these skills and dispositions, teachers must use digital tools consistently with students every year. Not every use of technology will meet all the standards at the same time, but just as teachers use Common Core or district standards to write academic goals, they need to be writing *technology goals* based on the ISTE Standards•S. With each unit of study and each technology-based activity, teachers should know and monitor which ISTE Standards•S are being developed or practiced. All teachers must seek ways to support students' growth in all the ISTE Standards•S learner domains.

As you read explanations of the ISTE Standards•S, keep the following guiding questions in mind:

> What lessons do I currently teach that help students meet this standard?

> How can I revise lessons to better incorporate the technology standards?

ISTE Standards•S

Standard 1: Creativity and Innovation

Students demonstrate creative thinking, construct knowledge, and develop innovative products and processes using technology.

> Teachers at every grade level already help students build creativity and innovation skills. The question to be considered is "How am I building these skills with *digital* tools?"

1a. **Students apply existing knowledge to generate new ideas, products, or processes.**

This statement pushes against the concept of teaching students to use specific software or hardware and encourages treating technology skills as tools for doing work. Consider teaching students how to use a ruler. Instruction on the use of a ruler is short and always connected to students doing the work of measurement with the tool of a ruler. When students graduate from rulers to yardsticks, they do not require new instruction on how to measure; we expect them to apply their measuring skills to new settings to accomplish new tasks.

Technology skills should be approached in the same way. Students should be able to use their knowledge of *technology* to generate new ideas, products, and processes with technology. They apply what they already know about how technologies work to new digital settings to accomplish meaningful work.

All students come to school with funds of knowledge based on their life experiences outside school. Often those experiences include knowledge of digital tools. Many toddlers have used their parents' phones and tablet devices; by elementary age, children may have had a lot of digital experience—or none. Whether students bring digital knowledge with them to the classroom or receive instruction at school, their technology-based assignments should tap into their knowledge of technology to generate new ideas, products, and processes across digital settings. For instance, students who have learned to use a digital camera and digitally insert pictures into programs can apply that knowledge to a number of digital platforms for book reviews, brochures, presentations, digital stories, and other products.

1b. **Students create original works as a means of personal or group expression.**

Allow yourself to think beyond the fine arts as examples of original works. Yes, students should express themselves through digitally based art, music, and creative writing, but these are not the only ways to define original works. Imagine students creating posters, multimedia slideshows, videos, infographics, and comic strips. Asking them to add dialogue bubbles to a photograph, such as an historical photo from the Library of Congress, provides an outlet for their originality in the form of personal or group expression.

1c. Students use models and simulations to explore complex systems and issues.

Models and simulations serve as powerful learning opportunities for all age groups. Think about pilots, surgeons, and even student drivers practicing in simulated digital environments prior to having the authentic experiences. Students can participate in simulated dissections as preparation for science experiments or, when money is tight, as substitutions. Virtual manipulatives often keep students engaged in math learning longer than hands-on experiences because of the immediate feedback. When students travel virtually through Google Maps or access live cams around the world, they see and experience places and cultures other than their own.

1d. Students identify trends and forecast possibilities.

Supporting this aspect of the standard might seem easier in the secondary grades than in elementary schools. If curriculum covers weather, students might apply their knowledge of weather elements with weather forecasting simulations, such as Edheads Weather (www.edheads.org/activities/weather) or Forecasting Under Pressure (http://urbanext.illinois.edu/treehouse/activity_pressure.cfm). More often, though, to identify trends and forecast possibilities, students need to collect and analyze data. Secondary students should have many opportunities to work with data. One way to involve all students with data collection and analysis is through participation in global science investigations for citizen scientists, such as those offered through Journey North: A Global Study of Wildlife Migration and Seasonal Change (www.learner.org/jnorth).

Standard 2: Communication and Collaboration

Students use digital media and environments to communicate and work collaboratively, including at a distance, to support individual learning and contribute to the learning of others.

The classroom has always replicated a community where students learn communication and collaboration skills. In fact, for some students, the classroom serves as the first training ground for social skills. In the past, though, the community stayed small, and many communities lacked diversity of cultures. In the digital world, educational communities often reach beyond classroom and even national walls, so communication and collaboration skills require more sophistication. Technology tools invite students to work together, create ways to deliver information, and learn about other cultures.

2a. Students interact, collaborate, and publish with peers, experts, or others employing a variety of digital environments and media.

Teachers have found an abundance of ways to involve their students in work with other students around the globe. These connections do not need to be expensive; many tools, such as Skype and wikis, are free to teachers. Finding partners is not difficult either; teachers can use professional development platforms to put out calls for collaborators. In fact, responses are often so fast and numerous that teachers have to sift through a list of potential partners. The more specific teachers can be in their requests for partners, the more likely they will find the right collaborators. What may be difficult in global communities is maintaining teacher-to-teacher communications when the school year gets busy or coordinating projects that meet the curricular goals for everyone involved.

2b. Students communicate information and ideas effectively to multiple audiences using a variety of media and formats.

Technology tools can deliver information and ideas to broad audiences. This requires more sophistication in communication skills than typically has been promoted in classrooms. Students need explicit instruction on how to communicate effectively through writing, the projects they create, and in audio or visual formats. When teachers are in a rush to get a project done so that the class can move on, it's tempting to skip quality control. Yet, the time spent front-loading instruction on what makes quality communication will benefit students throughout their lifetimes.

2c. Students develop cultural understanding and global awareness by engaging with learners of other cultures.

Many students lack the life experiences to imagine that people in other cultures live, behave, and believe differently. Online collaborations create authentic ways for students to learn about places they have never experienced. For instance, a cross-national sharing between elementary schools in different climates revealed that students in one school had questions about snow, which they had never seen, while the partner students were trying to imagine open-air, year-round schools. Minor differences are not minor to students who have never been exposed to any differences at all. Given that most students will, as adults, work in international markets, the more exposure they receive to different cultural patterns during school years, the more successfully they will make the transition as adults.

2d. Students contribute to project teams to produce original works or solve problems.

No one disputes that learning to work in teams is a desired life skill. In many organizations, digital teamwork is the standard operating procedure. Students can work with teammates in the same room or work at a distance. They can know one another well or be virtual teammates. They can even work with virtual mentors who are experts in a field. The goal is to give students experiences working digitally with others in authentic partnerships.

Standard 3: Research and Information Fluency

Students apply digital tools to gather, evaluate, and use information.

Traditionally, school librarians have addressed research and information fluency skills with or without classroom teachers' involvement. Unfortunately, many schools have lost their librarians to budget shortfalls. Educators now recognize that even in schools with full-time librarians, information literacy must be a whole school effort. Building library skills extends beyond library walls.

At this time, most classroom teachers have received little training on teaching research and information fluency skills, and few schools have identified ways to teach these skills most beneficially. To be effective, research skills need to be addressed and built cumulatively over the K–12 school years. While information literacy is not the focus of this book, resources for teaching aspects of information literacy are provided. Additionally, an excellent resource, including a matrix showing the correlation of the Big6 Skills and ISTE Standards•S, is available at www.janetsinfo.com/big6info.htm.

3a. Students plan strategies to guide inquiry.

In the lingo of the Big6 research model, this stage combines Step 1: Task Definition, and Step 2: Information Seeking Strategies. Students need to define the task they want to accomplish and plan strategies for finding the information. Students can create their own research questions for inquiry. Good questions may have no answer, which requires students to propose an answer, or many possible answers, which requires students to choose a stance and support it. Students must determine where they may find information that will enable them to become expert enough to present an argument for their answers. The development of the question and the plan for finding resources does not necessarily require the use of technology. However, if the inquiry is being done collaboratively, technology can be used to capture each person's ideas most effectively.

3b. Students locate, organize, analyze, evaluate, synthesize, and ethically use information from a variety of sources and media.

This aspect of research combines the Big6 Step 3: Location + Access and Step 4: Use of Information. These are not necessarily linear steps because students may find that they need to locate additional or different resources as they move through the process. However, digital resources play a large part in the location, access, and use of information for research projects. Students need explicit instruction on how to conduct effective online or database searches and how to evaluate the sources they find.

Note that the standard calls for ethical use of information as well. This is a critical aspect of teaching information literacy that is often overlooked. Teaching students how to take notes, identify copyright limits, and cite sources should begin in concert with the first information literacy lessons. Include lessons on how to find, evaluate, use, and cite digital photos as well! Students should learn that there is more leeway with copyrighted materials in educational settings than in a workplace or for personal use.

3c. Students evaluate and select information sources and digital tools based on their appropriateness to specific tasks.

When students used only printed library resources, selecting and evaluating information sources was less important than it is now with easy access online resources. Many students struggle to understand that online information might be slanted, inaccurate, or entirely bogus. Explicit instruction on evaluating sources is essential; several of the annotated resources in the next section of this chapter address that issue. Students may use digital tools such as word processors to capture notes and online citation makers to credit sources. They should also be thinking about appropriate digital tools for reporting their results.

3d. Students process data and report results.

A final step in conducting research is synthesis of the data and reporting the findings. With appropriate attention to the previous steps, this outcome should flow naturally. Throughout the research process, teachers need to encourage students to think about creative ways to report their answers. Tech tools provide numerous choices for reporting results, and students enjoy the freedom to use their creativity.

Information Literacy Resources

Information, media, and visual literacies should be taught at all levels of K–12. At the elementary level, teaching critical thinking skills prepares students to build on those skills as they mature. The following resources, chosen for their compliance with the COPPA laws for children under the age of 13, can help teachers convey the lessons of information literacy while students are young enough to internalize the concepts. Secondary teachers need to continue instruction on information literacy skills with more sophisticated support materials.

Digital Literacy and Citizenship Classroom Curriculum (www.common-sensemedia.org/educators/curriculum) is a free curriculum for elementary students. If your school does not have a plan for teaching digital literacy, this curriculum is certainly worth investigating. The eight categories of the curriculum, divided into K–2, 3–5, 6–8, 9–12, and Library, are Internet Safety, Privacy & Security, Relationships & Communications, Cyberbullying, Digital Footprint & Reputation, Self-Image & Identity, Information Literacy, and Creative Credit & Copyright.

MLA Elementary Citation Maker (http://oslis.org/@@mla-elementary) and Citation Machine (www.citationmachine.net) can help teachers and media specialists teach source citations. When students fill in forms, citations are created for them.

TV Smarts for Kids (http://mediaeducationlab.com/tv-smarts-kids) has three videos to demonstrate how TV manipulates watchers.

Standard 4: Critical Thinking, Problem Solving, and Decision Making

Students use critical thinking skills to plan and conduct research, manage projects, solve problems, and make informed decisions using appropriate digital tools and resources.

Critical thinking skills have become vital in students' media-driven world. Students of all ages are aware of world problems, face a bombardment of advertising and political opinions on all their digital devices, and believe they will need to solve global issues in their lifetimes. Today's students want to know the relevance of what they learn in school to what they will encounter as adults. Teaching critical thinking skills encourages students to seek answers to authentic problems.

4a. Students identify and define authentic problems and significant questions for investigation.

Students can be passionate advocates for justice when they have opportunities to identify authentic problems and propose solutions, particularly when those problems have local connections. When students look at their schools and neighborhoods with a critical lens, they often find issues, such as bullying, ADA access, or dangerous traffic flow patterns, they would like to tackle. They usually have to conduct preliminary research to formulate a significant question.

4b. Students plan and manage activities to develop a solution or complete a project.

Teams of students can use collaborative documents and spreadsheets to plan their investigations and track progress. As part of a unit on financial literacy, teams of students in a third grade class used Google Apps to develop plans collaboratively for donating to a charitable organization. The students used a calendar to make a timeline for conducting the investigations and spreadsheets to track the financial costs they would incur if they donated. Each team then offered its proposal for a class vote. Students took an intense interest in preparing viable, high-quality proposals, hoping that their charities would win.

4c. Students collect and analyze data to identify solutions and/or make informed decisions.

Technology makes collecting and analyzing data easier for students. Data may be accessible online, particularly if students are attempting to look at a community problem. What is the history of the problem? What solutions have been proposed in the past? Who makes the decisions? Using a collaborative space for the data allows everyone to be involved in analysis as well.

4d. Students use multiple processes and diverse perspectives to explore alternative solutions.

Students bring different levels of community knowledge to any project, and frequently one student will see an aspect of a solution that others missed. Sometimes what looks like an obvious solution turns out to affect others in unacceptable ways, and students learn about compromise. Connecting students to peers in foreign countries can reveal different perspectives on world problems. Teaching students to consider perspectives outside their own prepares them for living and competing in a global community. Students in the third grade class researching charitable giving had to convince three other classes to vote for their proposal. All four classes developed one-minute video clips to advocate for their choices.

Standard 5: Digital Citizenship

Students understand human, cultural, and societal issues related to technology and practice legal and ethical behavior.

In this domain, teachers help students understand practices that lead to becoming responsible, ethical, and safe digital citizens. Because so many students use technology, including accessing the internet even before they enter elementary school, teachers must start addressing these values in kindergarten or earlier. Child protection laws and district filtering policies protect students from many online threats while at school, but students are often vulnerable when they use computers at home. Even within the confines of protected spaces and classroom use, students can violate other students' privacy, erase or edit files, and treat peers poorly. Digital citizenship is only peripherally addressed in this book, but online resources (see Chapter 15, "COPPA, Internet Safety, and Copyright") can help teachers strengthen their instruction in this domain.

5a. Students advocate and practice safe, legal, and responsible use of information and technology.

One of the biggest areas of concern under this standard is cyberbullying. In an analysis of published research on cyberbullying, researchers found widely varying rates of cyberbullying (2.5% to 70%). The Cyberbullying Research Center (http://cyberbullying.us/facts/) indicated that the average rate of victimization among secondary students is 21%. In one of the few studies of cyberbullying among elementary students, Elizabeth Englander found that 30% of fifth graders admitted being cyberbullies and 46% reported being a cyberbully victim. Young people rarely realize the potential harm or the subsequent consequences of their behavior. This issue could easily be used as an authentic problem for students to research among their peers (Standard 4). Under this standard, students need to learn about how to choose credible information, avoid plagiarism, and cite sources. Responsible digital citizens treat technology tools in safe and responsible ways as well.

5b. Students exhibit a positive attitude toward using technology that supports collaboration, learning, and productivity.

This standard is a wonderful goal, but difficult to assess. In some ways, it is like setting a goal that all students will read for enjoyment. For those who love to read, it's hard to imagine that others find reading a chore. The same can be true of technology use. Occasionally, students do not embrace technology as a means for collaborating, learning, or producing. When technology has been primarily a source of entertainment, students may resist the transition to using technology for school work. Some students are self-conscious because their skills lag behind their peers'. Others reflect their parents' negative attitudes toward technologies. Teachers may not always know the cause of students' lack of interest in using technologies, and should, if student resist, offer alternative ways to accomplish the same tasks. Planning rich tasks that promote collaboration, learning, and productivity will likely lead to positive attitudes among students.

5c. Students demonstrate personal responsibility for lifelong learning.

A first grade teacher once expressed dismay that students had gone home after an online exploration in the computer lab and revisited that site. "They've ruined it because they've already seen what I wanted to show them," she told me. Actually, the teacher should have considered it high praise from students that a class activity with technology provoked curiosity to deepen their knowledge at home. Truly, taking the initiative to learn is what we want students to do—throughout their lives.

5d. Students exhibit leadership for digital citizenship.

Teaming students on technology tools allows them to support and encourage one another to use the tools responsibly. Listen to their conversations and acknowledge students when they remind others about digital citizenship responsibilities. Encourage students to work with technology across grade levels, too. One fourth grade teacher sends her students to primary classrooms to assist with technology projects. This encourages the older students to be mindful of modeling digital citizenship.

Standard 6: Technology Operations and Concepts

Students demonstrate a sound understanding of technology concepts, systems, and operations.

It's hard to remember when words for digital technology, such as mouse, screen, disc, cursor, and desktop, were not part of everyday vocabulary. Teachers no longer need to teach the vocabulary of the computer, but they can introduce students to computer skills that transfer from program to program. Since this domain of the ISTE Standards•S is about understanding how technology and digital tools work, students learn the information primarily through using technology, not through specific skills lessons. As they become proficient users, they unconsciously build competency in technology operations and concepts.

6a. Students understand and use technology systems.

At the elementary level, students might gain understanding of some systems, such as how digital cameras work, but typically they will not really understand the technical aspects of technology systems until secondary school. In an after-school technology program for fourth and fifth graders, students dismantled desktop CPUs, keyboards, and mice. Those students felt empowered by their explorations of the computer system. Today, when laptops have replaced desktops in many locations, providing such opportunities is more difficult. Often students gain knowledge of systems through their own explorations at home. How many parents have been dismayed when the ring tones on their phones were changed by their children!

6b. Students select and use applications effectively and productively.

During much of elementary school, students are just learning applications and often do not get to choose the applications they will use. However, intermediate and secondary students with a solid knowledge base about applications should be given increased responsibility for selecting their own tools and applications for demonstrating what they have learned. A teacher might offer three options and allow student teams to choose which ones would work for their presentations.

6c. Students troubleshoot systems and applications.

It can be helpful in any school to teach a cadre of students how to troubleshoot technology problems for their classmates and teachers. In one program, students worked in two-person teams, a fifth grader and a fourth grader, to support assigned classrooms. The pairs checked the classroom's computers at least once a week, solved simple problems, and referred more complex issues to the technologist. In their own classrooms, the student techies were instructed to suggest troubleshooting techniques or solutions to their peers but not solve the problems for them. This built competence among all the students and gave the techies great problem-solving experiences.

6d. Students transfer current knowledge to learning of new technologies.

If students explore a variety of applications, they will quickly see that some techniques transfer across different applications. First and second graders can learn the computer skills to save files to a server or cloud, insert pictures and clip art, type text, and type URLs. These techniques have become ubiquitous across applications and platforms.

For additional information about the ISTE Standards•S, explore the implementation wiki at http://nets-implementation.iste.wikispaces.net. Members have uploaded ideas, lesson plans, and links to support the implementation of the technology standards. This is also where you will find student-friendly names for the standards: Make It, Share It, Find It, Solve It, Protect It, and Use It.

CHAPTER 3

Paths to
Technology Integration

CLASSROOM INTEGRATION of technology requires a different level of thinking from personal tech use. First, teachers need to understand how technology tools can support the instructional goals of their curriculum. Educators have always used a variety of activities to help students further their understanding of curricular content: shared reading, experiments, writing, field trips, making posters, simulations, discussion, building dioramas, drawing, role playing, singing, kinesthetic movement, manipulatives, and so many others. Most of these activities can now be accomplished as effectively and, in some cases, *more* effectively with digital tools. The activities and projects discussed in this book will illustrate how the digital world aligns with curriculum.

In addition, teachers need to adapt to the changes that digital technologies bring to the classroom itself. Researchers have noted subtle shifts in classroom communities when teachers use computers and digital tools effectively. For instance, students generally consult classmates for assistance rather than tug on the teacher's sleeve. This raises the productive noise level of the class. Also, using technology takes longer than lectures and worksheets, but the payoff is increased student engagement, work quality, and depth of learning. As teachers integrate tech tools into instruction, they begin to view some of their "tried and true" instructional practices with new eyes. As Marie Tribur, who started teaching 34 years ago, said so well in Chapter 1, observing her students' increased enthusiasm for learning as she began to use tech tools has sold her on accommodating more noise for the sake of her students.

With the pressures of accountability testing and public censure, many teachers struggle to find time and support for taking the risk of introducing technology into their teaching days. Initially, teaching with tech tools takes longer than traditional styles of teaching, yet students demonstrate greater recall and deeper understanding when technology is used effectively. The struggle to balance accountability demands and students' needs for a differentiated digital-age learning experience is not easily resolved. Unfortunately, accountability testing has disheartened and, understandably, embittered battalions of teachers who face districtwide demands for lock-step adherence to pacing guides and even scripted curriculums.

Even when teachers agree with the ideas and philosophies of digital-age learning, many find it difficult to change the comfortable practices they've used successfully for years. Teachers know the level of students' achievement related to their current teaching methods. What if the time spent trying a new strategy that incorporates technology puts students further behind instead of ahead? How can a teacher recover the time invested in learning to use a tech tool if the change proved disastrous?

Successful change comes in small steps. Begin with short, simple ideas that can build flexibility and confidence, particularly if you are a novice with instructional technology. Once you and your students have mastered one innovation, you can look for another idea that will stretch your usual methods only a little. *Three adaptations to your technology use over one school year represent considerable work and some degree of risk.* Each year, you will be amazed at how much easier and fun using tech tools will be for your and your students.

If you are working collaboratively within your school to build instructional technology use, consider working with your colleagues at each grade level, so that each person takes responsibility for teaching one specific tool or skill to her/his students. At the elementary level, such a progression might start with drawing on the computer in year one, learning to put drawn pictures and text in presentation software in year two, and adding audio to slideshows in year three. In middle school, students should be able to work easily in word processing and presentation programs, so teachers might consider working with spreadsheets one year, creating multimedia digital stories another year, and working on videos the third.

VOICES OF EXPERIENCE

Candy Shively, director of K–12 initiatives, retired
The Source for Learning, Reston, Virginia
www.sourceforlearning.org

There are so many great tools and so little time to learn them all. Help students get past the novelty of new tools by implementing one new tool per grade level in your school. Each grade level can concentrate on one new tool, allowing students to become experts with it. With tool mastery, they will pay more attention to the content of their projects than to the glitz of the tool. Of course, the class will discover new features of their tool as the year goes on. Each teacher must learn only the one tool well, so he/she can also focus on what the students are saying, making, or writing in their various projects. Students enter each grade with tool experience from prior years, so they are able to choose from a growing repertoire of "old" or "new" tools for projects.

Parents can help at home more easily if they learn one tool each year, too. You could even host family "tool workshop" evenings by grade level and have student "experts" teach the moms and dads.

Students who move into the school will easily catch on to "old" tools from prior grade levels via the many in-class experts, so teachers are not the only tool masters.

Continued

As long as the tools remain free, they're great. If they are not free, your school can decide whether to purchase an institutional subscription or change to a different tool.

There is no perfect tool sequence. Many easy skills, such as copying URLs or uploading digital picture files, will transfer from tool to tool. Move from simpler, class-centered use of tools to group and independent use. An intentional tool sequence also lets schools incorporate basic internet safety and digital ethics, such as avoiding real names and abiding by the ethical use of images. Students will develop as technology consumers as they delve into new tools each year. In a world where technology changes constantly, it is important that we give students experience both mastering and selecting tools.

To learn many more ways the one-tool-per-year model can be used or adapted, see the article "Building Schoolwide Literacy with Free Web 2.0 Tools: A Grade by Grade Elementary Model" on the TeachersFirst website (www.teachersfirst.com/schoolwidelit).

As you become more comfortable using tech tools, try this experiment at elementary or middle school levels: After teachers and students have mastered their agreed-upon tools and/or skills, arrange for two classes to meet and work together. Your students will work with partners or in small groups with your colleague's students. Ask the students to teach each other their new tools or skills—first students from one class act as their peers' teachers, and then roles are reversed. You and your colleague can decide on a schedule that will be convenient for both of you. After each joint session, when you and your students are back in your own classroom, ask them to think about what worked well and what they plan to change during the next session as teachers or learners. Encourage students to devise creative lessons that do not necessarily mirror your own teaching methods. This co-teaching activity will fulfill several of the ISTE Standards for Students.

At the secondary level, this may mean first assessing students' competencies to determine what they know and building a plan to fill in the gaps. Teachers can then give students responsibility for designing their own projects, using the skills they have to learn more sophisticated skills. This works as a start-up model, and, as teachers and students gain experience, additional tech tools and higher-level skills can be incorporated.

Integration Approaches

Within the following chapters, you will read about so many wonderful ways to integrate tech tools into your teaching that you may find it hard to decide where to start. In fact, the possibilities may paralyze novice teachers. Every idea seems excellent. Which ones will make the biggest impact? Which will be successful? Which sound easier than they are in practice? How will I know I'm doing it right?

Be assured that no "right answers" apply to these techniques. Teachers begin with tools that best fit their styles, classroom contexts, level of confidence, and students' abilities. Almost any idea can be an entry point for increasing students' use or teachers' instructional use of technology. No teacher is an expert in all technologies. As individuals, we gravitate toward what interests us. Within a classroom, students may be interested in several different aspects of technology—and a teacher cannot possibly use them all in one year.

Instead, teachers can focus on the concept of backward design. What central ideas should my students know at the end of this unit? What activities, including those using tech tools, will enable them to master the big idea and express their mastery? What do they know now about the technology they will use? What will they need to experience in order to achieve success? If students need to build technical skills prior to jumping into a project, plan scaffolding experiences. If they already know how to use several tools, consider allowing them to choose one for their final products. At the end of the unit, evaluate what worked and what could be improved. Think about whether another tech tool would enhance the unit's purpose.

Evaluate this unit against the ISTE Standards•S. Did the unit advance one or more of the ISTE Standards•S categories? If not, how could the unit change to support the ISTE Standards•S? Teachers are in the best position to lead students as they become global citizens with polished, ethical digital skills. The ISTE Standards•S describe digital-age skills students need.

In the end, teachers will decide how to use various tech tools that best fit their students' needs and interests. If an idea in this book looks intriguing, try it!

Eventually, your and your students' experiences will narrow down the choices, but at the beginning, everything is a possibility. Some ideas may not work well, but we know that growth and learning arise from mishaps as well as from successes. When a lesson flops, confident teachers are honest with students—they admit their failure. In these situations, teach your students by example how to laugh at mistakes and persevere! The following ideas outline how teachers from various backgrounds have incorporated technology into their classrooms. I hope their experiences will be models for your consideration.

VOICES OF EXPERIENCE

Nicolette Vander Velde and Chris Moore, fifth grade teachers
East Elementary School, Littleton, Colorado

Nicolette and Chris team teach the fifth grade at their school; they often combine classes or switch students for lessons. Five years ago, they were part of a pilot program, funded through a grant, to use carts of netbook computers for writing instruction. The grant work included professional development on supporting writing through technology tools, as well as a cross-collaboration with teachers in another school district. Their work with their students has been documented in *Learning in the Cloud* (Warschauer, 2011). Nicolette and Chris cowrote this response to questions I sent them.

I'm particularly interested in your voice on how collaboration within a grade level works. You two do so much of it, and other teachers would like to hear how that happens—how do you plan collaboration?

The team aspect is something we aren't often asked about. It's made a huge difference for us and for our students. Having a teammate to work with, take risks with, and make mistakes with has been extremely important. Things would be very different if we didn't have each other. The learning process would be much slower, and there would be less risk-taking for sure. We'd have fewer opportunities to model learning for our students. They see us work with each other, and they see the positive and negative aspects of learning and working as part of a team.

How do you divide the responsibilities?

In the beginning, Chris ran the blog and Nicolette ran the wiki (PBWorks). Both of us struggled through the 1:1 (one computer for every student) computer laptop program and hardware issues. Once Google Apps came along, we both worked on that. We've definitely developed a bit of friendly competition as far as learning and using new tools and resources. These days, it's more of a shared responsibility because we both know how to do so much more. Again, this is because we have the team aspect going on. Currently, the responsibilities are divided as equally as possible based on who has time to work on certain things. We're both busy with family and kids, so we just do what we can and then share.

What got you started?

We were fortunate enough to be in on the ground level of the Littleton Public Schools (LPS) Inspired Writing Project, which included schools from LPS as well as Englewood. We were also fortunate to be able to go 1:1 right from the very beginning. Through professional development provided by the districts, we learned more about writing and the writing process with the netbooks (i.e., portable computers) and other web-based tools. We were extremely focused on writing, and we used the trial-and-error method of problem solving—a lot! We relied heavily on the students. They became the stars of the classroom as they solved problems and made improvements to nearly everything we did with the netbooks. Eventually, we began to branch out with new tools and quite a bit of science content. Since then, we've made technology and the netbooks central to our regular routine in all content areas. Our classroom culture has been completely changed by this work.

What did you do?

We opened the floodgates. We really let the students run with everything. We used the computers all day long right from the beginning. We had them for writing, but we also relied heavily on them for science content, and we allowed the students to use them at any time of the day. We used the PBworkspace (www.pbworks.com/education.html) and Blogger, which is now a Google App, as instructional tools, student showcases, and launchpads for our work in general. We focused on growing an audience and purpose for the work of our kids. We shared our students' work by using tools like Twitter to reach an interested audience.

Continued

Two things we noticed right away: Having an audience and purpose for their work makes all the difference to students, and they love to revise their work on the computers. This has been a total game changer for us.

How did sharing their work with different audiences affect the students?

It gave the students new and improved teachers! We had to change our teaching practices. We were really able to differentiate in so many new ways. We were able to provide much more and much better feedback. Students saw us writing, learning, and getting excited—and that was definitely contagious. Students became technology experts and problem solvers out of necessity; however, they just thought they were having a great time learning with their teachers.

We had an incredible group of kids that first year. Their scores and their writing were off the charts. Since then, writing scores have been evening out.

What made it work?

Our administration said (and still says) "yes" to us all the time. We're allowed to really go for it in terms of just about anything we want to do with the tools and resources we have available to us, and then we're encouraged to share what we do at every level—districtwide through internationally. Here are links where others can see our students' work: http://eastdragonden.blogspot.com and http://eastdragondentake2.pbworks.com.

Types of Integration Approaches

The paths to implement the use of technology with students can be categorized into a few types: instructional uses, software and websites, non-computer tools, technology centers, teacher-directed projects, Web 2.0 tools, collaborations with colleagues, and project-based learning. Novices and moderate tech users may advance more quickly in using technology with students if they first review the routes others have taken. This section will review the advantages and disadvantages of each option; future chapters will explore the possibilities more extensively.

Instructional Uses

For some teachers, the easiest entry to using technology is to model it first as an instructional tool and then advance to student demonstrations with technology. Ideas for instructional uses are presented in Chapter 4, Instructional Use of Technology.

One major advantage of beginning integration in this way is the low level of risk; when technology stays in the teachers' hands, malfunctions do not disrupt the entire lesson. Depending on how technology is used, lessons can stretch students' thinking as well. On the other hand, teachers' control of the technology frustrates students who want the freedom to express themselves using technology. While teachers' control of tech tools may make them feel comfortable, students are not building their tech skills. Teachers who begin with instructional tech uses should plan to transition to student demonstration use within a year and preferably sooner.

Software and Websites

For many teachers, the use of educational software and websites feels like the safest way to manage students on computers and even to incorporate technology into instruction. Many interactive websites provide rich experiences for students that can introduce, support, extend, or assess classroom instruction. The better sites provide simulations, where students manipulate online objects, such as math virtual manipulatives or science experiments. The worst of educational software or websites are those that emulate worksheets with drills on grammar or math facts, though students can learn through factual drill sites. Research has shown that students' memorization of basic facts improved with drill software. The problem is that fact drills are boring. Many websites lie between the best and worst. For instance, an online book may or may not require students to interact; however, when students are paired to listen to or read the online book, this activity has greater value in terms of student engagement than simple drills. Throughout this book, you will find descriptions of websites that engage students in higher levels of Bloom's taxonomy.

Using software and websites as an entry point for using tech tools in education has advantages and disadvantages. Advantages are the relative low risk of malfunction, the ease of having all students working on the same task simultaneously, the potential for high-level thinking if the site is a good match for students' skills, and the predictable length of time needed. On the other hand, this approach offers little differentiation, does not scaffold technology skills, and is not likely to engage all students. For students to experience higher levels of learning, consider having them work with partners to access websites, which encourages students to discuss their work. If a website is being used as a whole group experience, for example, to build background knowledge, let students control the mouse, if possible, and allow students' questions and observations to drive the experience.

Noncomputer Tools

Some teachers start students with noncomputer tools. Students may use digital cameras to capture photos related to themes, video cameras to tape presentations, or audio recorders for stories or books. Management of the digital files often falls to the teacher. This method is often used by teachers as an introductory experience until students have built the skills to manage some of the files themselves.

Students feel empowered by this approach because they can control the technology and make decisions about what is important to capture. Teachers become facilitators of the final products. If students are allowed to decide when to use a tool, they can share insights on how they view the classroom world. Disadvantages include the time it takes teachers to manage the files (upload, save, and share), the management of the tools themselves either for equity or safety, and the distribution of the final products, especially as students often want instant results. Chapter 7 gives ideas for the use of digital cameras.

Teacher-Directed Projects

Some teachers design projects that students can complete using technology. Teacher-directed projects should not be disparaged; they can be useful when students are building basic technology skills and need introductory experiences. Simple projects, such as drawing self-portraits on the computer or making basic slideshows with a program's templates, are scaffolds for future, more complex projects. Teacher-directed projects would be situated at the lower end of Bloom's taxonomy, even when they take several weeks instead of one day, because the teacher controls how and why students use the technology tools.

Advantages are the potential to scaffold technology skills, the similar end products to share with parents, and the likelihood that projects will reflect what students learned in the classroom. Disadvantages include the lower level of thinking skills required, lack of differentiation, and fast and slow finishers' potential frustration. Plan productive ways to engage fast finishers and support slow finishers.

Perhaps projects could also have varied levels of difficulty to address the need for differentiation.

Web 2.0 Tools

Some teachers prefer to start students with internet-based tools that allow them to be both consumers and producers of information. (See Chapter 12, Web 2.0 Tools, for more information.) Web 2.0 tools enable students to create content and publish it on the internet. These students may maintain blogs, contribute to wikis, or develop products that they post online. They collaborate with peers in their classrooms or across the globe. The collaborations may lead to email pals, teleconferencing, and virtual visits.

For teachers, the advantages include student engagement, authentic experiences with real audiences, and the potential to connect with other students and experts outside the classroom. On the other hand, Web 2.0 tools, even in protected environments, require significant monitoring. When students publish, comment on blogs, or send emails, their messages sometimes hurt others unintentionally. Teachers need to address appropriate language, messages, and tone *before* students begin using the tools and then monitor use during the experiences. Consider pairing students to monitor one another before any message is submitted to you for approval. Secondary teachers, of course, have more leeway than elementary teachers when students are using Web 2.0 tools, not only because the Children's Online Privacy Protection Act (COPPA) does not apply to youth over 13, but also because older students ought to have deeper understanding about how their words may affect others.

Technology Centers

Teachers who use learning centers in their classrooms can design complementary technology centers as well. Technology centers may be content-based with a combination of digital tools. Sometimes the center can involve a highly engaging website or the use of digital tools like cameras or audio recorders. Teachers should also plan multiple opportunities for students to communicate—writing online, creating a presentation, or contributing to a class site.

The advantages of classroom technology centers are that teachers can easily promote equitable access with limited access to technology, involve all students in using digital tools every day, support ongoing projects, and place students in charge of their own work. Disadvantages include the time required for advanced planning until the work becomes routine for the teacher and students, the need for students to take responsibility for troubleshooting (which can also be an advantage), and the need for monitoring students' work.

Table 3.1 illustrates the advantages and disadvantages of various instructional approaches to technology integration highlighted in this chapter.

Table 3.1 Technology Integration Instructional Approaches

INTEGRATION APPROACH	ADVANTAGES	DISADVANTAGES
Instructional Use Only	Comfortable starting point Low risk Teacher controls technology Can engage whole class at once Good for modeling	Passive for students Does not build student technology competency
Software/Websites	Fairly low risk Outcome dependent on quality of teacher's choice Students are active Pacing is consistent across student groups May engage students in simulations and problem solving May promote student-student talking May build students' conceptual skills	Limited differentiation May be boring May replicate basic fact drills Usually does not build students' technology competency Requires sufficient computer access
Noncomputer Tools (i.e., digital cameras, video cameras, audio recorders)	Low to moderate risk Possible familiarity Often student controlled Builds teamwork Encourages imagination Does not require much computer access	Teachers' management of equipment and products can be time-consuming Can become complicated with editing and production processes

Teacher-Directed Projects	Integrates technology with content	Greater risk of something going wrong
	Keeps students involved	Minimal differentiation
	Scaffolds technology skills	May have fast and slow finishers
	Keeps end products consistent	
Web 2.0 Tools	High student motivation	Needs significant monitoring
	Typically low learning curve	Needs explicit instruction and modeling for online communication
	Differentiated by content	
	Authentic interactions with others for authentic purposes	Must comply with COPPA (privacy laws)
		Requires sufficient computer access
Technology Centers	Equal access with limited equipment	Needs consistent planning
	Students control the technology	Requires students to troubleshoot
	Differentiated by student ability	Requires training students
	High student motivation	
Teacher Collaborations	Lowers risk of something going wrong	Dependent on good collaboration
	Distributes the work load of planning and implementation	Requires coordinated planning
	Builds capacity in teachers	
	May engage students in differentiated work	
	Builds students' technology skills	
Project-based Learning	High level of student autonomy	Higher risk
	Students control technology	Needs consistent monitoring
	Naturally differentiated	Students may end at different times
	Builds students' technology skills	End products may differ considerably

VOICES OF EXPERIENCE

Nancye Blair, technology and gifted specialist
The Schools of McKeel Academy, Lakeland, Florida

Over the last two decades, teachers began increasing the use of technology to design and deliver engaging lessons that integrate relevant multimedia. Within the last decade, teachers started working with students to create digital media projects in a variety of curriculum areas and settings. Yet, the most empowering uses of technology in the classroom are those that allow students to discover and create independently, especially when their discovery and products will be shared with an authentic audience.

Why are these activities so powerful? Daniel H. Pink shares in his book *Drive: The Surprising Truth About What Motivates Us* (2009) that true motivation stems from three elements—autonomy, mastery, and purpose. Through the implementation of meaningful technology-based centers that promote these three elements, students become intrinsically engaged and motivated to excel and create. Moreover, by providing tasks that give students autonomy, mastery, and purpose, we are telling them that their work and voices matter, that they are capable of learning, creating, and achieving far beyond their wildest dreams. These powerful messages instill a basis for lifelong learning in our students.

Best Practices

Four strategies foster a smooth shift to independent technology learning centers and cultivate the most significant student successes:

1. Introduce a new technology tool through a high-quality model in whole group instruction to invoke student excitement about its capabilities.

2. Work together with students to use the new tool to create a collaborative class piece. During this activity, set students up for success by teaching basic skills they will need when using the tech tool independently. This step can be repeated or expanded to small group activities until students are confident with the new tool.

3. Plan tech learning center activities that enhance or extend class curriculum through web research and digital media creation. Provide all directions and a sample project, when possible, at the center. Consider using color-coded instructions to provide differentiation for diverse ability levels, interests, and learning styles.

4. Share the student work and discoveries with an authentic audience through class presentations, school websites, blogs, Skype, or other means.

Samantha Lewis, a first grade teacher at South McKeel Academy in Lakeland, Florida, uses independent technology centers on a daily basis with her students. When students participate in tech centers, Lewis says, "the quality of student work doubles because they are excited and know everyone is going to see their finished work." Technology centers can become a foundational part of daily educational practices in elementary classrooms. When the centers are used regularly, they offer students authentic opportunities to demonstrate knowledge and mastery of curricular content and technical objectives.

Six Types of Powerful Technology Centers

In the digital age, the tools that can be used for technology learning centers are seemingly limitless. Nevertheless, there are six categories of center activities that have proved to be exceptionally effective at the elementary level.

1. **Digital Storytelling Center.** Whether young students are using My StoryMaker (www.clpgh.org/kids/storymaker/embed.cfm) to write and illustrate their own books or fifth graders are writing collaborative stories with their parents on Storybird.com (http://storybird.com), digital storytelling allows students to create compelling, interactive pieces that captivate readers.

2. **Blogging Center.** Digital-age writing skills fuse with authentic audiences as students use blogging to post their original writing, explain scientific concepts, write responses to critical thinking prompts, or exhibit artwork.

Continued

3. **Podcasting Center.** Audacity (http://audacity.sourceforge.net); GarageBand (www.apple.com/support/mac-apps/garageband); and Vocaroo (http://vocaroo.com) are kid-friendly applications for practicing reading, sharing original poetry, learning to play or share music, and designing informational news broadcasts across curriculum areas.

4. **Movie Making Center.** Even our youngest students can use digital media software like Windows Movie Maker; iMovie for iOS; or Animoto (https://animoto.com) to classify, analyze and sequence images. Students can also use the simple video recording features of a webcam, Sony's Bloggie, or a document camera to showcase reading fluency or explanations of math problems.

5. **Presentation Center.** Various presentation software programs make great platforms for students to display information they research while in the center. Some good ones are Microsoft PowerPoint, Open Office Presentation, and Apple Keynote.

6. **Desktop Publishing Center.** By using Microsoft Publisher, word processing templates, or Web 2.0 tools, students can demonstrate knowledge and solve real-world problems by creating posters, brochures, and newsletters.

Independent technology centers can truly empower students, inspiring them to explore the full capabilities of technology to enrich learning, communication, and creation. In the process, students can engage in creative problem solving, share work with authentic audiences, and begin to reach their unique potentials.

Collaborations with Colleagues

Rather than flying solo in using technology, many teachers partner with colleagues to plan for, implement, and evaluate technology use. In some schools, grade level teachers have combined their classes for technology experiences, while others have combined older and younger students as "buddy classes." Schools with teacher/librarians or teacher/technologists often encourage coteaching. In fact, at schools lucky enough to have media specialists or technologists, teachers will enjoy initiating partner teaching if it is not already in place. This gives classroom teachers planning partners as well as coteachers. At one school, a team of second, third, and fourth grade teachers plans technology-based experiences that build over three years. Sometimes parents and community members express interest in helping with technology in a classroom, particularly if they have expertise that complements the teachers' skills. Teachers have invited high school or college students with interest in teaching or technology to become extra sets of hands in the classrooms.

VOICES OF EXPERIENCE

Lauren Brannan, former technology support teacher
J. E. Turner Elementary School, Wilmer, Alabama

Technology integration at our school is a fairly new concept. In the past, teachers were used to bringing their kids to the computer lab to play commercial games. Moving away from those commercial activities has been a challenge for us, but we are seeing more results from authentic, integrated lessons.

This year our classes were scheduled to visit the lab once per week for 30 or 45 minutes. I built my lab schedule around the schedule of the teachers. I have a weekly scheduled planning time with each grade level. This allows for time to plan integrated lessons. This collaboration has allowed our students to learn so much more this year. Not only are they learning useful technology skills, but they are also learning to use the new content in real-world situations.

Blogging allows our students to have a real audience to provide feedback about their work. Using a green screen for digital storytelling allows our students to place themselves in the setting of a story, a time in history, or raging weather. Integrating technology into the curriculum has motivated our students to learn and apply what they have learned.

Collaborations divide the work and time spent on tasks while increasing teachers' technology capacities. Novice teachers gain management tips through observing how experienced partners work. When problems arise, one partner can trouble-shoot while the other keeps the class moving ahead. When the collaboration works, it works well for everyone.

When collaborations do not work smoothly, partners may give students mixed or frustrating messages. Alternatively, partners may not agree on who bears which responsibilities. Consider creating a planning sheet that outlines the responsibilities for each partner. Later, after several experiences, the planning may not need to be as detailed. If your personalities clash when you try to work together, both of you need to find different partners. Try to find someone whose personal qualities and technical expertise better complement yours.

Project-Based Learning

Project-based learning (PBL) is a specific learning approach that engages teams of students in investigating and responding to complex questions or challenges.

Thomas (2000) defined project-based learning as having five components:

1. The projects are central to the curriculum, not peripheral.

2. The problems or challenges drive students to encounter and struggle with the essential concepts and principles of the content area.

3. Students construct new understandings through their investigations.

4. The projects are, to a large extent, driven by students, not prescribed.

5. The projects are realistic and authentic.

Students are given driving, intriguing problem-solving projects, such as, "Design a study, including the best destination, for you and your colleagues to research how giraffes communicate" (i.e, use any problem that will involve students' meeting curricular objectives while researching material they find compelling). Another one might be something like this: "On Hawaii Island, Kilauea continues to erupt. Scientists think the park should be closed, but tour operators and restaurants are concerned closing the park will decrease tourism. Homeowners near Hilo and the Puna Coast are worried about whether they need to evacuate. County officials are requesting advice." Teams research, consult, and develop ways to convey their answers to authentic audiences. These studies may take days or even months, and technology can be involved at any and all phases. Projects often involve several content areas, illustrating to students that acquiring knowledge is an exciting process that relies upon expertise in many areas. Typically, project-based learning that incorporates technology supports multiple ISTE Standards•S.

Project-based learning is at the high end of Bloom's taxonomy and is highly constructivist and differentiated. Because students have timelines to meet, another advantage is that students have a responsibility to complete their work at the same time. Disadvantages include the difficulty of finding balance between teacher direction and student autonomy, the potential that students will tackle technology tools for which they do not have the skills, and the challenge of monitoring group work. For PBL to be effective, teachers need to schedule regular conferences with each team to manage the social relationships, academic requirements, and timeline demands.

VOICES OF EXPERIENCE

Linda Jones, fourth grade teacher
Lois Lenski Elementary School, Centennial, Colorado

I have 29 students in my fourth grade classroom with a computer for every student. This gives me the opportunity to have them work on computers two to three hours daily, working on writing assignments, research, and group collaboration. My use of computers started about twelve years ago with the use of only one computer. Gradually, as students were exposed to computers, learning took on a new look. Students were more interested in their assignments and learning became fun! Over time, we acquired enough computers so that each student could work with his/her own computer.

In my class, most projects start as reading assignments for science or social studies, then writing assignments, and finally oral presentations. Here's an example from early in the year: Animal reports (Science) combined with life zones of Colorado (Social Studies).

Continued

1. We start out with a whole class study of bighorn sheep. Every student is taught how to highlight the topic of each paragraph, ask questions, and give answers. We start with an essential question. Students decided on "Why is the bighorn sheep our state animal?" Using a nonfiction passage about bighorn, students consider one paragraph at a time. First, they highlight the topic of the paragraph in yellow. We read each paragraph and ask, "What question is it answering?" Second, they write the question in the margin. And, third, they highlight the answer in pink. We continue throughout the article. Example: If the paragraph is talking about the bighorn's coat (yellow highlight), the question could be as simple as, "What does the coat look like?" (The answer will be highlighted in pink.) Because our school uses Step Up to Writing color coding, students are used to thinking about the topic in yellow and details in pink (The Step Up to Writing program can be found at www.voyagersopris.com/curriculum/subject/literacy/step-up-to-writing-fourth-edition).

2. We organize our questions into categories such as description, adaptations, habitat, and protection. Students come up with basic organization ideas that fit their interest levels.

3. On the computer, I teach them to put their highlighting into three-column note form. Every category has its own box in column one.

Description with question (yellow)	Notes (pink)	Interesting facts (blue)
What does the coat look like?	Thick Double-layered Tan Shed in spring	The undercoat hairs are hollow for warmth.
Adaptations What adaptations do bighorns have for the mountain habitat?		

4. After students complete their notes, they write and type their essays.

5. We use a particular revision strategy, which colleagues and I invented, that ensures students will make significant revisions on their writing. Using Microsoft Word, students convert their essays to one-column tables with each sentence in its own row. This enables students to easily assess their work for organization (Do sentences support the main idea of the paragraph and flow logically?); sentence variety (Do sentences have varied beginnings, lengths, and subject-predicate structures?); word choice (Is the language rich and varied? Have I created mental images?); and, finally, conventions (Have I used correct spelling, punctuation, and grammar?)

6. In its final form, the essay has titles and subtitles, pictures, and a bibliography. We answer the essential question in the conclusion.

After this whole group experience, students pick individual Colorado animals to research. Using books and reputable websites for research, they take notes on their computers.

1. For research on the web, they copy only information answering their question and paste in a word processing document, making sure that the website is cited. Students print their web research and, as they were taught, highlight and take notes.

2. After they accumulate notes, they are ready to write individual reports and revise multiple times to ensure the text is lively. Students give the animals personalities and write as though the animals were keeping journals. Students use pictures (cited) and write captions for them to enliven the text.

3. They use Citation Machine (www.citationmachine.net) to cite their bibliographies.

At the end of this assignment, each student is responsible for an oral presentation. Each slide for their presentations can have only three main points with lots of pictures. They think of presentations as similar to their writing: an attention grabber, introduction, organization, stories, use of vocabulary, and conclusion. In their presentations, they embed

- Blabberize (http://blabberize.com) as an introduction

Continued

- Photo Story 3 (www.microsoft.com/download/en/details.aspx?id=11132) or Microsoft Movie Maker (http://windows.microsoft.com/en-us/windows-live/movie-maker) with pictures and their voices. Students are responsible for their own scripts.

A final note: This assignment is the catalyst for all projects in collaborative groups throughout the rest of the year. I start with individual projects first so when they are working in groups, I know they can contribute.

How you integrate technology is your choice. Others can assist you along the journey, but you control your classroom. The remaining chapters of this book provide ideas and projects. Browse until you find something that appeals to you that will enhance students' experiences in your classroom.

CHAPTER 4

Instructional Use of Technology

ONE WAY TO BEGIN to integrate technology into a class-room—and meet the needs of students with different learning preferences—is to use digital tools for instruction. Teachers can quickly begin to introduce more visual and kinesthetic/tactile materials into their instruction with a computer linked to a digital projector. Additional equipment can enhance instruction even more.

Instructional use of technology represents an initially easy, low-risk change to teaching methods. When teachers use instructional tools (digital equipment), teachers control how and when the tools are used. Because one of the current goals for K–12 education is that students will learn to manage and work with technology, this chapter can serve as a transitional step for teachers to gain confidence with tech tools. Ideally, instructional use of digital equipment becomes a shared experience, as students may make some decisions about what they would like to explore with the teacher's equipment setup.

Making a Case for Classroom Setups

The education world has not agreed on what constitutes a basic technology setup for teachers. At this point, most elementary teachers have at least one computer in their rooms for attending to the clerical aspects of education, such as taking attendance and entering grades. With just one computer, teachers are limited instructionally because gathering all the students around one computer is difficult at best. This setup does not meet teachers' or students' basic needs as they use tech tools to help with instruction.

At a minimum, the teacher's computer needs to be attached to a digital projector. With the addition of a projector linked to a computer, a teacher can show downloaded video clips, pull up primary source photographs and documents, and demonstrate websites. In some schools, teachers may need to share projectors on rolling carts. Ideally, schools will couple all teachers' computers with projectors as a minimal setup for each classroom. Once a computer image can be projected for everyone to see, students are likely to suggest that teachers help them look up words and verify facts. Most students already know how to do these things for themselves. Wise teachers will encourage these students to give their classmates impromptu lessons on how to navigate a website and use the computer's and projector's tools.

A third piece of equipment for a basic equipment setup is a document camera. Not all administrators see the value of document cameras; however, of all the digital tools, document cameras can transform instruction quickly for teachers who have hesitated to use technology. The stages of transformation often follow a linear path. Because document cameras are similar to overhead projectors, though more convenient, teachers quickly learn how to use them.

Then, as teachers discover how to toggle between the document camera and the computer, they begin to experience the convenience of alternating between computer-based materials and document camera materials, such as students' work, books, 3D objects, and pictures. Eventually, teachers are pleased to learn how easy it is to use the document camera as a camera and as a low-powered microscope. In a school where teachers had been using document cameras less than one week, one instructional coach could not find a single teacher willing to give up the document camera for a one-day demonstration at another school!

Choosing a Document Camera

Document cameras, or visual presenters, are priced between $250 and $1,700, depending on the features you choose. The following features are common on document cameras:

- **Ability to toggle between computer and document camera for projector.** Some low-end document cameras require switching the projector cord from the computer to the document camera and back. This is inconvenient, and teachers are less likely to take full advantage of the ability to project the computer screen if they have to keep changing cords. Given the choice, opt to keep the document camera hooked up to the projector.

- **Document bed.** Some document cameras come with an attached bed. The bed adds to the cost but is convenient because the dimensions of the bed define the viewing image. Beds typically also have lighting from beneath so transparent items can be viewed. However, most document cameras do not have beds, and teachers can still use them successfully.

- **Lighting.** To be most effective, document cameras should have a light source so that teachers are not dependent on the lighting in their classrooms, which may be poorly arranged for this purpose.

- **Portability.** This is only important if you present often at conferences or in professional development sites where you need to provide your own equipment and want to carry your camera with you.

- **Flexibility.** The document camera should bend and swivel because you may be trying to show items that either will not fit beneath it or need a close-up view.

- **Capacity to take pictures.** Though not necessary, when the document camera can capture pictures, teachers can digitize students' written work and drawings, as well as illustrations in books, science experiment steps, and many other things that might be of value for projects or sharing with parents. One teacher used this capacity to email photos of students' work to their parents.

Continued

■ **Magnification.** If you do not have a digital microscope in the classroom, it's handy to have one through the document camera. Document cameras can usually bend quite close to 3D objects, and magnifications of two or three times (2x or 3x) can fill the screen with details. Magnification is generally a feature of these cameras.

■ **Connection type.** Make sure that the connector will work with your computer and projector. Some document cameras have USB connectors, and some have monitor ports.

IPEVO (www.ipevo.com) sells a USB portable document camera for under $100. The IPEVO is versatile because it has a convenient camera button and comes with an attachment so that you can connect it as a webcam on a computer monitor. The document camera lacks a light source, which can be problematic in rooms with irregular lighting or glare. I bought the IPEVO document camera with a case and stand extender (otherwise, it projects only half a page) for a conference presentation. It was small, easy to carry, and, once I purchased a light to work with it, quite convenient. Other manufacturers are likely to create similar products.

When the opportunity presents itself to expand your basic classroom setup, other useful equipment to consider would be webcams (although the document camera can be swiveled to act as a webcam), headsets/microphones, and wireless mice with built-in laser pointers. Digital cameras and video cameras also expand the possibilities for instruction and student use.

Instructional Technology Ideas

How teachers use instructional technology is more important than what equipment is used. The following ideas for instruction should be applied when teachers are working with classes in large groups. Whole class work is appropriate at times but should not be teachers' only approach to instruction. Remember that some activities listed as instructional uses can just as easily be adapted for small groups, activity centers, or project-based learning.

VOICES OF EXPERIENCE

Diane E. Vyhnalek, retired first grade teacher
Lois Lenski Elementary School, Centennial, Colorado

A Day in the Life of a Document Camera in First Grade

I was introduced to using a document camera as an instructional tool in my classroom almost nine years ago by Boni Hamilton, then my school technology advisor. Now, the document camera has become my strongest partner for integrating technology and for empowering my students to be responsible for their learning. In order for me to have high expectations for my students' academic growth, as well as teaching them to self-assess, the document camera allows students to have independent practice along with my explicit teaching. Students need to see that we, as educators, do believe in them and their abilities to learn. Allowing them to use the document camera to show their learning allows students to have a voice.

Starting with daily orientation activities, the document camera greets students. I use it to model and clarify directions for seatwork. It serves as a model for demonstrating correct letter formation during handwriting practice and for showing how to write our numbers with the use of instructional poems. It is used for the morning message and calendar time. A daily cartoon from the comics is presented on the document camera. The message is covered, and students use their background knowledge merged with picture inference skills to determine what a possible caption might be. Students are given an opportunity to predict their thinking before seeing the artist's message.

The document camera is used to present lessons for daily phonics lessons. Students use the document camera to create words for their word work. Tile letters may be moved on the camera to show understanding of building words. The document camera helps all students, especially visual learners, to acquire skills and strategies needed to be successful readers.

Continued

The document camera is used during the reading block to create story webs, make chapter frames, build discussion webs together, and allow applications of different strategies needed for success in the genre studies. It allows for visually teaching the features of an informational text, so the students may then write their own informational texts on topics of their choice.

During the writing block, students are encouraged to work together to create story elements and participate in class editing of sample paragraphs. Students are invited to share their writing samples on the document camera, as well as present orally from their daily journals.

The document camera is connected to the projector through my computer. This connection allows for a scaffolding of activities that were not available before document cameras. It also allows us to access the computer lab via our school server, where students have their folders. In this way, students' folders are available for our classroom use, and parents are allowed access to their children's folders for conferences. Students often give their own PowerPoint presentations in our classroom, present research on science topics, and share poetry and other creative writing projects. In addition, this toggle connection allows me to share enrichment videos for all subject areas from our Discovery Education account.

The math instructional time becomes engaging with the document camera, as students model their thinking, demonstrate steps to solve problems, and use a variety of math manipulatives, such as discs, coins, rulers, and geometric shapes. When we discuss measuring the weather, the computer may be toggled with the document camera to share the current temperature, wind velocity, and forecast.

Social studies and science units are highlighted with the use of a document camera. In social studies, students share their self-authored books about family traditions, and as a class we look at the features of maps. Some of our favorite activities involve the class in talking and thinking about science. Science experiments and other science units of study are enhanced when the document camera zooms in to show exact body details of insects or pictorial captions and diagrams in nonfiction texts. Of course, the computer allows access to websites about animals, which can be projected for classroom discussions and brought up on students' individual computers.

The art teacher instructs weekly in our classroom, so she frequently uses the document camera for her instruction. The camera might be used to model the shapes students are using for their five-minute sketches or as a tool to model the steps needed for a particular art lesson. An art show is created when students share their work on the document camera.

As you can see, the possibilities of using the document camera in primary classrooms are limitless, as we educators become informed about this and the many other uses of technology to support our teaching.

A portion of every elementary school day involves whole class activities. The purposes of the activities may be to:

- Develop background knowledge prior to studying a unit
- Model an activity or skill
- Read
- Demonstrate
- Solve a problem
- Explore
- Review information
- Respond to or critique an idea or sample
- Appeal to other senses
- Engage students in thinking about and discussing an idea
- Reach outside the walls of the classroom.

While the use of technology may not be essential for every whole class activity, the addition of instructional tech tools adds to teachers' capacity to engage all students. The basic setup enables teachers to expand the use of visual and kinesthetic/tactile experiences, even during large group activities. Consider the following examples of how teachers can enhance instruction by using technology tools.

Develop Background Knowledge

When students lack background knowledge about a subject, they struggle to comprehend the concepts. The use of pictures can make content come alive for students. For example, to introduce a novel set in Venice, a fifth grade teacher used Google Earth and online photographs. Students were then better able to comprehend the novel's context because they could visualize it. A primary teacher used personal photos and zoo memorabilia to prepare her students for a field trip to the zoo. A first grade teacher toggled among an actual dragonfly carcass on the document camera, a website with photos of dragonflies, and a video clip to introduce a unit on insects. By incorporating web resources and real objects to introduce units, teachers can give all students simultaneous visual, auditory, and tactile experiences before units begin.

Model an Activity or Skill

Students have more success with new processes when teachers model the skills. A first grade teacher not only modeled how to write the month on lined paper, but also invited students to compare their writing to hers. Because she used the same paper as they did, students could set their work next to the teacher's for comparison. Interactive writing of paragraphs has gained popularity in classrooms; most teachers have used large chart paper for this. Using a piece of lined, student paper on a document camera can accomplish the same goal. Students and teachers have access to the teacher's sample after the lesson is done. In math, students can place their solutions on the document camera and explain their thinking. Video clips can model a procedure, such as graphing. As reported in Chapter 3, Linda Jones models how to take notes, first by projecting a nonfiction article and highlighting important information, and then by entering the notes into a three-column table in a word processing file.

Read

Primary students often read chorally from big books. However, big books are expensive, and not all school or classroom libraries have extensive collections. Teachers can project the pages of a book onto a screen and invite students to read in unison. When teachers have access to only one copy of a book, that copy can be placed on a document camera or scanned into slideshows. Teachers of older students can project the pages of a book during a mini-lesson so that students can pay attention to writing conventions or stylistic choices. When learning test-taking skills, classes can read sample instructions or test questions to analyze the tasks. Reading story problems together can build students' skills as well. One of my favorite reading activities for elementary classrooms is accessing online stories or songs (which typically last 3–5 minutes) for transitions between activities. Singing a song or listening to a story podcast can motivate students to move quickly and quietly during cleanup or when they are lining up for supplemental classes such as music, art, or physical education.

Demonstrate

Science teachers, in particular, despair of having every child see a demonstration of a lab procedure when students crowd around their teachers. When document cameras are used, students stay seated, and the teacher projects the steps of the experiment for all to see. One fifth grade teacher conducted the experiment in advance of class, captured each step with the document camera's photography interface, and placed the photos in a slideshow. During the experiment, student teams completed each step simultaneously, and the teacher projected the slides to demonstrate what they should see. Equipped with a wireless mouse and a laser pointer, the teacher circulated among the teams, advanced the slides, and used the laser to highlight particular sections of photographs.

Solve a Problem

Although we may think of problems primarily in terms of math, consider the variety of problems students may encounter during school days. A counselor showed students video clips and photographs of conflicts at school, then invited the students to discuss how they could solve the problems. A writing teacher showed the class a student's well-written paper and asked the students to suggest where the writer could expand the text with additional examples. Classmates came up with three places where the writer could append additional text to a hand-written paper without having to erase and rewrite the rest of the sentences.

Explore

Numerous websites lend themselves to whole group exploration, discovery, and engagement: consider a series of video clips from NASA; a preliminary visit to a visual manipulatives site, such as http://nlvm.usu.edu/en/nav/vlibrary.html; or a literacy site with good content written at a higher reading level than the students can manage, for example, www.magickeys.com/books. A third grade teacher combined an exploration of the Scholastic Interactive Tour of Ellis Island site (http://teacher.scholastic.com/activities/immigration/tour) with a series of primary source photographs of immigrant families to trigger rich conversations about what students noticed. Placing a 3D object on a document camera allows students to examine its details simultaneously. For instance, one teacher brought a series of rocks and gems to class, placed them on the document camera, and asked students to identify and classify them.

Review Information

Some teachers like to download or create games for whole class reviews of content, especially before a test or to teach test-taking skills. Students can also create their own electronic K-W-L (What I Know, What I Wonder, and What I Learned) charts and revisit them every week or so to update their accomplishments. In one classroom, after students master material in a particular unit, the teacher periodically displays the pretest questions and asks students to answer them; this shows them how much they have learned and encourages them to continue learning. A group of teachers uses student-created slideshows to review vocabulary words.

Respond to or Critique an Idea or Sample

Having trouble getting students to work toward excellence in their projects? Show an example from an earlier year or one you've made, and have students create a rubric based on their critique of the sample. Writing lessons lend themselves to critique; with a student's permission, teachers can show a sample and ask the class to discuss the strengths of the work along with ideas for improvement. In kindergarten, a teacher used the document camera to magnify students' show-and-tell objects. All students could see and respond to the samples without waiting for the objects to be passed around.

Appeal to Other Senses

While most students can learn from several modes of instruction, some students crave visuals or hands-on experiences because their most effective learning styles are visual or kinesthetic. Talking with these students fails to keep their minds engaged. Of course, auditory learners understand best when they are listening to speech, music, or other sounds. Teachers can reinforce learning through visual or multimedia stimuli, such as video clips. Interactive websites, students' demonstrations of their work, the study of 3D objects, and complementary activities that require students to work at their desks or in teams to check against what is on the screen (i.e., using manipulatives, finding main ideas, solving problems, and creating art) make learning more active for students.

Engage Students in Thinking about and Discussing Ideas

As a warm-up for teaching thinking skills, a teacher showed one-panel comics and asked students to think about what was happening to the characters in the comic, as well as outside the comic, that is, what actions might have occurred before and what actions could occur later, as a result of the comic. Comics can teach inference, vocabulary, punctuation conventions, visual literacy, and sometimes even cultural references.

Another teacher often used provocative editorials for students to analyze. They considered where and why the arguments were strong, misleading, or misinformed. The goal was critical thinking about persuasive writing, and students loved the activity.

Concept cartoons are excellent ways to generate conversations and tease out possible misconceptions. In a concept cartoon, characters make statements about a concept, one that the teacher is introducing or one that the students are studying. Each character takes a different point of view, with several characters stating misconceptions that students may have. Students think about the statements and align themselves with one viewpoint. Through discussion, students eliminate incorrect or illogical ideas to identify the correct concept.

A variation of the concept cartoon would show characters making statements representing various points of view about a topic on which students have different opinions. For instance, the comic characters could disagree about a decision made by a character in a book they have studied, or the disagreement could be a debate on the best location for NASA's next exploration. This type of dialogue helps students learn about and understand valid points of view that may differ from their own.

Figure 4.1 Concept cartoon created by Boni Hamilton in Comic Creator at ReadWriteThink (www.readwritethink.org/files/resources/interactives/comic)

Reach beyond School Walls

If you want students to be excited about learning, use the internet to connect with someone in another location, even a classroom down the hall. Skype is the most common way teachers facilitate communication outside the classroom, and anyone with an internet connection can use Skype for free. The potential for teleconferencing boggles the mind. Students can talk to experts, students in other classrooms, and individuals who are exploring unusual places or creating fascinating objects. In one school, students kept in contact with a young man as he hiked across several countries. Many classes correspond with others through email and then participate in face-to-face teleconferences. The Skype an Author Network (http://skypeanauthor.wikifoundry.com) connects students with authors and illustrators who enjoy discussing their writing and artistic processes. One teacher used Skype as a classroom management reward: When students earned enough good behavior points, they called the teacher's mother and met the teacher's dogs.

Presentation Slideshows as Instructional Material

After teaching preservice teachers for the past few years, I've become aware of how much presentation slideshows, such as PowerPoint, have saturated the education world. Almost every preservice teacher considered slideshows the best way to teach with technology. Unfortunately, typical bulleted slideshows replicate a lecturer writing notes on the board—a great way to lull your students to sleep. If you would like to use slideshows as effective instructional tools in your classroom, consider the following guidelines.

Use photos, not bulleted notes or clip art. In visual presentations, bulleted notes signal that students do not have to listen or participate, just copy. A good photo will trigger emotion in the viewer. Students' responses open doors for conversations about what is and is not in pictures. When students learn to read pictures or illustrations, they strengthen their inference, critical thinking and visual literacy skills. By identifying details of objects, individuals, and environments, they learn to draw inferences. In addition, they retain what they see longer than what they hear, and become more conscious of how visuals contribute to understanding of ideas.

Want to spark students' motivation to acquire background knowledge? Project relevant pictures and let students infer what the pictures mean. Want to provoke deeper thinking? Show pictures of student work and have students analyze them. Teaching internet safety and responsible use? Capture screenshots of online forms or webpages for students to discuss as safe or unsafe. Cartoons and humor can make new information memorable as well. A concept cartoon can capture any controversial or many-sided topic on which students may have differing opinions or understandings. Clip art, categorized by one astute student as "the lowest bid art," looks like a decoration and rarely elicits an emotional response other than derision.

Stop talking. Each time a new slide appears, presenters need to give the audience at least 30 seconds to scan the visual and think about the new idea. Then, if explanations are needed, ask questions: What do you notice? How does this relate to what we are studying? Let students construct shared knowledge. Encourage them to disagree, question, press a viewpoint, and be willing to

Continued

change their thinking. Even if the slideshow is a demonstration of an experiment, students will learn more if they construct an explanation based on the picture than if the teacher tells them what they should notice.

Skip the animations and transitions. Animations and transitions in slideshows expose presenters as beginners. Such tricks either annoy or distract audiences. The goal is to convey meaning, not entertain.

Be clear about the message. When the slideshows end, audiences (students) should have a clear understanding of why teachers created the shows. Creating a show should not take more time than learning from it. Use slideshows to provoke student discussions. They learn more from listening and reacting to one another than from hearing a teacher's interpretations.

Peripheral Instructional Tools

Not every instructional technology use requires a projector, computer, and document camera. In fact, some of the most powerful instructional tools cost less than a computer. Typically, these tools work best for small group or one-on-one instructional purposes.

Digital Audio Recorders

Digital audio recorders cost $40 and up, depending on the features you choose. While students will find many uses for recorders in their work, teachers can benefit from using recorders as well. An important instructional use for recorders occurs during reading assessments. Teachers can record students' reading assessments for multiple purposes. First, novices in administering reading assessments can check their original notes against the recordings or can use the recordings to practice running records. A first-year third grade teacher reported that knowing she had recordings relieved the stress of assessing her readers, while she built her skills in administering an individualized reading inventory. Because her students expressed curiosity about the recordings, she allowed them to listen to themselves—and discovered additional purposes for the recordings. The students compared what they had read into the recorder with the original text. They not only caught decoding mistakes, but also recognized when they were not reading fluently. Students became more purposeful in attending to their oral reading, and some students asked to record subsequent readings to determine whether they had improved. These digital recordings became portfolios to document students' improvements. The teacher could email the files to parents, play them at parent-teacher conferences, and have students listen to the files to see how much their reading had improved. By having access to the digital recordings, students felt empowered as monitors of their reading growth.

A speech and language teacher used digital recordings of her students to document their improvements in producing problematic speech sounds. Like the third grade teacher, she found that students valued and gained confidence from auditory evidence that their speech was improving in clarity.

Digital Audio Recorders

A digital audio recorder is a fancy way of referring to a modern voice recorder. In the past, we used the term "tape recorder" because those devices collected sounds on spooled or cassette tapes; modern recorders collect files digitally. Typically, a digital audio recorder looks like a miniature cassette recorder but attaches to a computer through a USB (universal serial bus) connector. A digital audio recorder typically contains multiple folders to organize hours of recordings. When a digital audio recorder's USB connector is attached to a computer's USB port, digital files can be transferred easily. When a USB connector on any peripheral device (such as a digital audio recorder, camera, flash drive, printer, or scanner) is plugged into a computer's USB port, the computer automatically reads the files stored on the peripheral device. All you have to do is create and label separate file folders on your computer where you can save this material for easy access.

MP3 Players

Although an MP3 player can be used as a digital audio recorder, many MP3 players can also manage videos and pictures. Teachers often think first of iPods as the only brand of MP3 player and despair of affording them, but reasonably robust, 4G MP3 players are available for less than $50.

Loading materials onto any MP3 player follows essentially the same procedures, so teachers do not need high levels of technology expertise. The greater challenge is figuring out how to access the loaded material for playback, but students typically solve that problem much faster and more intuitively than adults do. As instructional tools, MP3 players provide versatility because teachers can load audio files, music, pictures, and videos. Each has its own value.

Audio files might include the reading assessment, a student's storytelling performance, or podcasts of books. A kindergarten teacher asked upper-grade students to create podcasts of books her students would read in guided reading. She loaded the stories onto MP3 players and sent the books and players home with struggling readers and English language learners (ELLs). They and their parents listened to the stories and followed along in the books. Not only did having familiarity with the books improve students' confidence the following day, but parents of the ELL students also acquired higher-level English skills. On the teacher's computer, she has a collection of audio files to send home with students at any time. Annually, she recruits new readers to increase her podcast collection.

Websites sometimes offer podcasts, and local libraries have downloadable audio files of books. Students who read below grade level can feel left out when their peers discuss books. Giving these students audio books of popular grade-level texts allows them to get excited about books and join the conversations.

Music files at the elementary level may include songs used in music classes for performances; ditties that review content (the alphabet, numbers, or science content, such as the water cycle); or classroom routine songs, such as cleanup time, that make chores more fun. Students enjoy listening to recordings of their classmates and themselves as well.

If teachers own music CDs and are using them for educational purposes, they can load the songs onto players for use with students without violating copyright. Use music recordings to enhance poetry or songwriting units, build background knowledge about a historic period, familiarize students with famous composers, or introduce a culture.

Picture files of classroom activities can be loaded to initiate conversations within families and keep parents informed and involved. Teachers who want students to practice picture-reading skills may also provide pictures that the students and their families can 'read' together. This may give teachers insights about the differences among families and cultures.

When videos came only as 30- to 45-minute movies, and sometimes in reels rather than cassettes, sending a video home to build background knowledge was difficult, if not impossible. Today teachers can access downloadable video clips that students can watch and discuss with their families. When students struggle to learn visually (as I do), the chance for repeated viewing of video clips improves mastery of the material.

VOICES OF EXPERIENCE

Sally Brown, associate professor of literacy
Georgia Southern University, Statesboro, Georgia

Would you like to renew your students' interest in and enjoyment of reading? The Nook is just one tool that will reengage students with reading. E-readers can motivate and excite students through unique features that are not possible with paper books. I chose the Nook e-readers to use along with a diverse group of primary readers because they are cost-effective and offer picture books in color. Specifically, the Nook offers read-to-me and read-and-play books. The read-and-play books offer interactive activities, like floating the cursor over pictures to see the word in print. The Nook uses the EPUB format with ebooks, allowing you to have access to many more books than an e-reader like the Kindle, which uses its own format.

I purchased six Nooks to use with students in small groups for guided reading and literature circles. Below are some insights based on my experiences using Nooks with young readers.

Continued

■ Make wise choices about the ebooks you purchase. There are many ebooks available for less than a dollar. Most of these books are low quality and do not connect to students' interests. Instead, spend more money to get quality children's literature. It is worth the investment. With the Nook you can pay for an ebook once and upload it to six Nooks at no additional charge.

■ Many ebooks for the Nook offer a "read to me" section. This allows students who may be struggling readers to listen to a story in advance of reading it. Students can also listen to a story after reading it themselves to enhance fluency. The newest version of the Nook allows students to record themselves reading an ebook.

■ At the chapter book level, the Nook offers multiple features that young readers find helpful. For example, students can operate the bookmarking, dictionary, note-taking, highlighting, and multiple font size features.

■ One advantage of the e-reader is the anonymity of the books being read. No one knows what you are reading when you are using an e-reader. This is important for students who may be reading below grade level. As these students may be embarrassed about the books they can read independently, the e-reader allows them to conceal this information.

■ I recommend purchasing some type of skin or covering and screen protectors for your nooks. Nooks seem to be pretty durable with an added layer of protection. These are relatively inexpensive and worth the investment.

■ Nooks have Wi-Fi, so they can connect to the internet. This has been an asset because it allows students to engage with technology in ways other than e-reading. Just know that obtaining permission for these devices to connect to the internet on a school district server may involve overcoming some hurdles. Even if you do not want students to use the internet, you will need access to download your ebooks and update the Nooks. You can disable the Wi-Fi application to prevent students from surfing the internet.

E-readers

E-readers are becoming more cost-effective as tools for the classroom. Teachers can borrow texts from public libraries for e-readers when school libraries lack high-interest books for specific students. Alternatively, teachers can buy digital books and download them onto one to six readers (according to most e-reader agreements) for studying a book. Most e-readers offer note taking, text highlighting, text-to-speech capability, text resizing, and built-in dictionaries. Teachers can use the note-taking feature to reinforce prereading strategies or to initiate reading purposes by asking questions. Another benefit is that what students read is private; students with lower or higher reading levels or those who need large print versions are not stigmatized by the thickness of the book.

Digital Cameras

Although students will use digital cameras for their work more often than teachers will (see Chapter 7, Digital Still Cameras), teachers can use pictures for instructional purposes. For instance, when students are prereaders, photos can reinforce expectations, such as how the room should look at the end of the day, the procedures for borrowing a book from the classroom library, where things belong in the classroom, the equipment that goes into each bin, and other managerial tasks. Teachers can also reinforce appropriate behavior by snapping photos of students doing things well—as long as the photos capture different students and, eventually, all students. Younger students may need picture reminders of important people in the school, including janitors, playground supervisors, and bus drivers.

Photos also provide visual ways for bilingual children to "see" concepts under study as they are building academic language. For instance, teachers can take photos of a bread slice in stages of decomposition to demonstrate "change over time". Showing the photos illustrates the concept in a memorable way. Develop an eye for photo opportunities that illustrate curricular concepts and keep your camera handy.

Documentation panels serve as another excellent instructional use for digital cameras. Documentation panels can be made at any grade level by students, as teacher-student collaborations, or by the teacher alone. The purpose of the panels is to illustrate various facets of the students' learning in process. The photos show students as they are engaged in learning activities, including progressive steps of creating artifacts, such as writings, drawings, diagrams, charts, slideshows, videos, and 3D objects.

Photographs and objects are arranged in sequence on a panel, such as a science fair trifold, a bulletin board, or poster board, so that viewers can see at a glance how students went about acquiring knowledge related to a learning goal. The learning goal should be stated at the top and the sequence of photos and artifacts numbered. Picture captions and/or quotations from students throughout their learning finish off the panel.

When posted, panels should be self-explanatory. Teachers can use them to communicate to parents, administrators, and visitors how learning happens in the classroom. Students can make documentation panels of how-to sequences or the stages of an experiment. Whatever the topic, documentation panels make the learning process visible.

Documentation Panels

Documentation panels show how the process of learning unfolds in school. Although originally used for preschools, documentation panels fit into all classrooms. Teachers or students can create documentation panels on poster boards or bulletin boards to illustrate the learning process. Documenters post digital photos with captions that show the stages or steps of learning and may include student quotes and artifacts, such as drawings or charts.

For instance, at the primary level, observers may think of library visits as fun times for students—listening to the librarian or teacher reading books aloud and checking out their own books—but not as learning experiences. To demonstrate how library visits comprise effective education, librarians can show evidence of student learning by creating a documentation panel that illustrates the following:

Photos of students learning from activities	Captions about what students learn during library activities	Students' quotes about what they learned from library activities
Students listening to a story	While listening to stories, students imagine, make predictions about, and connect to children's literature.	"I liked acting out the story during story time. It was a fun book."

Librarian holding several books during a book talk	Students learn about books and authors new to them.	"I like it when the librarian tells us about new books."
Students at bookshelves	Students learn how to locate fiction and nonfiction books on library shelves.	"I want a book about snakes. That's nonfiction, and I can find it on these shelves."
Student using a shelf marker while looking at a book	Students place a marker on the shelf when they remove a book. If they decide not to check out the book, they'll remember where it goes.	"You have to put a marker to save your place so if you don't want the book, you can put it back."
Student using the five-finger method to choose an appropriate book	Students learn how to tell if a book is just right for them.	"I like chapter books, but some are too hard for me."
Students at a puppet area or a listening station	Students discover other learning possibilities in the library.	"I like borrowing puppets to play at home."
Students at the checkout desk	Students learn to take responsibility for books they borrow and return them on time.	"This hole is where the books go when you return them."
Students sitting and reading	Students read while they wait patiently for their classmates.	"I found my book fast, so I can start reading right away!"

By documenting the learning that happens during a library visit, the librarian makes the high educational value of a library program public. Parents and visitors can scan the panel quickly and comprehend the types of learning experiences children have.

Whether documentation panels are created by teachers, librarians, or students, the processes of collecting pictures, quotes, and artifacts, as well as developing short, informative captions cause the documenter to reflect on what was important and to communicate it to an audience.

Video Cameras

Although primarily student tools, video cameras can be used instructionally as well. For instance, teachers can videotape students' class presentations so that the students can self-assess and set goals for future presentations. Just as teachers do not know how they appear to students (a video of me showed a nervous habit of putting my hand on my head while I spoke), students cannot tell how they perform for audiences. As videos can be viewed and viewed again, they benefit the presenters.

One teacher videotaped students as they told and acted out stories they wanted to write. The class responded to each story with compliments and suggestions for improvement. The storyteller immediately retold the story, which was again video-taped. The two videos served the purposes of capturing models for future events, allowing the storyteller to see both performances, and providing auditory and visual details the storyteller could include in a written representation of the story.

VOICES OF EXPERIENCE

Ayana Jackson, kindergarten teacher
Garrison Elementary, Washington, District of Columbia
ayana.jackson@dc.gov

I am a first-year kindergarten teacher at an urban school in Washington, DC. I am working in a school that has adopted the Tools of the Mind curriculum for early childhood learners. The Tools of the Mind curriculum focuses heavily on using dramatization among students as a way for them to comprehend texts and connect with each other.

Our first theme in the beginning of the year was fairy tales. We would spend one week per fairy tale. Each day after reading the story, the students were respon-sible for going to our centers and acting out the story in a group. After the first week, I found that many of my students had no idea what role playing should look like. So, after going over this skill, I noticed a new problem. By the end of the week, the students were unmotivated and bored with acting out the same story.

That weekend I went home and thought about how I could help the students enjoy our dramatization activity. What was it that could motivate them to work harder to become better actors? That Monday I went to school and told the students that we would start to have recording days, when they would come in the front of the class and act out the story to make a movie. I showed the students the camera that I would be using and how they would be able to see themselves on the computer when they were done.

I told students that each day I would be coming around and that only the groups that were working hard at practicing their roles would be able to make a movie at the end of the week. When I decided on this plan, I did not imagine that it would have the success it had in my classroom. My students went from hating acting to begging me for more time. When Friday came and I announced it was our first recording day, the class was flooded with excitement. There were five groups, each with three to four students. Each group was given two minutes to go in front of the class to make its movie. At the end of the day, we watched all of the movies on my computer.

I must admit that choosing to incorporate this technology into my classroom had many more benefits than I had originally intended. I decided to add this "recording day" just as a way to help students stop being miserable in acting. But that actually became the smallest of my victories. Students learned to work together in a way that no formal lesson could ever have taught them. They learned to hold themselves and their classmates accountable. They surpassed my goals by going above and beyond the original standards of dramatization. And I have none other than a little ol' digital camera to thank for that.

Think of the video camera as a visual learning tool. When teachers tell students what to do, students may comprehend something quite different from the teachers' intentions. When students see what to do, teachers know that students are less likely to get different messages. One teacher showed a video of a book discussion in a middle school class to demonstrate to current students her expectations for their discussions. Teachers have videotaped science experiments, math problem solving, social studies reenactments, student performances, and other group events to share with future classes or with current parents. Elementary teachers can tape students during transition times, in the cafeteria, or on the playground to generate conversations with students or parents about behaviors that are working well and others that need to change.

The effective use of instructional technology encourages active participation by students, which keeps them involved and places much of the learning load on them. From my experiences and those of other teachers, learning to use instructional technology tools takes an initial commitment of time and energy. We now know that our willingness to use these tools results in students' deeper understanding and greater excitement about learning. If you are not using instructional technology, please find a simple idea in this chapter and implement it. Test the results. You may find new energy in your classroom—your students' and your own.

CHAPTER 5

Downloadable Software

SCHOOLS TODAY have less use for downloadable software than in the past. Yet some software programs make life easier or engage students in tasks that stretch them academically without straining the budget. For teachers who want to use learning centers, some of these downloadable software packages might be worth installing on classroom computers.

Productivity Software

Computers do not need productivity software loaded on them when students can use Google Apps for Education to create documents, spreadsheets, and presentations, but I find that Google Apps are not always enough for what students and teachers may want to do. Additionally, if the network crashes, students cannot log on to Google Apps or other online programs. As OpenOffice has a similar look to Microsoft Office with many of the same capabilities, schools can choose this free productivity suite for computers as a supplement to Google products. At the primary level in particular, using Google Apps may not be feasible. Schools could start young children out with OpenOffice for Kids (OOo4Kids) instead.

OpenOffice for Kids (OOo4Kids) (www.unixmen.com/openoffice-for-kids-ooo4kids) not only is a free office productivity suite for kids, but has also simplified everything about introducing kids to productivity software. The software is available for all platforms. (The OOo4Kids link is in English. The developer's site, http://educoo.org, is written in French.) This product resulted from OpenOffice.org's education project, which had the goal of creating a productivity suite that would span ages 7–12 with simplified interfaces. The opening screen is icon-driven and uncluttered. Students pick which of the four types of programs they want to open: document, spreadsheet, presentation, or drawing. Setting the user experience to one of three levels, from novice to expert, restricts or expands the toolbars while students learn navigation of the program. This may replace elementary school student versions of Microsoft Office without anyone complaining.

OpenOffice (www.openoffice.org) is the adult version of the free productivity software. For the typical tasks that older students and adults accomplish in productivity software, OpenOffice has the same functions as Microsoft Office at no cost to the consumer. If schools use OpenOffice for Kids as an introductory program, OpenOffice will feel more intuitive for older students than any other productivity suite.

Complementary Tools Software

Sometimes software packages extend the capacity of computers as tools. Students can access dictionaries and thesauri online, but sometimes teachers want an off-line tool that will offer the same service without hitting the internet. Or, and this is important at the elementary level, students need help reading text that is presented to them either online or in files on their computers.

WordWeb (http://wordweb.info/free) is a free download, although there is a paid pro version. The software embeds a dictionary/thesaurus with audio pronunciation of 5,000 words on your computer. Although the same features can be accessed through several online services, installing WordWeb gives better functionality to older computers or those not accessing the internet. This software package is specific to Windows, although a Mac OS X version is available through its App store (see www.wordwebsoftware.com/mac for more information).

NaturalReader (www.naturalreaders.com), available for both Windows and Mac computers, is a text-to-speech software that reads aloud highlighted text with natural sounding voices. This free, read-aloud program enables students to listen to texts that might be above their reading levels. A floating NaturalReader toolbar can sit on the desktop and be activated at any time. NaturalReader reads aloud any written text, such as webpages, PDF files, word processed documents, and emails. NaturalReader's optical character recognition (OCR) function works with a scanner to convert printed characters into digital text, allowing users to listen to texts on their computers or edit texts in a word-processing program. Although a pro version is available, the free version has sufficient capacity for most students.

Supplemental Project Tools

When teachers begin projects, such as podcasting and digital storytelling, they might not immediately find all the tools they need online. Many of us have found that using the following free tools makes creating higher-level projects much easier.

Audacity (http://audacity.sourceforge.net) is free audio editing software for all operating systems. Audacity has online manuals and tips, but I've never seen students access them. Instead, students are far more likely to experiment with software and share their expertise with peers. Audacity can be used for sound in movies and for podcasts. Tutorials on how to use Audacity are available through Teacher Training Videos by Russell Stannard (www.teachertrainingvideos.com).

Photo Story 3 (www.microsoft.com/en-us/download/details.aspx?id=11132) can still be downloaded at Microsoft. Although it is listed as suitable for computers running Windows XP or earlier versions, I loaded it on my Windows 7 computer without any difficulty. This software is Windows' best option right now for digital storytelling, because the step-by-step software is easy to use with students and can be made simple or complex to fit students' skills and available time. Students in second through sixth grades can usually master the basic features in less than an hour, although younger students may need support recording their voices, depending on their experience.

Format Factory (www.formatoz.com) is a free file converter for Windows. If you need to convert audio, video, picture, or document files so that they can be used on other devices, this software makes it easy. Though other free converters are available and may be just as efficient, Format Factory is the conversion freeware I use.

Mobipocket Creator 4.2 (www.mobipocket.com/en/downloadSoft/ ProductDetailsCreator.asp) is free software that converts PDF, .doc, or .html files into fully formatted ebook files that will run on any .mobi-enabled e-readers, like Kindle. The free Mobipocket eBook Reader can be downloaded onto mobile devices. Students can also create illustrated books, save them as PDF files, and use the software to convert them.

Student Resources

Software that encourages students to imagine, experiment, solve problems, think critically, and create original work cannot be ignored. These skills are exactly the ones we want students to develop. The following software packages may keep curiosity alive in some students for the rest of their lives. Another joy of these software packages is that they are free for students to download at home. So, while students may get only a cursory exposure to the programs at school, they can use the programs in after-school settings and at home for further explorations.

Google Earth (www.google.com/earth) is familiar to teachers, but in its infancy it was rather clunky to use. Now many schools have the bandwidth to manage Google Earth smoothly. Explore the Google Earth educator community for lesson plans and tips (www.google.com/earth/educators).

Tux Paint (www.tuxpaint.org) turns students into digital artists. A free, computer art program for students ages 3–12, the software works on all platforms as well as with older computers. The program can be set to print or not, as desired. Download the additional stamp package if any of your students like stamps. The program has some coloring pages, but my preference is that students create original pictures.

Paint.NET (www.getpaint.net) is a free image and photo editing software program for Windows only (including Windows 7). The features of the program probably surpass the needs of elementary student photographers, but the program might work well for secondary students.

Interactive Learning Software

Most of the learning software listed here is appropriate for elementary students who need guidance in using computers. Software for more mature computer users, such as for programming and robotics, appear in the chapters where those skills are discussed.

Sebran (www.wartoft.se/software/sebran) sits somewhere between skill drill software and discovery, which means my reaction is lukewarm. Meant for PK–1 students, some activities seem simply to drill students on skills like alphabet and number recognition, but others push students to make connections that generally come at higher grade levels, such as computation. The graphic designs, music, sound effects, and games are pleasing and fun, and the program comes in several languages. Specific to Windows computers, Sebran's exploration software can stretch young students' knowledge of letters and numbers, especially when teachers are looking for much more than drill software.

Seterra 4.0 (www.seterra.net) is freeware that teaches and assesses geography knowledge and is specific to Windows computers. This geography quiz game, developed by the same creator as Sebran, receives the same lukewarm response from me for the same reason. Though Seterra has the potential to give students geography awareness through trial and error, I am concerned that it will be used only as a map memorization game in too many classrooms.

Free software for computers, except for iPad and phone applications, has decreased because providing services over the internet has increased. In fact, most of the software packages discussed in this chapter could be emulated at some level online. The difference is that the software, once downloaded, can be run even when the network crashes. Since that happens occasionally, loading computers with these software programs may feel like a blessing on a very tough day.

Downloadable Software Highlighted in this Chapter

PROGRAM	PLATFORM	FOCUS	GRADE LEVEL	COMMENTS
Audacity	All	Audio editor	3+	
Format Factory	Windows	Converts audio, video, pictures, & documents	3+	Easy to use, need to pay attention to where files save
Google Earth	All	World map	All	Join the community for lesson ideas
Mobipocket Creator	Windows	Create ebooks	3+	
Natural Reader	Windows & Mac	Text reader	All	Reads any text aloud
OpenOffice	All	Productivity	All	Adult version, saves in other formats
OpenOffice for Kids (OOo4Kids)	All	Productivity	K–5	Three levels of complexity
Paint.NET	Windows	Photo editing	3+	Powerful enough for adults
Photo Story 3	Windows	Digital storytelling	2+	Is no longer supported by Microsoft but still works well
Sebran	Windows	Content variety	PK–1	Be selective; some aspects are drill, some discovery
Seterra	Windows	Geography	K–4	Use for gaining knowledge, not map memorization
Tux Paint	All	Drawing	All	Pay attention to where files save
WordWeb	Windows & Mac	Dictionary	All	5,000 pronunciations, many more words

CHAPTER 6

Interactive Internet

INTERACTIVE WEBSITES for students can play significant roles in building students' knowledge and skills. Websites are often particularly useful for activity centers and computer lab experiences when teachers are not using technology tools for project-supported learning.

On the following pages, you will not find websites that simply drill students on facts or skills. Too many schools waste scarce funds by loading expensive software onto classroom computers only for students to drill math facts, punctuation marks, spelling mastery, basic reading skills, and so forth. Exactly the same types of drills are available free on the internet; however, drills for memorization are rarely effective interventions. Students who have already mastered the skills don't need them, and those who struggle do too much guessing that reinforces their misconceptions. The internet has many other, much more engaging sites for students.

Students can build background knowledge, extend their learning, reinforce their understanding, or assess themselves through interactive websites. These websites are worth bookmarking when they fit with your curricular goals. The following websites are primarily geared to elementary students, as secondary students have much more independence in selecting and using website resources.

Multiple Content Area Interactives

The word "interactives" is an abbreviated term used to refer to interactive media, interactive systems, or interactive devices. When products and services on digital, computer-based systems respond to (i.e., interact with) individual user's input with specialized content, such as text, graphics, animation, video, and audio (or any combination of these), these devices or software are categorized as interactive.

Johnnie's Story Page (http://jstorypage.com) and Johnnie's Math Page (http://jmathpage.com) aggregate literacy and math resources for young students at primary and intermediate grade levels. The story pages hold links to video stories on several websites across the internet. Story links are sorted into Stories for Beginning Readers, Classic Stories for All Readers, and Stories for Older Readers. This is a more convenient way for getting to stories than bookmarking the separate websites. However, not all online stories appear in this aggregator site, so use it as only one source for online stories. The math pages are sorted by math strands and math for interactive whiteboards. Like the stories, math links are available sorted into primary and intermediate grade levels.

Toy Theater (www.toytheater.com) may have been designed as a safe garden of activities for preschool and primary children, though some activities will challenge adults' problem-solving skills! Some areas, like reading and math, have activities one would expect for young students, but other areas, such as puzzles and art, tap into all students' potentials for stretching their creativity and problem-solving skills.

UpToTen (www.uptoten.com), a site in English created by French developers, offers many areas of exploration for children ages zero through 10. Simple computer tasks like learning to double-click or drag and drop are enfolded in educational games. With hundreds of games and activities, lots of audio support, and a wide array of educational content, this site can keep young children and primary students engaged and learning. Although the site offers subscriptions, parents and schools can have free access.

Language Arts Interactives

Bookshare (www.bookshare.org), sponsored by the U.S. Department of Education's Office of Special Education Programs, limits membership to individuals who can document print disabilities with physical causes, such as visual impairment or inability to hold a book, that make reading difficult. This service does not extend to students with nonphysical causes for reading disabilities, such as autism, emotional/behavioral problems, or English Language Learners. While eligible users may be only a small number of students in a school, if you teach students with those print disabilities, accessing to up to one hundred books per month from the library of digital texts, including periodicals, makes a critical difference in their education. Bookshare has updated its site to improve content and services, "from learning how to download your first book to using advanced features, accessing training, and getting more involved in the Bookshare community." Core services have not changed.

Starfall (www.starfall.com) may be the best free reading website on the internet for prereaders through students in PK–2, plus special needs students, ELLs, and homeschooled students. The site offers stories, games, videos, many download-able books, and a few elementary math games. A new program focuses on a PK curriculum. Initiated "in 2002 as a free public service, Starfall has been teaching children to read with phonics ever since." Parents, teachers, classrooms, and schools may also purchase one-year memberships that include many more choices for prereaders and young students.

Mrs. P.'s Magic Library (www.mrsp.com) stars TV actress Kathy Kinney, who tells stories and reads books to children. This free site sponsors writing contests, and winners' books are added to the site. It's a warm and wonderful place to visit. For students who have never snuggled on a lap to listen to a book, this site creates virtual experiences with a cozy interface and Kinney's warm, conversational tone. Most of the site's titles are available on YouTube (www.youtube.com/user/MrsPStorytime); a few categories are Happily Ever Afters; Bullies: Once Upon a Classic and Modern Tales; and Read Along with Mrs. P–4 Favorite Fairy Tales.

Phil Shapiro Websequiturs (www.his.com/~pshapiro/websequiturs) looks very basic, so it may or may not engage students who are used to fancy sites. On this site, students choose from among three phrases to compile the sequence of a story. The task requires paying attention to where the previous phrase ended. It may have ended with a period or anywhere within a sentence. If students make incorrect choices, the story does not sound right. Both fiction and nonfiction are offered. I found the first story about the astronauts fascinating, although it was long. If intermediate or middle school students struggle with comprehension because they do not use context clues or do not reread, the exercises on this site may help them improve. See www.cict.co.uk/textoys/pricing.php for classroom pricing of the software.

Zinger Tales (www.cmlibrary.org/bookhive/zingertales/zingertales.asp) is part of the Charlotte Mecklenburg Library site and features videos of storytellers. If you teach storytelling, students will definitely want to see and hear professionals to develop ideas for how they can tell their own stories more compellingly.

Instant Poetry Forms (http://ettcweb.lr.k12.nj.us/forms/newpoem.htm) keeps students engaged in the creative work of poetry writing without getting bogged down in extra typing. Standardized wording of poems appear pretyped in many different forms, such as "If I were in charge of the world, I'd ... "; students then devise their own endings for the lines. After students complete a selected form, the entire poem appears. Students can print or copy the poem and paste it into a word processing program.

Audio/Video Books for Young Students

Reading is a critical life skill. Fostering a love of reading becomes of paramount importance at the elementary level, because without pleasure in learning from and imagining through books, students may not develop adequate reading skills. Many adults can point to the one particular book that turned them on to reading. But finding that one book for each child is a massive task, so elementary teachers expose students to many books. And, for many students, the best book may not be solely in print form; instead, audio and video can bring life to text.

Multimedia books expand the potential for engaging students' imaginations as they learn to read and to enjoy books. When online books become shared reading experiences, teachers open doors to students' conversations among themselves about the delights of reading. Consider times when you might use the following audio/video online books for students to learn in new, imaginative, creative ways.

In **Storyline Online** (www.storylineonline.net), members of the Screen Actors Guild tell stories beautifully. Students will relate to the readers. The online stories include illustrations from the texts, so no texts are necessary, but because the books on the site are common in libraries, teachers could have the texts available in the classroom for independent reading. This lets students know that the books exist as print materials; quite a few may be enticed to relive enjoyable multimedia experiences by reading the books.

Robert Munsch (http://robertmunsch.com/books), beloved Canadian children's author and poet, reads his books aloud and permits MP3 downloads of the stories. Consider pairing MP3 stories with print copies of the books for listen-and-read sets. Munsch has a dramatic storyteller's voice. Most of his best-selling books are based on true stories, such as *Love You Forever*. A strong advocate of literacy, Munsch believes that literacy begins in families, well before children attend school.

Speakaboos (www.speakaboos.com/stories) has more than one hundred free multi-media stories and some songs. Additional materials are available to members. The stories include many with space race, Arthur (star of the PBS Kids GO! "Arthur" show), and Gustafer Yellowgold (friendly alien in animated music videos and live concerts) themes, as well as fables, fairy tales, and stories en Español. Some titles may also be available in school or classroom libraries.

Kindersite (www.kindersite.org) is an aggregator of links to other websites for free stories, songs, and games for prereaders and young students. This site is designed for teachers and parents of children in preschool through kindergarten, as well as young ELLs; age ranges for each link are provided.

We Do Listen Foundation (https://wedolisten.org) has free online songs and animated books for primary students to enjoy. Great messages relate to students' lives to bolster self-worth, teach effective communication skills, and build conflict resolution expertise.

Scholastic Listen and Read Books (http://teacher.scholastic.com/commclub) has 15 nonfiction books, sorted by subject, for young students. Students can read each page or click on the speaker to hear the text read aloud.

Childtopia (http://childtopia.com) has stories with comprehension questions translated into multiple languages. See the Listen and Reading Comprehension link and the Classic Tales (with six stories) link. Students can listen and take a quiz or read and take a quiz. Though Childtopia offers a premium membership with more activities, the free side of the site has plenty to keep students engaged.

eStories by Story Teller (www.prattlibrary.org/home/storyIndex.aspx) is a collection of more than fifty videos of storytellers telling folk tales from various countries' traditions. Lengths range from 2 to 8 minutes. The stories and storytellers are compelling although when I watched, the audio was slightly out of sync with the video.

The Story Museum (www.storymuseum.org.uk/1001stories) is a British site aiming to collect 1001 audio files of stories from around the world. Stories are sortable by age, theme, or country of origin. The audio files include links to story maps (cartoonish illustrations of the story on one page—great for retelling the story) and story texts (audio files are not word-for-word readings). This wonderful resource is growing.

Curious George Stories (www.curiousgeorge.com/kids-stories-books) is a Houghton Mifflin Harcourt site with four Curious George audio picture books plus games and activities. Words are highlighted as they are read to encourage students to read along.

Martha Speaks True Stories (http://pbskids.org/martha/stories/truestories) tackles science, technology, engineering, and math with four books for each content area. Based on the PBS television show aimed at children between ages 4 and 7, the online nonfiction books feature voice-print match as well as child-friendly definitions for harder vocabulary on each page. Martha Speaks nonfiction books teach academic vocabulary in context and are appropriate for students who are beginning to learn English.

Professor Garfield Toon Book Reader (www.professorgarfield.org/toon_book_reader) allows early readers to hear cartoons in five different languages. Although the words in the stories are highlighted as they are read, students must click on the Read To Me icon for every page. Many other choices are available on the site, including Brain Busters, Comics Lab Extreme (for students to create their own comics), the Music Bot, and Math Games. Upper-level elementary and middle school students will enjoy these funny, engaging learning activities.

Story Time For Me (http://storytimeforme.com/series) invites authors to submit narrated and animated books to the site, which then makes them available for sale. All the books are free for students to read. The animated books feature voice-print match and are sorted for ages 1–4 and 4–8.

At **KidsSpace: Toronto Public Library** (http://kidsspace.torontopubliclibrary.ca/genStoryArchive_Age_6-12_1.html), students in elementary and middle school can listen to twenty audio stories in English and access some multimedia stories. Limited audio stories are also available in French, Italian, Polish, Urdu, Mandarin, Korean, and Russian. The site also lists many other valuable websites and offers materials for parents to use with preschool children.

Browser Books (http://staff.prairiesouth.ca/~cassidy.kathy/browserbooks) was created by teacher Kathy Cassidy so that students in her first grade class in Saskatchewan could read books created by other students on their web browsers. When students are unsure of a word, they click on it to hear a child's voice read the word.

Not all fables listed at **Aesop's Fables** (www.aesopfables.com) have audio, but those that do are marked with an audio speaker icon. Many curricula call for students to learn about fables, and all Aesop's Fables are presented on this site with texts. Recently, 127 fairy tales by Hans Christian Andersen were added to the site.

Public libraries are great sources for audio and video materials. Check your local library and, if permitted in your area, libraries in surrounding communities. In Colorado, for instance, if a resident has a library card in one location and that library is part of the state system, the card may be used for materials at other libraries in the state. Many libraries subscribe to online book sites, such as TumbleBookLibrary (www.tumblebooks.com/library), or online research databases for students.

Math Interactives

National Library of Virtual Manipulatives (NLVM) (http://nlvm.usu.edu/en/nav/vlibrary.html) rates at the top as a virtual experience with math concepts for all grade levels. Students manipulate virtual shapes, color patterns, puzzles, abacuses, 3D blocks, and more to solve problems, experiment, or explore concepts. The advantages of virtual manipulatives are instant feedback and student engagement; students know immediately if they have done the work correctly. When whole classes work with virtual manipulatives in lab or laptop situations, teachers can spot students with misconceptions and work one-on-one with them while other students continue with higher levels of the concepts. This is not a drill-and-skill program; students use manipulatives to understand how math concepts work.

Mathlanding (www.mathlanding.org/content/about-mathlanding) is an online information exchange service for elementary math teachers. A wide range of math topics and resources are aligned with the Common Core State Standards for Mathematics and the National Council of Teachers of Mathematics Focal Points. All content has been reviewed and evaluated by experts, including lessons, interactive media, activities, games, articles, and more. This site is an aggregator, so a search will bring up links to a variety of resources. With registration, teachers can save their favorites in folders for quick access. Grade level content goes from PK through 6+.

Other math manipulative sites include **Interactivate** (www.shodor.org/interactivate/activities/byAudience); **Illuminations** by the National Council of Teachers of Mathematics (http://illuminations.nctm.org); and **Glencoe Virtual Manipulatives** for teacher-directed activities (www.glencoe.com/sites/common_assets/mathematics/ebook_assets/vmf/VMF-Interface.html).

Freudenthal Institute: Games for Mathematics Education (www.fisme.science.uu.nl/publicaties/subsets/rekenweb_en), formerly called Kids Kount, has math activities for ages 4–17. This site in the Netherlands offers games that challenge students to think about strategies and spatial sense. Some activities require two students working together, and for many activities, paired practice would help students be successful.

Kids and Cookies (www.teacherlink.org/content/math/interactive/flash/kidsandcookies/kidcookie.php) is a one-purpose simulation activity to practice fractions in a real context. Students choose friends and a number of cookies and then try to share the cookies evenly among the friends. Students will generally realize the benefit of few friends and lots of cookies.

Science Interactives

NASA's Space Place (http://spaceplace.nasa.gov/menu) uses tabs to organize a wealth of science and technology activities. Top-level tabs are Space, Sun, Earth, Solar System, People & Technology, and Parents & Educators. For each section, tabs allow users to sort the resources by All, Explore, Do, and Play. The site encourages learning through doing and playing.

The **learning science.org** site (http://learningscience.org) is a free, open learning community, framed by the National Science Education Standards, that helps teachers and students locate excellent interactives and resources worldwide.

Planet Arcade Games (http://games.noaa.gov), sponsored by the National Oceanic and Atmospheric Administration (NOAA), has collected science games students can play to explore science topics. An aggregator, NOAA also has collected child-appropriate science games from several other government sites. Activities are suited for late elementary and higher grade levels. Some links go to activities on subscription-only sites.

Edheads (www.edheads.org) offers virtual science, health, and math activities for students in grades PK–12. For example, students can choose from Simple Machines, Virtual Knee Surgery, and Stem Cell Heart Repair. Math skills are aligned to Common Core State Standards.

Social Studies Interactives

Digital History (www.digitalhistory.uh.edu) is, in my opinion, the only history site for students in late elementary and secondary classes that has a student-friendly interface in addition to a wealth of U.S. history content. The site's home page captures students', teachers', and parents' interests immediately with a Timeline from pre–1492 through 2012. Users may also select material from four main areas: Eras, Topics, Resources, and References. History teachers will find this treasure trove to be a valued learning tool.

Mission US: A Revolutionary Way to Learn History (www.mission-us.org) simulates U.S. historical periods as games for grades 5–8. The options are For Crown or Colony (Revolutionary War), Flight to Freedom (Slavery), and A Cheyenne Odyssey

(Westward Expansion). Additional missions are planned. Teachers can register to create class accounts and track students' progress through the games. Helpful supportive materials are found at the site.

Information Literacy Interactives

Boolify (www.web2teachingtools.com/boolify.html) acts as a visual search engine for teaching students to narrow Boolean searches. Students can use puzzle pieces to create searches and see, at the bottom of the page, the results in a search engine. Using the visual tools makes students aware of how to focus keyword searches and how to eliminate unrelated results. Though designed for elementary and middle school students, Boolify can help students of all ages to visualize the logic behind their searches. Some educators feel that Boolify has become outdated as search engines have improved, but since libraries often use Boolean logic for their collections, this can still be a useful site.

Admongo (www.admongo.gov), sponsored by the Federal Trade Commission and developed with assistance from Scholastic, teaches advertising literacy and critical thinking skills to students in grades 5–6, though the site reports successful use for students in grades 3–9. Presented as a game, the site helps raise students' awareness of the ubiquity of advertising and how ads are designed to influence people of all ages. Students learn to ask themselves these questions: "Who is responsible for the ad? What is the ad actually saying? What does the ad want me to do?" Teachers' materials (www.admongo.gov/teachers.aspx) and a noncomputer version of the game are also available.

Critical Thinking and Problem Solving Interactives

Zoopz (www.zoopz.com) has incredibly engaging problems for young children through adults, appearing as increasingly difficult games with challenges to solve. Zoopz will stretch students' and teachers' thinking and problem-solving skills. The site does not keep data on players.

Clearly, this chapter's list of website resources for teachers does not exhaust the possibilities of useful learning tools available on the internet. A good place to search for ideas is **TeachersFirst** (www.teachersfirst.com), a free resource written and edited by experienced educators. You can do a keyword search to find many potentially usable sites. Teachers who are beginning to use tech tools can learn a lot by browsing the site's sample units and lessons. Free membership allows you to customize your start page, tag your favorite resources, and share resources with students and families.

Before beginning an internet search, you can save time by determining your criteria. To hasten the process of sorting through any list of resources, ask yourself the following questions:

- Does the site require registration? Because of the Children's Online Privacy and Protection Act (COPPA), sites are not allowed to collect identifiable information from elementary students. (Chapter 15 of this book, "COPPA, Internet Safety, and Copyright," addresses the basic concepts of responsible, ethical, and safe use. Teachers also need to seek more fully developed materials to support their instruction on these topics. An excellent resource, **How to Protect Kids' Privacy Online: A Guide for Teachers** (www.education-newyork.com/files/teachersFTC.pdf), can be downloaded.)

  If the site has a registration requirement, read the terms of service and privacy policy to determine whether young students are even allowed on the site. This is not a concern for teachers whose students are 14 or older.

- Does the activity on the site build background knowledge, reinforce instruction, extend conceptual understanding, or assess student knowledge?

- Does the activity engage students for more than drilling basic skills?

- Is the activity appropriate for all students or targeted to just a few students in my class? The answer to this question will determine how you use the site.

- For primary students, does the site have audio support? For older students, is the text within students' reading ranges?

- Are interactive sites visually appealing? Can students who don't read well figure out how to use the site based on visuals, audio, or video tutorials?

Text-heavy sites "tell" students information rather than "show" them how to use it.

■ Is there any accountability for students' time? How will students show evidence that they have worked on the site? Many teachers find that creating their own tracking pages for accountability purposes helps them keep up with each individual's progress. Pinterest's **Tracking Student Progress** shows lots of ways to do this (www.pinterest.com/ explore/tracking-student-progress).

■ Is this an activity that should be shared/paired, or is it better completed by individuals?

■ Does doing this activity on a computer have any advantage over in-class, hands-on work?

Plan to use interactive websites at the best times to complement students' learning processes. At times, you may find that student-created physical manipulatives are more effective than virtual ones online—and vice versa. For instance, when teachers use physical/kinesthetic manipulatives in classrooms for activities like fractions, they may not be able to get to all students quickly enough to check for misconceptions. Nor may they have time for sufficient practice so that students build comprehension of the concepts. Online virtual manipulatives can solve this and other problems.

For example, if teachers lack supplies for science experiments with electrical currents, virtual experiences that teach electrical currents, especially when students work together, clarify content that students otherwise would have missed. Students in primary grades may not have books at home, or their family members may not be capable, for various reasons, of reading to them. Showing multimedia books on a document camera while students cool down after recess (or at other transitional times during the day) can give them satisfying, supportive reading experiences they miss out on at home.

Be thoughtful and selective about the online interactive experiences your students may access at school. Many students already play plenty of games, even educational games, at home. The purpose of using websites at school is to stretch students' experiences as they learn and to provide differentiated learning to fit individuals' needs. Most often, these goals will be accomplished through projects and collaborations—some with and others without websites.

Websites Highlighted in this Chapter

WEBSITE	TYPE	GRADE LEVELS	FOCUS	COMMENTS
Admongo	Government	3–5	Media Literacy	Game about advertising literacy
Aesop's Fables		3–7	Reading	Texts and some audio
Bookshare		K–adult	Reading, audio books	Limited to students with physical print disabilities
Boolify		3–5	Information Literacy	Visual search engine trainer
Browser Books	School	K–1	Reading	Book ideas for young students to create
Childtopia		PK–3	Reading	Stories with comprehension quizzes
Curious George	Publisher	K–3	Multimedia books	Curious George books as multimedia texts
Digital History		K–12	Social Studies	Comprehensive history links
Edheads		3–12	Science	Simulations and explorations
eStories by Storyteller	Library	K–5	Reading	Storytellers, multicultural
Glencoe Virtual Manipulatives	Publisher	K–5	Math	All activities teacher planned and directed
Illuminations	NCTM	K–12	Math	Many online activities
Instant Poetry Forms		2–5	Writing	Poetry frames
Interactivate		3–12	Math	Most manipulatives geared to middle school
Johnny's Math Page	Aggregator	K–12	Math	Excellent resource for centers
Johnny's Story Page	Aggregator	K–3	Multimedia books	Excellent resource for centers

Continued

WEBSITE	TYPE	GRADE LEVELS	FOCUS	COMMENTS
Kids and Cookies		3–5	Math (Fractions)	Fractions as fair share
Freudenthal Math		K–5	Math	Challenges, activities good for centers and paired work
KidsSpace	Toronto Public Library	PK–6	Multimedia books	Audio and multimedia books
Kindersite	Aggregator	PK–3	Books, songs & games	Age ranges provided; to age 9
learning science.org	Aggregator	K–12	Science	Links to interactive science sites
Mathlanding	Aggregator	PK-6+	Math	Links to math resources aligned with Common Core
Mission: US		5–8	Social Studies	Specific to Revolutionary War
Mrs. P.'s Magic Library		PK–4	Multimedia books	Read aloud with Kathy Kinney
NASA's Space Place	NASA	2–12	Science	Explorations of space topics
National Library of Virtual Manipulatives		K–12	Math	Many virtual manipulatives
Planet Arcade	NOAA	3–12	Science	Links to science sites
Professor Garfield's Toon Book Reader	Publisher	K–5	Multimedia books	Cartoon books, voice-print match; must click for audio
Robert Munsch	Author site	K–5	Multimedia books	Audio books read by author, life lessons with humor
Scholastic Listen and Read	Publisher	PK–1	Multimedia books	All nonfiction texts, Levels A & B

WEBSITE	TYPE	GRADE LEVELS	FOCUS	COMMENTS
Speakaboos		K–5	Multimedia books	Includes songs
Starfall		PK–2	Reading	The best early literacy site, printables available
The Story Museum		K–5	Reading	Audio stories with story maps and original story text
Storyline Online		K–5	Multimedia books	Multimedia books read by actors
Story Time for Me	Publisher	K–2	Multimedia books	Animated books
Teachers First	Aggregator	Teachers	Resource finder	Free, teacher-friendly database of interactive websites, lessons, tips
Toy Theater		PK–1	Comprehensive	Wide range of challenge
UpToTen		PK–2	Comprehensive	Audio supported
We Do Listen		PK	Multimedia books	Positive values, conflict-resolution skills, raising self-esteem
Websequiturs		4–7	Reading	Build a story, comprehension practice
Zinger Tales	Library	K–5	Reading	Storytellers
Zoopz		2–12+	Critical Thinking	Games that get increasingly difficult

CHAPTER 7

Digital Still Cameras

ONE OF THE MOST AFFORDABLE technologies available to schools today is the digital camera. Not only have the prices for cameras dropped significantly, but the affordability means that many families update their equipment and end up with usable cameras they can donate to schools, especially as school donations are tax deductible. Additionally, many students use cell phones with embedded cameras. The technology of digital cameras has evolved so that even preschoolers can take usable photos.

When young students use digital cameras, their photos often differ dramatically from pictures taken by teachers and parents. Adults tend to snap pictures of *children* in settings where they are learning; students take pictures of *what they are learning*. Perhaps pictures also tell you about values: the teachers value the students; the students value the new information and experiences in the present moment.

Secondary students use photos for many purposes and will find any projects requiring photography easy to accomplish, especially as most have cell phones.

VOICES OF EXPERIENCE

Boni Hamilton, Ed.D., Ph.D. Doctoral Student
University of Colorado Denver, Denver, CO

I bought a camera designed for kids because it was digital, cheap, and sturdy. I liked the idea of putting cameras into students' hands, but I didn't want to invest much money until I saw whether it would work. I could think of plenty of things that could go wrong. Most kids wouldn't know how to take a good picture with a camera, so their photos might be blurry or off-center. There was always the chance that they'd just take shots of their friends or of kids goofing off. At least with a digital, I could erase bad pictures without spending extra money. When my now-adult offspring had used cameras as kids, I wasted a lot of money getting really bad pictures developed.

I handed the camera over to several students in the school's daycare program when they were going to the aquarium. I hadn't realized how challenging the task would be for them. The camera had no flash, so much of the time their pictures were dark. Then, too, all the photos had to be taken through glass, which had glare from spotlights. Yet, the students came back excited about their pictures and full of detailed stories about each shot. And they had not broken the camera!

A few weeks later, I convinced fourth grade teachers to let their students take several inexpensive digital cameras on a field trip. The cameras had no viewing screens. Students had to look through an eyepiece, click, and hope. The next day, the student photographers watched me download their pictures from the cameras. As I paged through the pictures, they nudged one another and talked about each shot. I stopped at one that seemed to be mostly tan with a few semicircles of white. "Oops!" I said. "That looks like a mistake. We can delete it." A student immediately cried out, "Don't delete it. It's important!" What the student had shot was a close-up of how the pioneers carried china plates in covered wagons. The tan area was a heap of dried corn in a barrel; the white semicircular pieces were the edges of the china.

In all the years classes had taken that field trip, no teacher had ever photo-graphed the barrel of corn. They didn't think it was important. Teachers photographed students in front of the tepee, students standing next to the covered wagon, students riding on the hay wagon, and students sitting on logs to listen to a storyteller. What students photographed, besides the corn barrel, were the two horses pulling the hay wagon, the stakes of the tepee, the rolled-up side canvas of the covered wagon, and other aspects of the field trip that they found fascinating. The pictures changed the conversations students had about the trip as well; the student photographers' pictures generated more detailed memories.

When students take pictures of what they deem worthy of photographing, teachers see the events through children's eyes. That's worth a lot more than the price of a digital camera!

This chapter will focus on photos. Keep in mind that many options for students' use of digital photos can also be applied to digital videos, which will be covered in another chapter. Overall, teachers and students need fewer skills and less prepara-tion for using digital photos than for incorporating digital videos into their tech toolkits. Kindergarteners have successfully filmed with video cameras!

Picture File Options

Advancements in technology prevent nearly all problems that were once so common with cameras. Now, cameras often have USB recharging capacity, so teachers no longer need a case of replacement batteries or different chargers for each camera brand. Many cameras take secure digital (SD) cards, which increase the camera's capacity to store photos; downloading pictures becomes a simple plug-and-play matter. Most cameras also do not need specialized software to view the photos.

The cost of printing pictures, particularly in color, remains significant. Now that pictures are digital, teachers have options for using photos without printing them.

They can upload the pictures and projects to websites or email them to parents. However, a critical issue remains: picture file size.

Picture Compression and Quality

The primary concern with photo extensions is the compressibility of the photos. Compression decreases the amount of required memory, but it also may affect the sharpness of pictures when they are enlarged. For elementary students, pictures should be compressed to ensure that their projects do not become so big they cannot be emailed or posted online.

Photos can be saved as files with different extensions and each extension has its own characteristics. The following are the four most common digital image extensions you might encounter when using digital cameras.

.bmp—This file extension is a standard in Microsoft Paint. Students should be encouraged to change this extension to .jpg before they save their drawings. As .bmp files are huge and high quality, they are difficult to compress without losing quality, so they take much more memory than other files.

.gif—Popular for websites, .gif files compress without losing quality and can store animations. Their large file sizes make them more suitable for professional web design than classroom projects.

.jpg or .jpeg—This file extension is favored for internet use and should be the file extension of choice for elementary students. Because .jpg files are compressed (a 10%–20% compression is usually enough), they lose quality, but unless they are highly compressed (60% or more), the change in quality is negligible. The .jpg files are easily interchangeable among operating system platforms, such as Windows, Mac, and Linux. Pictures on Macs should be in .jpg if students want to export them to any other platform.

.tif or .tiff—This file extension is typically used by professional artists and photographers and for files in commercial programs, such as Adobe Photoshop or Corel Painter, so that they retain high quality. The files are huge, even when compressed, and typically are not necessary for student projects. Only the smallest .tif files can be emailed.

Changing File Extensions and Resizing Pictures

Sometimes setting a camera to good, rather than best, quality decreases picture file size as well. Yet, if students are placing a lot of photos in one file, as in a collage or slideshow, the combination of pictures, even when taken at good quality settings and compressed as .jpg files, may still take too much memory for the file to be emailed or posted online. In that case, pictures need to be resized to reduce their memory requirements. Resizing is not the same as dragging the edges of a picture to make it look smaller on a page. Resizing requires using a photo editing software application to change the image.

Here's how to change an image from a .bmp, .tif, or.gif file to a smaller.jpg file:

When the picture is open in a photo management or editing application, choose "Save As...." When the dialog box opens, look toward the bottom of the box for a phrase like "Save as type...." This will have a drop-down arrow on the right of the box. Use the drop-down to scroll to .jpg and click. The file will save as a .jpg and will require less disk space.

Large pictures require a lot of memory. Shrinking their appearance by dragging the corners does not make the file size smaller. In a slideshow or digital story with many pictures, the large file size of the project can end up too big to upload or email.

To resize the photo to decrease the file size, you have several options:

- Open the picture in a basic photo editing application, such as Microsoft Office Picture Manager, iPhoto, Picasa, or PhotoScape. Among the editing tools will be a command to "Resize." Choose the dimension you want for the picture. Often a size in the 3"–5" range will be sufficient.

- **Web Photo Resizer** (http://webresizer.com), a free online photo resizer and optimizer, requires no registration. Not only can you resize photos, but you can crop, sharpen, add borders to, and rotate photos. You can even change them from color to black and white. Once you open this site, after 60 minutes of inactivity, your session will end, and your pictures will automatically be deleted from the site. This is an easy site for elementary students to navigate.

- **Pic Resize** (www.picresize.com) resizes and offers special effects tools to enhance photos. This site will also capture, crop, and resize photos from websites, which does not violate copyright law when the images are used for educational purposes. Photos are deleted 20 minutes after previewing the final picture.

Key Skills for Camera Use

Using digital photos is a great way to meet visual learners' needs while giving all students multimodal experiences. Essentially, teachers can replicate any drawing activity with photography. The difference, though, is that students taking photos will likely be out of their seats and consulting with one another, and students typically stay seated in one place for drawing. Prior to starting photo projects, teachers may need to devote time to teaching students about the cameras. First, familiarize students with the camera's functions and camera care.

Getting to Know Cameras

While it may seem desirable to have multiple identical cameras, if you depend on donations, you'll have different brands, sizes, and capabilities. Most cameras work in similar ways, and students often adapt to slight differences better than adults do. Plan at least one session for students to explore how cameras function.

Plan to set parameters for elementary students' use of the cameras. For instance, students need to know how to zoom, review pictures, and delete unsatisfactory shots. Otherwise, general camera settings are probably sufficient for the work students will do. No need to try close-up or high-quality settings with young students, although secondary students should explore all the options.

How you organize activities for getting students familiar with digital cameras will differ among classrooms and grade levels. In secondary schools, students can be given perfunctory instructions and access to a manual. They will inevitably look up hints on the internet or have experience with phone cameras.

At the elementary level, teachers should think about the best ways to ensure that students know how to care for a camera. In some schools, librarians work collaboratively with the classroom teachers to help students learn about cameras. In other schools, teachers work alone. Camera lessons for novice photographers may be structured either as small group explorations or as development of in-class experts.

Small group explorations allow all students to feel confident with all the classroom's cameras and provide the most flexibility when it's time to take pictures. In this activity, groups of four to six students share one camera. Under the teacher's direction, each group explores the buttons and functions of one particular camera. If you have more than one camera model, have groups exchange the cameras for further exploration. Encourage comparisons. Continue exchanging the cameras until students express confidence about how the cameras work.

After students are familiar with the various cameras' features, groups explore picture taking by photographing people and items in the classroom. At minimum, students should try taking pictures at a distance and then with the zoom. Depending on your plans for camera use, students could also try indoor and outdoor shots. If you plan to introduce projects that require advanced photography skills, invite a photographer, either a professional or a skilled hobbyist, to share tips with students. Otherwise, an introduction to basic skills will suffice.

Another way to get students acquainted with cameras is to designate a few individual students as experts for each camera. The designated experts work individually with the teacher or librarian to learn about specific cameras. The student experts then teach their classmates about the cameras and are consultants when anyone else is taking pictures. While this activity saves class time, it limits the depth of knowledge other students gain prior to their first picture-taking experiences.

Depending on your students' backgrounds, a combination of these approaches could be an effective way to differentiate learning. As you begin to discuss cameras, you'll see which students are already knowledgeable and note others who are enthusiastic. After some basic, whole class instruction, consider partnering camera-savvy students with less computer-savvy students who show enthusiasm about the cameras (i.e., kinesthetic learners who prefer hands-on activities to reading) and asking these teams to serve as peer tutors for the others. As the less knowledgeable students become confident experts, partners can split up to work one-on-one with those who need help.

Camera Accidents

When cameras are in students' hands, accidents will happen. Decide in advance how to handle these incidents. I tend to be more merciful than punitive because I don't want students to be afraid of technology or of making mistakes. Of course, it's easier to be merciful when the camera was donated than when its cost came out of your budget.

You can minimize the likelihood of accidents by taking the following precautions:

- If possible, replace wrist straps with neck straps. A student once accidentally dipped a camera into water several times as he panned for gold. Fortunately, the bath did not permanently harm the camera.

- To avoid tussles among students over one camera, design an equitable sharing plan before they begin taking pictures.

- On field trips, keep cameras in a common basket or carrying case during travel.

- Label all cameras and memory cards—memory cards, in particular, can easily be misplaced or mixed up. Identifiers that match cameras to cards help.

- Designate specific physical locations in your classroom or the library for downloading pictures, removing memory cards, recharging cameras, and storing the equipment, so parts are less likely to be lost or knocked over accidentally.

Camera Care

At the elementary level, teachers need to teach camera care. At the secondary level, students are generally aware of the fragility of cameras and need only a brief reminder.

If cameras are housed in the elementary classroom, students will have better access than if they have to check cameras out from the library. Ask students to compile a list of expectations for camera care, based on your situation. Topics might include:

Camera storage. Where will cameras be housed? How will students gain access? How and where will cameras be returned?

Camera charging. When will cameras be charged? Who will monitor the charging?

Camera use. Who will carry the camera and how? Who will take the pictures? How will the photographer know which pictures to take?

Photo downloading. Who will download the pictures? Where will photos be stored? When and where will downloading take place?

Camera problems. How will students report accidents with cameras? What consequences are appropriate if someone intentionally abuses a camera or acts inappropriately as the photographer? What happens if someone takes improper pictures?

The expectations may change slightly, depending on the purpose of the picture taking. Taking photos on field trips differs from documenting in-school events, such as Dinosaur Day, or finding pictures for figurative language units. An occasional review of expectations throughout the year is worthwhile.

Key Skills for Using Pictures

Students should learn technical skills before embarking on picture-taking projects. These crucial skills include downloading, storing, and accessing pictures; manipulating pictures; and using pictures in other applications.

Downloading, Storing and Accessing Pictures

Over time, the practicalities of downloading and storing digital pictures have been simplified. In many schools and districts, technology specialists can teach students how to store photos so that the pictures are accessible from a common file. Ideally, students have access to a common storage folder on a school or district server.

Online photo storage is also available. Elementary teachers need to use online photo services that do not require registration if they want students to upload and download from the site. Secondary teachers have many options, provided access to the sites is allowed through district filtering software.

Note: Before you ask students to use any photo editing or hosting site, be sure to check all the tabs on the site yourself to avoid students' accessing any with inappropriate photos. Material on these sites changes frequently. In fact, in the preparation of this book, on one occasion a site had a suggestive photo on its main page, and innocuous photos a few days later. Exercise due diligence.

If a district uses Google Apps for Education, Google's **Picasa** (http://picasa.google.com), a photo editing software with web albums may be an option. The following free online photo hosting sites are examples that could be explored by teachers; they are not necessarily the best or most educator-friendly. These are new services I explored as possibilities. As with all technology, if these disappear from the internet, other similar services can be found through an online search.

Share.Pho.to (http://share.pho.to) does not require registration, allows batch uploads, and provides short URL codes where the photos are housed. The site also offers embed codes so that photos can be shared on blogs and other websites.

Image Upper.com (http://imageupper.com) makes registration optional. Batch upload up to 50 pictures at once, and you'll have a gallery page with thumbnails of the pictures. The site offers to optimize images for faster download.

Use.com (www.use.com) also has an optional registration and unlimited free image hosting without registration. The site also provides a photo editor that allows you to add captions and speech bubbles. On this site, you can set privacy levels, so if the photos are of students, teachers may want to make the page private. An embed code enables placing the gallery on websites.

Manipulating Pictures with Photo Editing Software

Except for picture extensions and resizing, most photos can be used as they are. Older students may manipulate pictures by cropping, correcting the color, or applying special effects. To accomplish such changes to photographs, students must use photo editing software. Each software package differs in ease of use and sophistication, but essentially, they all have the same tools for simple manipulation. With access to many easy and free photo editing applications, elementary schools do not need to buy licenses for high-quality commercial graphic applications, such as CorelDraw, Adobe Photoshop, or Quark. Such excellent software packages have more complexity and capacity than elementary students typically need.

At the elementary level, students can accomplish photo editing with free software. With any of the following applications, students can rotate, crop, resize, correct color, or apply special effects to photos.

In Microsoft Office suite versions 2003–2010, the tools for most photographic tasks students will undertake are installed as the **Office Picture Manager,** located under Microsoft Office Accessories. The interface for the tools is fairly intuitive. However, in the 2013 version of Microsoft Office, Office Picture Manager was removed from the suite. A Microsoft adviser suggests using **Windows Live Photo Gallery** (http://windows.microsoft.com/en-us/windows-live/photo-gallery), which is a program-specific picture editing tool.

Apple Macintosh computers have **iPhoto** (https://www.apple.com/mac/iphoto), formerly part of the iLife suite, which has been renamed **Apple Creativity Apps** (https://www.apple.com/creativity-apps/mac/up-to-date), a suite of software applications for Mac OS X and iOS. The Apple Creativity Apps suite includes iPhoto, as well as iMovie and GarageBand. As is typical with Macs, the graphic elements and tools rate high user satisfaction.

PhotoScape (www.photoscape.org) is another free photo editing software to download, available either for Mac or Windows. The site has videos to demonstrate how the software works.

Web Photo Resizer (http://webresizer.com), a free online photo resizer and optimizer, requires no registration. Not only can you resize photos, but you can crop, sharpen, add borders to, and rotate photos. You can even change them from color to black and white. Once you open this site, after 60 minutes of inactivity, your session will end, and your pictures will automatically be deleted from the site. This is an easy site for elementary students to navigate.

Pic Resize (www.picresize.com) resizes and offers special effects tools to enhance photos. This site will also capture, crop, and resize photos from websites, which does not violate copyright law when the images are used for educational purposes. Photos are deleted 20 minutes after previewing the final picture.

Digitizing Pictures and Print Photos

Sometimes students have picture prints at home or illustrations in books that they want to use in projects. Digitizing is easy with any of the following tools:

Digital camera. Students can always take a picture of a picture. During the camera exploration activity, students might try taking pictures of pictures to learn effective techniques, such as squaring the camera to the picture, reducing glare, and/or using a tripod to steady the camera.

Document camera. Any document camera that connects to a computer is capable of taking pictures of items placed under the lens. This system is particularly effective for taking pictures of drawings, print photos, and book illustrations because students can see exactly what the photo will look like before snapping.

Scanner. Multifunction printers often have scanners. Digitizing is more automated when scanners are used, so this may be the easiest system, but schools are less likely to have scanners available for student use.

Using Pictures in Other Applications

Pictures can tie into any curricular unit or special event. The following ideas refer to particular curricular units but can be adapted to fit the circumstances of your school. Keep in mind that printing pictures, particularly color pictures, can strain a budget quickly. One way to reduce costs is to upload students' projects, including projects using photos, to the school's website or a blog or wiki. Another option is to email projects to parents so they can, in turn, forward them to other family members. Students with computers at home can copy projects onto flash drives or CDs to show at home.

Developing Themes

Students create slideshows that present specific themes. These may range from colors or numbers to mathematics, vocabulary, or habitat studies. One teacher guided preschool children to develop a theme of emotion. The children generated a list of emotions. Each one then chose an emotion to demonstrate through facial expressions, and the teacher took separate pictures of them. The assembled book of emotions was available for the students to read and proved helpful when they did not know how to label what they were feeling. A kindergarten teacher had her students contribute to books about colors, counting, and collections. Small groups or individuals could also accomplish this project. Depending on the levels of independence teachers grant, as well as the scopes of the initiatives individual students undertake to create themes and take photos, this project can range across all levels of Bloom's taxonomy.

VOICES OF EXPERIENCE

Laura Herring Dariola, second grade teacher
Sheridan School, Washington, District of Columbia

Note: Laura's project reminds us that disposable cameras are also technology tools that can transform students' experiences.

Inspired by Wendy Ewald's book, *I Wanna Take Me a Picture,* I created a unit for my second graders called "Exploring Identity Through Photography."

When considering how to bring this project to life, I was also driven by the idea of creating a "third space," as Jackie Marsh discusses in *Popular Culture, New Media and Digital Literacy in Early Childhood* (2005). Marsh writes, "She (McCarthey, 2002) suggests that students who are able, when teachers allow, to transform their identities within classroom contexts can create a 'third space' (Gutierrez, Baquedano-Lopez, & Turner, 1997) in which schooled norms and student lived experience can meet and ensure that children have agency and voice" (p. 30). The notion of students' identities outside of school uniting in a meaningful way with their in-school identities carried this project forward in my mind. A second focus was to understand others' perspectives.

We began by reading images: "What is the photographer's message?" "What can I learn from this photograph?" This work led to interesting discussions about perspective. Student Sita observed, "If everyone saw stuff in the same ways, it wouldn't be interesting. Perspectives kind of matter."

Continued

I distributed disposable black and white cameras, assigned five self-portraits, five family pictures, five pictures of culture, one picture of a tree, and, based on a suggestion made during a personal conversation with Vivian Vasquez, one picture of "fair." The cameras went home, and the photographers got busy.

The room buzzed with a wide array of excited reactions when the developed film was distributed. Soon, students began writing poetry about their photos. After a week or so of writing poems in their writer's notebooks, it was time to choose "the one." This would be the photo and poem to be scanned, enlarged, and mounted on stock paper for display at the annual second grade assembly.

It was evident by both the vibes and the conversations throughout this unit that my students brought their "outside of school" identities into the classroom in meaningful ways. Using cameras made these moments, people, and places accessible, as the images captured indisputable fodder for conversation.

One area of this project that deserved more attention, in hindsight, was the question of what "fair" looks like. Most of the kids took pictures of even amounts of things. For example, "My brother and I have the same amount of cider. That's fair." I breezed through these responses, thinking they were simpler than what I'd sought—though I'm not sure exactly what I was looking for. As a result, this part of the project kind of fizzled. If I were to do it again, I'd think more deeply about how to investigate the idea that if everyone has the same thing, it's fair. This concept could extend to the resources schools in our city have or could be used to explore homelessness. In my haste, I believe an opportunity was lost.

Scrapbooks

When students have pictures on a particular theme, they may choose to make scrapbooks of their visuals. This can be done digitally in Microsoft Office PowerPoint. Students place several AutoShapes on a page. They then format each shape separately and replace the background color of the shape with a picture. Writing captions for each photo reinforces two literacy skills: becoming aware of the roles captions can play in nonfiction structures and writing concisely. While only Microsoft Office supports using a picture as background for a shape, students can simulate the same effect by simply placing photos on any presentation slide and using lines, colors, and visual styles around the pictures to enhance them. Without using Microsoft Office, students can add frames to photos in **Web Photo Resizer** (http://webresizer.com) or **Pic Resize** (www.picresize.com) to produce photo albums. In any version of the project, captions can be added as text boxes.

Capturing Experiences

Teachers plan field trips and invite guest speakers to make learning experiences more personal for students. Capture what students learn by having them photograph the events. They can then select photos to illustrate essays about the experiences. Visuals often spur more details in writing. This activity requires students to attend to several skills. Photographers make decisions about what is important to capture, and writers reflect on what they remember about the experience so that they can write about it.

Illustrating Procedures

To help students remember school and classroom procedures, ask students to document them through photos and to write captions for each one. Then post the results. School procedures that most kids find boring, such as fire drills, bad weather accommodations, playground safety rules, and courteous lunch room routines, will suddenly take on more significant meanings. And essential learning procedures, such as the scientific method's steps, problem-solving scaffolds, and computer use steps, will become more deeply embedded into students' long-term memories. Such combinations of pictures and captions make the information more accessible and meaningful to students. These activities, located on Bloom's taxonomy along the range of comprehension levels, will give students practice in thinking sequentially, systematically, and logically. Furthermore, the ability to visualize and recall these procedures will become valuable, lifelong skills. Think about intelligent adults you've observed who are handicapped professionally and personally because they were never taught how to think logically or to solve problems systematically.

Documenting Sequences

Similar to illustrating procedures, photographs can be used to document a sequence of steps students use during a research or science investigation. Students can use the sequence of photos to create documentation panels/posters that lead an audience through the experience. Learning to document sequences prepares students for creating science projects and for careers in science, technology, engineering, and mathematics (STEM), as well as in writing, teaching, inventing, marketing, and the arts. If students are simply documenting steps based on a teacher's plan, this project falls low on Bloom's thinking levels, but when students are asked, either individually or as groups, to come up with the steps in a sequence, their work fits Bloom's third level, applying.

Highlighting Patterns

Recognizing and creating patterns is a crucial early step in mastering mathematics, so this activity is probably most suitable for primary students. Students can photograph patterns they've created or they've found in the environment. In one class, students were given random collections of buttons and asked to sort and graph them by pattern. Students used shape, color, size, number of thread holes, texture, and other characteristics for sorting. In another classroom, students were asked to create patterns of colored beads for neck chains. Photographing the results and giving each child a chance to write a caption about the pattern provided opportunities to assess students' understandings informally. In these projects, students apply their knowledge of patterns to new situations.

Reenactments

After students have read a book or studied an event in history, they can photograph themselves reenacting the experiences or draw a series of pictures that retells the events. The process of retelling through reenactment embeds learning into long-term memory. Reenactments emphasize evaluation and analysis skills because students need to figure out how to communicate main ideas.

Composing with Visuals

Using visuals to spark or complement writing is valuable at all grade levels. The field trip pictures, for instance, may trigger an idea for comparing life today with how people lived in another era or can become the basis for a persuasive essay on why a particular field trip should or should not be repeated the following year. Students can also write first and then draw or take photos to enhance what they've written.

Students can be assigned to study a value, such as loyalty, by taking a photo to illustrate it and writing a poem or essay about the value. Even better, ask several students to take photos that depict a value or emotion, and then pair them up to compare or contrast the ideas. Visual stimuli can be particularly effective in sparking creativity in poetry and figurative language. Ask students to choose two photos of dissimilar objects or people and to write similes and metaphors describing how the two are similar.

VOICES OF EXPERIENCE

Tracy Coskie, associate professor
Western Washington University, Bellingham, Washington

Michelle Hornof, fifth grade teacher
Alderwood Elementary School, Bellingham, Washington

Tracy and Michelle have a long-standing collaborative partnership. For more than 10 years, Tracy, a university professor, and Michelle, a fifth grade teacher, have teamed on projects in Michelle's classroom.

Little did our fifth grade students know what they were in for when they took home digital class cameras during the first week of school. We certainly didn't tell them that their photos would later be used for a full-fledged, thesis-wielding, detail-loaded photo essay! Students rarely asked what to take pictures of. They just naturally took photos of things and people in their lives that were important to them, which were topics that later motivated them to write. These self-chosen topics eventually turned into their personal photo essays.

Once we got started, our photo essay unit took four weeks. We began by reading photo essays with the class so that they would have a vision of the genre. We analyzed these essays by identifying the thesis and supporting details in both photos and text. Students started writing about their own photos in Microsoft Word, learning how to insert photos and text boxes, cut and paste text, format text, add clip art, save and move files, undo mistakes, and many other computer skills new to our students.

Students then chose a working thesis: an idea or an opinion, not a fact or a question. They made sure they had enough photos to support their theses, and if they didn't, they took a camera home again or changed the thesis. They added text, making sure to include details in the writing that was not in the photos, ensuring

Continued

that they were writing a coherent essay, not just captions. We then taught them how to write an introductory and a concluding paragraph and transitions between paragraphs. Students revised and edited with partners. They then reflected on their learning and goals. Finally, all students in the class published their photo essays by posting them in a hallway and inviting parents, siblings, and other classes to view their gallery and meet the authors.

Three Tech Tips for Making Photo Essays Work

1. **Students need time to explore the snazzy formatting features that computer programs allow before they can concentrate on the content of their writing.** When we get frustrated watching students spend so much time "playing around" with formatting instead of writing, we try to remember that when we were first learning how to use Microsoft Word, we were also fascinated by all these fancy features—WordArt, page color, fancy fonts, clip art, and so on. And just like our students, we spent a lot of time just fooling around. Students should all be allowed this time of free exploration, especially if they do not have access to computers at home.

2. **Each one teaches one.** Teach one student a technology skill and then designate that student as the "tech expert" for that skill, responsible for teaching it to the other students, as needed. Conferring the title tech expert helps spread technology skills rapidly across the classroom, enhances students' confidence, and helps maintain smooth classroom management.

3. **Plan to have two mini-lessons for the day: a writing lesson and a tech lesson.** We usually taught a writing mini-lesson at the beginning of the writing time, for example, how to narrow your focus or add transitions. Then students described the lesson in their own writing. Then about halfway through writing time, we called the students together to demonstrate a new technology lesson. Sometimes we had a preplanned tech lesson, but sometimes the skill was based on the questions that naturally arose as students did their new writing for the day. Students then returned to their computers to finish writing. Both mini-lessons needed to be short because we did not want to take students away from their writing time.

Why We Taught (and Will Continue to Teach) Photo Essays

- **Students experienced the photo essays as exciting ways of understanding more about each other and themselves.** They loved learning more about fellow students by reading their essays and studying their photos. They learned about themselves, such as Mark, who learned from writing his essay about building that he wants to be an engineer when he grows up. The essays also held poignant memories, like Betty's beloved guinea pig that died during the writing process.

- **Students learned about writing a thesis and a focused essay in a concrete manner because they used photos.** For example, when they checked their essays to see if all of their writing matched the thesis, they could easily see whether each photo pertained to the thesis or was off topic. These skills transferred to other writing projects later in the year—and to the rest of their writing careers, we can hope!

- **Students became engaged in writing and editing their essays.** Students were so engaged that they stayed in from recess, chose to write more photo essays after the unit was over, and only complained about writing when we did not have writing time. Even with a large class size and wide range of student writing abilities, hardly any discipline problems occurred, and every child was successful.

Dog Days
By Kaelin

Love reading? Love dogs? Dog days is a good combination for you then. Dog Days is a good way for kids in the Elementary age to learn to read. Don't know what Dog Days is? Read my piece and you will find out what Dog Days is.

Dog Days is a program where you go to the library and read to a dog from the Humane Society. (The Humane Society is an animal center

Zuzu

This is a picture of Zuzu laying down. Zuzu is a Laberdodle. He is a very kind dog except he will want to kiss you. (Be careful)! Not kidding. (He has almost kissed me before)!

Bonnie

Zuzu

This is Bonnie and Zuzu

where they use donations to help animals.) On the top is a picture of Zuzu at the Bellingham Public Library. I went there to read to Zuzu for a program called Dog Days.

Figure 7.1 Kaelin, a fifth grade student, created her photo essay about a public library experience.

Continued

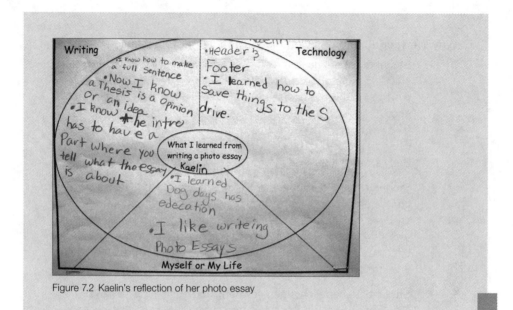

Figure 7.2 Kaelin's reflection of her photo essay

Reimagining Shapes

Students can photograph shapes in their environment. This may be as simple as recreating the alphabet with photographic illustrations (for example, a photo of a child's rake on its side with the tines forming the letter E) and as complex as finding advanced geometric shapes in architecture. Reimagining shapes excites students' imaginations and makes them aware of how marketing teams reimage shapes in advertising. A popular ad showed common objects such as car grills and parking meters as though they were smiling faces. Students' visual creativity is sparked when they reimagine one thing as representing another. For this project, students must synthesize and create, which sits at a very high level in Bloom's taxonomy.

Building Vocabulary

For regular vocabulary instruction, asking students to draw a visual representation of a word can be an efficient and effective strategy for building vocabulary. Occasionally, teachers may ask them to take photographs instead. One teacher knew that her students would find it difficult to draw or describe landform terms, such as arroyo and butte, critical for understanding geology texts, so she asked them to find photographs of Western landscapes and label their features.

In another school, fifth graders celebrated Visual Vocabulary Day and came to school dressed as words. The activity automatically provided differentiation, as students were encouraged to choose words they considered new, unusual, or hard to remember. Students were photographed in their costumes and then created individual dictionary pages that featured their photos. The dictionary pages were printed for an in-class book project and collected into a digital slideshow to share with parents.

As with several other projects using visuals, teachers will need to assess the project's design to determine its level according to Bloom's taxonomy. Generally, the more teachers are involved in directing and controlling a project, the lower the project's requirements for students' higher-level thinking will be on the taxonomy. In contrast, increased student planning and control push the project to higher levels of thinking.

Creating Photo Essays

Photo essays are collections of pictures that tell a story. The story may be one of experience, dreams, advocacy for a cause, history, a science experiment, a day in the life of a person or animal, a nature observation, or any other topic that captures a student's interest. Typically, photo essays, whether digital or made as a poster, include text in the form of captions that explain, expand on, or enhance the photos. These projects are excellent outlets for students who struggle to express meaning through writing, while pushing students into the highest levels of Bloom's taxonomy. Students synthesize what they know or imagine about a topic to create and communicate the story through pictures and words.

You can gather more ideas and information about photo essays from the following resources:

Thompson, S. C., & Williams, K. (2009). *Telling stories with photo essays: A guide for PreK–5 teachers,* Thousand Oaks, CA: Corwin Press.

Thompson and Williams give multiple examples of and ideas for nine types of photo essays: historical event, personal history, nature experience, field trip, overcoming traumatic events, career, content integration, advocacy, and historical event interpretation. In the following explanation, these authors convey how students' photo essays capture their thoughts and experiences in ways that writing by itself cannot:

> Photography is a very powerful medium for expression. Individual photos speak to a reader in ways that words cannot. When a caption or short narrative is added, additional information and the photographer's intent in taking the photo become more available to the reader. In this way, children's photographs are like windows into their experiences and thoughts.
>
> A photo essay is a series of photographs that tells a story. One photographer can take the photographs that make up the essay, or several children can contribute to the collection.... Photo essays can document many things, including a historical event, a family's history, science experiments, a day in a career, observations in nature, personal experiences and interests, journeys, and field trips. When children create photo essays, they communicate their experiences and thoughts with readers in authentic and very personal ways. As readers, this personal communication helps us to better understand children, their stories, and their ideas (Thompson & Williams, 2009, p. 7).

Chick, K. A. (2006). Using family and community history to foster historical inquiry in the elementary grades. *Social Studies Research and Practice, 1*(2), 233–241. Retrieved from www.socstrpr.org/files/Vol 1/Issue 2 - Summer, 2006/Practice/1.2.6.pdf.

In this article, Chick discusses the use of family and community history to foster critical inquiry. Learning about the past from conversations with older adults, students collect their participants' historical pictures and record quotations—by taking notes or, preferably, using audio or videotape with storytellers' permissions—to create photo essays. These projects, Chick says, allow students to experience history as real people and events.

Recording Growth, Processes, or Change

Some processes, such as plant growth, evaporation, or seasonal change, are hard to see on a day-to-day basis. Photographs taken over time elaborate in a concrete way what the statistical data show with numbers. This type of project is an excellent experience in the classroom, and it can be extended through free, online collaborative projects at Annenberg Learner's Journey North site (www.learner.org/jnorth).

When teachers and students participate in collaborative data gathering and analysis projects such as these, students use higher-order thinking skills and become excited about math and science.

Digital Storytelling

Students can create digital stories that combine pictures, text, and voice. After writing stories, which could be retelling historic stories, students take photos or draw pictures that they digitize to illustrate the stories. The pictures can be imported into slideshows or storytelling software, such as Photo Story 3. Students add titles, credits, and citations, if needed. As a final step, students divide their written text to match the story's illustrations. They then record themselves reading the story with the pictures. The final product is a multimedia narrative that can be shared. An excellent resource, Educational Uses of Digital Storytelling, is hosted by the University of Houston (http://digitalstorytelling.coe.uh.edu). Under the "How To" tab, a useful diagram by Samantha Morra illustrates the eight steps of digital storytelling. In addition to samples and lesson plans in many content areas, the site also covers fair use under copyright law, software options, storyboarding, and other related topics.

Students as young as second graders can master the process of digital storytelling, but with young children, this project takes a lot of instruction and supervision, so novices need to build up to it. Simpler projects in this chapter can help students gain the skills they need for digital storytelling, which requires teachers to show them how to synthesize skills and content. For six years, students in a middle school converted their own prize-winning short stories into digital storytelling projects for a local contest. Instruction on the process of using Photo Story 3 took less than an hour; completing the retelling of the stories took 3–4 hours, depending on the perfectionism of the students. The final products were acceptable, but better equipment and more time to review and revise would have improved their storytelling.

Teachers have several free software options for digital storytelling:

OpenOffice Impress can be downloaded as part of the free OpenOffice productivity suite. As basic presentation software, Impress will import photos, accommodate text, and record audio for digital storytelling.

Microsoft PowerPoint or **Apple Keynote** productivity suites have to be purchased, but many schools provide them for students. Like Impress, either presentation software can make a multimedia slideshow.

Photo Story 3 (www.microsoft.com/en-us/download/details.aspx?id=11132) is a free Microsoft download for Windows XP only. Photo Story is a simple, intuitive tool for making stories come alive. Although Photo Story is Windows-only, the finished stories can be converted to other formats. Good instructions on how to use Photo Story 3 can be accessed through the "How" hotlink at Book Trailers–Movies for Literacy, Mark Geary's web collection of book trailers created in Photo Story 3 (www.homepages.dsu.edu/mgeary/booktrailers). The "How" link is a photocopy of Geary's article, Phun with Photo Story 3, *Florida Educational Leadership,* Spring 2008 (www.homepages.dsu.edu/mgeary/vita/Phun_w_Photostory3.pdf). Geary teaches technology and literacy at Dakota State University, Madison, SD.

PrimaryAccess (www.primaryaccess.org) is a free, online digital authoring tool for K–12 students and teachers. Users learn how to create digital storyboards, rebus stories, and documentary movies and film clips, based on primary source documents. Authors narrate their films in their own voices. The University of Virginia and the Virginia Center for Digital History developed the project in collaboration with the Smithsonian and other organizations, with the purpose of involving students in demonstrating their understanding of history. Teachers can register for accounts and manage class lists. A sample digital story movie can be viewed at www.primaryaccess.org/show.php?id=271.

Myths and Legends (http://myths.e2bn.org) is a British site available to U.S. schools for a $99 subscription fee. Once a school's identity is confirmed for registration, students in every class can sign in through their teachers' accounts and create digital stories with Story Creator 2 or upload text stories. Although geared primarily to encourage the telling of myths and legends in the students' cultures, samples on the site include timelines and current fiction. The tools are intuitive for students, and all finished stories go to their teachers for approval before publication on the site.

VOICES OF EXPERIENCE

Tracey Flores, third and fourth grade
English Language Development teacher
Landmark School, Glendale, Arizona

As a teacher of language minority students, I have had the wonderful experience of working with phenomenal families who truly care about their children and their education. During my six years in the classroom, we have come together each year as a true community of learners to work as a team to allow for their children to achieve success, both socially and academically. There have been many gallery nights of shared writing projects, poetry readings, and end-of-the-year classroom celebrations. These family involvement experiences have allowed me to connect with parents and create important relationships that have opened the lines of communication between my families and me. However, although these experiences did get parents "involved in their child's learning" and brought families "into the classroom," I wanted to expand the types of family involvement opportunities that I was offering to my students and their families.

The family writing/literacy project that I envisioned would transform my practices from the past and create a safe space for families to come together to participate in a weekly writing workshop. The family writing/literacy project would create equitable experiences for parents to support their child academically by engaging parents in authentic reading and writing experiences that honored their cultural backgrounds and heritage languages. Each family's home literacy practices would be explored and used as a foundation for reading and writing experiences that we would share as a community of readers and writers.

As part of the school's efforts to bring the community together and my own interest in helping to acclimate my students and their families into the Landmark School community, I created and implemented The Family Writing Project as part of my classroom learning community. It started at the beginning of January and lasted until the end of March. It convened for ten weeks, once a week for an hour and a half after school. The participants were students in my third and fourth grade English Language Development (ELD) classroom and their families.

Continued

Each writing workshop began with a mini-lesson, writing and drawing time, and an author share time. Mini-lessons consisted of drawing neighborhood maps to elicit stories from their lives, reading mentor texts to make connections within their lives, and sharing ideas for creating stories using sensory details. Every family writing workshop took place in English and Spanish, with parents helping to translate for the entire group, and students translating for their parents in their writing partnership. Families were encouraged to read and write in the language that was most comfortable to them, and all attempts at writing were honored.

Participants chose one piece of their writing to take through the writing process. With the support of their family writing partnership, which was facilitated as part of The Family Writing Project, their self-selected writing pieces were revised, edited, and then published on the computer, using Microsoft Word. Then, all writers worked with Frames, a digital storytelling program, to create images using various media to accompany their stories. Writers were encouraged to choose from the program's premade backgrounds, bank of images, and sound media. However, many choose to start from scratch and invent a unique digital story with images of their own creation.

The program was very accessible to each participant, and with the support of the computer teacher and myself, writers designed a variety of scenes for their digital stories that also included their recorded voices telling their stories.

Digital Mashups

Mashups are original creations that combine multiple resources. Students can combine their drawings with photographs or clip art to create original illustrations. For instance, a fifth grade teacher asked students to create a picture of a crime scene as part of a mystery unit. Students saved copyright-free background pictures that they took with classroom cameras or found on the web, for example, **Public Domain Image.com** (www.public-domain-image.com) or **morguefile** (http://morguefile.com/archive). In a drawing program, such as Paint.net, they used their photos as backgrounds and layered clipart to create scenes. After importing the pictures into a slideshow software as backgrounds for the slides, they added shapes, dialog boxes, and other objects to finish the illustrations. They also added text boxes at the bottom of the slides where they wrote summaries of the crime scene. These mashups showed the chronology of the crime mystery (opening scene for setting, crime, investigation, and resolution) through pictures. Students were, in essence, outlining the plots of mystery stories and practicing the vocabulary to demonstrate their understanding of the genre. This technology activity hits the highest level of Bloom's taxonomy because students are combining elements to create a new picture. Students need a mix of skills to create a good mashup, so this project would not suit beginners.

The police roadblock, set up in response to a downed airplane, disrupted the criminal's plan to abscond with the money and drugs he'd stolen. Not only was he delayed, but the dog alerted the police to the presence of drugs in his car. The criminal tried to claim he'd been framed, but his fingerprints on the drug packets were evidence that he'd been involved in a crime.

Figure 7.3 This sample mashup was started in Paint.net with a personal photograph as a background for the picture. The cars and figures were extracted from clipart photos and layered over the background. The picture was then imported into Microsoft Powerpoint where additional clip art, dialog boxes, and text were added.

Often students waste time searching the web for the "right" pictures, only to find that nothing fits exactly what they imagined. When students realize they can create their own, more specific pictures with digital still cameras, they free their imaginations from depending on images from the web. They can stage photographs that have all the elements they had imagined. Encourage the most eager students to explore the possibilities of photography, and soon they'll be leading the whole class into new ways of using digital cameras!

Fifteen Fabulous Ways to Use Photos

Photo essay. Collect pictures on a theme and mount them with captions.

Scrapbook. Make a slideshow of pictures with captions.

Documentation panel. Document a learning process.

Science notebook. Photograph each step of an experiment.

Visual calendar. Plot the activities of the day/week with photos.

Geometry poster. Find shapes in the environment.

Story map. Reenact scenes from a story, book, or play.

Digital story. Tell a fiction or nonfiction story.

Visual vocabulary cards. Post vocabulary words with visual examples.

Books. Use pictures to prompt an idea for or to illustrate a book.

Dance map. Illustrate the steps of a dance.

Process poster. Show the stages of a process.

Figurative language slideshow. Write similes, metaphors, and analogies.

Illustrated poem. Use a photo as the poems' inspiration and background.

Cultural slideshow. Show your family's traditions and foods.

CHAPTER 8

Leveraging Technology for Visual Learning

VISUAL LEARNERS PREFER to work with images, such as pictures, charts, maps, drawings, and graphs. Studies indicate that about two-thirds of adults show visual preferences for learning. Elementary classrooms tend to have more visual stimuli than secondary classrooms, but a quick scan of an elementary classroom will show that the visuals are often colorful borders or backgrounds on bulletin boards or posters. The text that predominates on classroom walls appeals more to read/write learners, rather than visual learners.

In contrast, aural learners prefer to listen to instruction or other students and to and discuss what they have learned. Kinesthetic learners like to use all their senses, preferring hands-on experiences and learning from real-life case studies. Fleming, who developed the VAK (*visual, aural* (auditory), and *kinesthetic* learning preferences model) in 1987 (Education.com, 2013), later expanded the model to include a fourth major preference, read/write. Students who are *read/write* learners do best when reading and writing visual text. "They prefer lectures, diagrams, pictures, charts, and scientific concepts to be explained using written language. They are often fast readers and skillful writers" (p. 2, www.education.com/reference/article/ Ref_Teaching_Tips). For more information on VARK learning preferences, see the VARK site (http://vark-learn.com/introduction-to-vark).

For the purposes of this book, activities for *read/write* preference have been dispersed across this chapter on visual learning (reading and creating with graphics) and Chapter 9 on aural learning (reading and writing text). Chapter 10 discusses the kinesthetic learning preference, and Chapter 11 focuses on methods that work well for teaching English language learners.

Any activity in this chapter will probably please all students, not just visual and read/write learners. The activities highlight visual projects suitable for labs and classrooms that students complete with computers. This chapter will not address the use of digital still or video cameras, as they are covered in other chapters.

Drawings

When technology is defined simply as the use of any tool, the act of drawing is probably children's introduction to creating visuals with tools. Early childhood teachers encourage students to draw to communicate ideas, and children draw pictures to plan what they will write as they learn to compose.

Like reading and spelling, drawing skills progress through predictable stages. A chart titled "Drawing Development in Children" by Viktor Lowenfeld and Betty Edwards, adapted from teacher in-service materials by Susan Donley (1987), outlines the stages of drawing skills well (www.learningdesign.com/Portfolio/ DrawDev/kiddrawing.html). The goal is not to identify students in particular stages, but to understand that students progress through predictable stages at differing rates. Thus, their work should be compared only to previous work they have done. Portfolios of drawings throughout the year can illustrate each student's growth in visual representation. Certainly, secondary art teachers value visual portfolios!

Although replicating pencil-and-paper tasks with a computer is not typically recommended as a good instructional use of technology, drawing on a computer proves to be the exception. Drawing software has tools and options that make pictures more aesthetically pleasing than most children can produce with physical drawing materials. For instance, drawing tools in software can create symmetrical figures, flood figures or backgrounds with solid colors, and produce varied line thicknesses, all of which are challenging or time-consuming with physical drawing materials. Additionally, if students want to start over, they can refresh the screen without wasting materials. They also use problem-solving skills when they correct mistakes, such as finding the hole in a figure from which color is escaping, or when they want to access certain features, such as layering or resizing objects. Other good reasons for using this software are to encourage students who are not talented at representational drawing to enjoy drawing and to allow all students to express themselves artistically in a judgment-free environment.

How often should students use computers to draw? Opinions will vary. My rules of thumb are that PK–1 students draw at least twice a month if they use computers weekly, that is, roughly half the time they use computers. If they draw less often, children need to be reintroduced to tools and processes. If they draw with computer tools more often, they could be missing out on learning how to use other valuable computer tools. At higher grade levels, drawing may be more sporadic, based on projects. When students use original drawings or photos in their projects instead of clip-art or pictures taken from the internet, they do not have to be concerned with copyright issues. Students can also combine clip-art, photographs, and drawings to create original artwork. Secondary students also benefit from drawing occasionally.

Young children might need two drawing opportunities for the same project. The first opportunity provides practice for the final creation. During the practice session, introduce any program features students might use and then release the students to draw. Near the end of the drawing time, stop the students and conduct a gallery walk so that they can look at and appreciate one another's drawings. The child who has struggled to come up with an idea may grasp a concept for the next session, and all students enjoy seeing their peers' work. Too often in classes, the only persons to see the finished drawings are the student-artists, teachers, and parents. If possible, save practice drawings. Then, if a child is absent for the next session, the practice drawing can be used for the project.

Drawing Software

Drawing capability is standard on any computer. For Windows computers, **Paint** can be found in the Accessories menu; it has simple tools that students can master quickly. Mac computers no longer come with a simple drawing program, but **MacPaint X** (www.macupdate.com/app/mac/29848/macpaint-x) is a free download that imitates the Windows Paint program. Computers using OpenOffice (www.openoffice.org), a free, open source productivity suite, have drawing tools embedded in the software suite, so that students can draw as part of any word processing or slideshow presentation application or can use **OpenDraw** for a picture canvas. These simple drawing programs typically have basic drawing tools (not extras like stamps, sound effects, and slideshows). Students with advanced skills can paste pictures or clip-art into the programs and alter them with drawing tools to create original art.

Add-on software is also available. For years, the leader in drawing programs was the commercially developed Kid Pix, which is sold by numerous software retailers. With significantly more features than the built-in drawing programs, **Kid Pix** is a bitmap program some teachers love and others find distract students from the purposes of drawing. The newest product, **Kid Pix Deluxe 4**, was designed with input from teachers and students and has Spanish language support. The Utah Education Network collected a list of links to Kid Pix lesson ideas, samples, and templates (www.uen.org/k12educator/kidpix.shtml#LessonPlans) for elementary grades. These ideas may be worth exploring, no matter what drawing program you use, to see how they could be adapted for your students.

An international drawing software favorite and hot competitor with Kid Pix is **Tux Paint** (www.tuxpaint.org), a free, open source download. Designed for PK–6 students, Tux Paint has many of the same features as Kid Pix (minus the bomb feature) and is available for all operating system platforms from one website. Stamps are a separate free download. Because Tux Paint is free and supported by volunteers, the program seems to be upgraded to work with new operating systems more often than commercial products. The iPad app for Tux Paint is no longer free but is inexpensive.

Project Ideas for Drawing

Allow the following projects to serve as springboards for your own ideas. Think about how these ideas for drawing might be adapted to fit your curricular objectives.

Self-Portraits

Open the year and introduce the drawing program for young students with self-portraits. These pictures can be saved as part of a digital portfolio or emailed to parents. If the self-portrait project is repeated near the end of the year, parents will have direct evidence of their children's growth in self-awareness and drawing skills. Although a simple activity, the act of creating a self-portrait sits high in Bloom's taxonomy because it requires students to think abstractly about their bodies, which they see only in reflections, and to create a representation.

Favorites

The possibilities of favorites extend into students' personal lives as well as their classroom recall of content. For instance, personal favorites may be holidays, foods, sports, hobbies, summer activities, animals, or books. Students could also draw favorite academic choices: book characters, science topics, historic figures, scenes from a read-aloud, or activities at school. Such drawings, accompanied by captions, show the variety of personalities in a classroom.

Labeled Drawings

Have students generate pictures of content concepts, such as an insect, types of rocks, or cross-section of an eye. Ask them to label the parts, either from a word bank or with best-guess spelling. This is a much better assessment of understanding than a worksheet with blank lines for writing labels. On a worksheet where students label parts, processes, or events, students only need to recall information. With teacher-provided worksheets, teachers can tell only if responses are right or wrong; teachers do not know students' thinking behind their word choices. Students may have used the process of elimination or may simply not understand. However, when students draw their own representations and label them, the drawings reveal the depth of their knowledge as well as misconceptions they may have. This task is appropriate for all grade levels because secondary students study systems, vocabulary, and other assessable concepts that can be drawn. Asking students to draw their representations of things, processes, or events raises the activity's thinking level on Bloom's taxonomy from remembering to applying.

Illustrations

Drawings can illustrate other projects. When students create illustrations, they can insert the pictures into ongoing projects, such as desktop publishing, slideshows, or online projects. Students have used self-created pictures as decorations on thank you and holiday cards; re-creations of what they've seen under a microscope for science reports; illustrations for stories, books, and reports; clues for riddles; and replacements for words in rebuses. Because students own the rights to their original works, they can publish the illustrations online or in printed materials.

Math Animals

Explore the **How to Draw Funny Cartoons** (www.how-to-draw-funny-cartoons.com/draw-animals.html) website section for intermediate students on drawing animals. The animals are basically made with rectangles, triangles, and circles. The website offers tutorials for each animal. To make sure students understand how the tutorials work, lead them through a tutorial on drawing one of the animals. Then encourage them to try one on their own. They should keep count of the numbers of each shape they use. Then they can create riddle cards. The outside flap would say something like: "What do you have when you add 1 rectangle, 1 square, 5 triangles, and 2 circles? Not just 9 shapes but..." inside, "...a penguin!" The 'How to draw' tutorials could be used for multiple projects across grade levels. Some tutorials are quite advanced and may interest art students.

Timed Sequences

Similar to the previous project, elementary students can use visuals to demonstrate their understandings of a sequence of events. If students are also asked to include labels in their drawings, teachers can assess what they know and what may need to be retaught. This process would work for steps of an experiment, the water cycle, a model of how to do a math problem, the seasons, migration patterns, or a crosscut of the eruption of a volcano.

If the cycle or process is sequential and each step has a different drawing, then students can work independently. An example would be the water cycle. Students could draw the phases of the water cycle with one phase per slide in presentation software and complete the work independently. The slides could then be set to advance in a timed sequence of 3 seconds to show how the water cycle works.

If, however, the sequence builds by adding on to an original slide, such as with the life cycle of a plant where the sequence of events happens in the same place but each event is distinct, students may not be able to work independently. The teacher may need to guide students through each step.

For instance, the life cycle of a butterfly can be depicted as happening in one specific tree, but the stages of the butterfly's life are distinctly different. To illustrate the life cycle of a butterfly, have students follow these guidelines:

1. Create a master picture with trees and other landscape features. Label the features. Save the master pictures.

2. Open the master picture and save a copy as "eggs." Draw butterflies and butterfly eggs on tree leaves. Label the new features. Save.

3. Open the master picture again and save a copy as "pupae." Draw pupae on leaves to show them munching. Label the picture. Save.

4. Open the master picture and save a copy as "chrysalises." Draw the chrysalises hanging from branches. Add labels. Save.

5. Open the master picture and save a copy as "butterflies." Draw the butterflies hatched from the chrysalises. Add labels. Save.

6. Import the series of pictures into a slideshow. Use the auto timer to advance the slides every 2–3 seconds. The resultant slideshow demonstrates the life cycle of a butterfly.

Some sequences build on one another and might be considered cumulative. An example would be the life cycle of a plant. As with the life cycle of the butterfly, the background picture for a plant stays the same, but each stage of the plant's life adds additional details onto a master picture. Each stage (seeds, roots, stems, etc.) simply advances the process cumulatively.

Other events are cumulative as well, such as the mathematical model of exponential growth or the scientific model of heredity through generations of a family tree. To illustrate exponential growth, have students follow these guidelines:

1. Draw a dot. Save as "picture 1."

2. Using the same one-dot picture, save again as "picture 2." Now "double" the dot by copying and pasting once so the picture has two dots. Save.

3. Save the same two-dot picture as "picture 3." Double the objects by copying and pasting. The picture will have four dots. Save.

4. Repeat step three, increasing the file name by one, and doubling the objects each time. Decide when students should stop.

5. Import the pictures into a slideshow and set the automatic timer to 2–3 seconds. The pictures will appear to grow magically.

An extension to this lesson would be to show students that the concept of dividing is related to multiplication by importing the pictures in reverse order. The number of dots will diminish at the same rate as they increased.

An alternative way to do sequences for grades K–5 is through ABCya (www.abcya. com/animate.htm), an animation website discussed later in this chapter.

Visual Representations

Combining words and pictures increases students' retention of concepts. For instance, when students are learning vocabulary, retention rates increase when they not only use definitions but also have pictures that illustrate the words. Students can create vocabulary books with each word defined, illustrated, and used in a sentence that relates to the picture. Visual representations can also be powerful for conveying content vocabulary in math, science, and social studies. Words like archipelago or convex can be understood and remembered most effectively when they are accompanied by drawings that make the concepts visible.

Figurative aspects of language, such as similes, metaphors, and idioms, become more understandable and concrete when students create drawings to illustrate comparisons embedded in the language. One classroom of English language learners created a dictionary of idioms with an illustrated page for each idiom.

Other Visual Activities

Pictures and drawings are not the only visual media students create. Charts, graphs, and graphic organizers also help students visualize ideas.

Avatars

On some websites, such as wikis, blogs, or VoiceThread (http://voicethread.com), students may want to post "pictures" of themselves as identifiers. Online safety eliminates photos of students under the age of 13, so elementary students need other sources for avatars. One option is for students to draw self-portraits in a drawing program and save their portraits. Another option is to use an avatar creator site. **Portrait Illustration Maker** (http://illustmaker.abi-station.com/index_en.shtml) does not require registration and lets students make choices about hair, eyes, face outlines, eyebrows, nose, mouth, and skin color. The icons students create are downloadable as files. The saved files can then be uploaded to documents or to online profiles. Note: Because registration is not required, students must complete their avatars in one sitting. Similarly, the **Mini-Mizer** (http://reasonablyclever.com/mini/flash/minifig.swf) uses forms that look like Lego pieces to create characters. Students will need to use the Print Screen options to save their pictures.

Word Clouds

Students enjoy taking their writing pieces and creating word clouds based on frequency counts. **WordSift** (www.wordsift.com) and **Wordle** (www.wordle.net) generate word clouds based on text entered into the text box on the site. The sizes of words in the clouds are based on their frequency counts in the text, minus the most commonly words such as "the." Word clouds can be especially helpful for ELLs; students can readily see which words are most important in a text.

Teachers have generated lots of ideas for using word clouds with students. One classroom teacher had middle school students write on the topic "Honoring Veterans." After students had finished their essays, they pasted their texts into Wordle to create word clouds. They then were challenged to be thoughtful about the colors, fonts, and shapes they chose for their clouds. For their end products, they created slides of the word clouds with explanations of their choices, followed by slides of the essays themselves. When the slideshows of all students in the class were combined, students could see how the words in their clouds reflected different themes in their essays. The final project can be accessed at the class blog (http://nsdedwards.blogspot.com/2011/11/writing-class-veterans-paragraph.html). This project turned a fun tech tool into a higher-level thinking tool.

As a research project in a graduate program, a team of students compared websites by pasting the texts of the home pages into a word cloud. The word clouds helped them see what the webpage owners valued.

Figure 8.1 This visual, created by the author in **Wordle** (www.wordle.net), captures the most common words used in the current chapter on leveraging visual technologies. Words in the visual are sized by frequency of use and suggest what is most important in the text.

Graphic Organizers

Visual students build their understanding of content through visual organizers, and these are easy to create on computers. Examples of graphic organizers can be found in any internet search. In addition to the common spider web graphic, students can try cause-and-effect charts, story maps, bubble maps, t-charts, and compare-contrast graphs.

Some teachers use commercial graphic organizer software, but students can use shapes in any presentation software or word processor to create graphic organizers. In Microsoft Office, AutoShapes with connectors work better in PowerPoint than in Word.

Students can also use an online graphic organizer, such as **Bubbl.us** (https://bubbl. us), for creating mind maps and brainstorming. The site does not require sign-up, although you can register for a free account if users want to save their maps online. Teachers and secondary students can have accounts; elementary students cannot. Graphic organizers can be saved on the computer as an image (.jpg or .png) or, in some cases, printed. (Note: Portable Network Graphics [.png or PNG, pronounced ping] is the most frequently used, lossless image compression format on the internet; it was created as an improvement on GIF graphic files.) The advantage of student-designed graphic organizers over predesigned ones is that students can better represent their thinking when they control the design. In fact, one goal of using graphic organizers is to stimulate students to independently design visual diagrams as thinking tools.

ReadWriteThink also has several graphic organizer tools. **The Webbing Tool** (http://rwtinteractives.ncte.org/view_interactive.aspx?id=127) can make cluster, cause and effect, and hierarchy webs. Typically, tools from ReadWriteThink are student-friendly and can be printed or saved. Lessons plans for using the ReadWriteThink Webbing Tool span grades 3–12.

Although students can use graphic organizers as a planning step for projects, consider making mind maps or webs the final products. In one third grade classroom, students in study groups researched immigration from different countries. The teacher ended the study by using the jigsaw method to make expert teams with one child from each study group. The expert teams then created diagrams to compare and contrast the immigrants from the countries they'd studied. The conversations students had as they designed their diagrams surpassed any whole group discussions during the unit, and the teacher never could have settled on only one design that would have honored the divergent thinking within her class.

Flow Charts

Introduce students to engineering by teaching them to make decision-making flow charts. These graphic organizers give students practice with analysis, which is at the fourth of six levels of Bloom's taxonomy. Using *Shapes* in any productivity suite such as Microsoft Office or OpenOffice, students can design flow charts. Big questions are used as titles. Smaller questions are written on diamond shapes, and possible answers on individual squares or rectangles. Arrows connect the diamonds and squares. Answers may consist of yes/no or may be specific to the situation. If there are conditions that influence the decision, the conditions can be written on the arrowed lines. An answer may easily lead to a second question, which has several possible answers. Sample big questions for flow charts include the following:

- What are the steps for solving a math word problem?

- How can you tell living from nonliving things?

- How do you know whether you can use an image in a slideshow that will be made public?

- How do you troubleshoot a computer problem?

- What are the implications of a decision (on any topic)?

- How do you choose an independent reading book?

- How do you respond to a bully?

Flowcharts can also be made with free digital tools. With **Gliffy** (www.gliffy.com/uses/flowchart-software), students can make flowcharts, graphic organizers, and other technical drawings. Users are not required to register. NCH Software offers free, downloadable **ClickCharts** diagram and flowchart software (www.nchsoftware.com/chart).

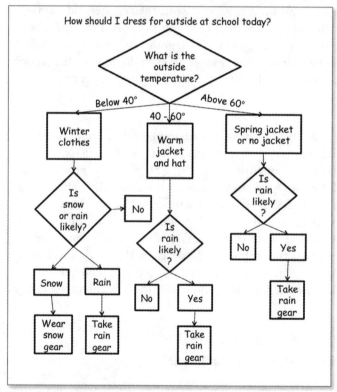

Figure 8.2 Decision Flowchart

Timelines

Students can use timelines to track the sequence of events in books or historic events. On other occasions, teachers may want students to make connections among events that seem disparate. Timelines can help. For instance, students in one class were reading biographies of famous people; they used a class timeline to look for overlaps of their subjects' lifespans. Students in another class used timelines to plot the events of the colonization of America. To dramatize an event, students can combine dates, photos, audio, and video clips in a slideshow. To view a professional example, see The Sesame Street Timeline (www.youtube.com/watch?v=Cz4JPszHnZM).

Commercial timeline software never seemed worth the price at my school because teachers simply did not create enough timelines for the software to pay for itself. Online timeline generators suitable for elementary students, however, have limitations that make them less attractive than commercial software. The really good, free, online timeline generators restrict users to individuals over the age of 13. Secondary students have many choices of good timelines generators.

Consider having students create timelines in word processor tables, spreadsheets, or presentation software. In the following list of resources, free timeline websites come first, followed by online help for creating timelines.

The National Council of Teachers of English provides a number of interactive tools for students at ReadWriteThink. The **Timeline** interactive (www.readwritethink.org/files/resources/interactives/timeline_2) is particularly easy to use with students who have limited technology skills. Two features limit the tool: students can use words but not pictures in their timelines, and the timelines cannot be saved, so they have to be finished in one sitting. Students can print their timelines horizontally or vertically.

Teach-nology (www.teach-nology.com/web_tools/materials/timelines) provides two simple timeline tools: a vertical timeline that shows up to nine events and a horizontal timeline that shows up to six events. This tool has the same limitations as those developed by ReadWriteThink.

Microsoft Office Timeline (www.officetimeline.com/free) is a free, downloadable add-on to PowerPoint for creating timelines in Windows. Microsoft also offers an Excel Timeline Template (http://office.microsoft.com/en-us/templates/timeline-TC001016266.aspx). Both come with instructions and allow timelines with pictures and unlimited entries to be saved on the local computer to be resumed at a later time.

Preceden for Teachers (www.preceden.com/teachers) has free teacher accounts, but this is one of the rare occasions when I advocate paying the $29 annual subscription fee. With subscriptions, teachers can create student accounts, have unlimited numbers of timelines with unlimited entries and photos, and save student work. The step-by-step instructions on how to use the entirely web-based site are excellent; all you need is access to the internet. You can even layer multiple timelines so that students can see how the events and dates on their timelines intersect with other timelines. Of all the timeline software options, this one provides the greatest flexibility.

How to Make a Timeline, an article at Social Studies for Kids (www.socialstudiesforkids.com/articles/howtomakeatimeline1.htm), explains how to make a vertical timeline. The second part of the article explains creating an historical timeline. The instructions could be adapted to office productivity software as well.

Spreadsheet Graphing

Teachers are not as likely to have experience with spreadsheets as with other productivity software, but spreadsheets are not difficult to master. For beginner graphing experiences, classes often use colored candies or cereal. Students sort their small containers of bits by color and enter the data in a table. The table can then be converted to a graph. The exercise itself has little need for a graph because students generally can tell from looking at the data table which color is more plentiful. To extend the activity, ask students to predict what the results will be if they combine all the data into one graph. Which colors will predominate? Which will be less common? Then collate and graph the students' data. How did the greater total number of objects affect the graph results? If a teacher combines data from another class to increase the total number again, students can predict the final outcome and then test their hypotheses. In collaborative spreadsheets, such as Google Docs, students can simultaneously enter their data individually onto separate columns. The rows of the data table can then be added and the data totals graphed.

Furbles are colored shapes with moveable eyes that help students visualize statistics and data by creating bar, pie, and tally charts and Venn and Carroll diagrams. For a demo of what Furbles look like, go to (www.ptolemy.co.uk/furbles08).

Furbles is a program for PCs and Macs that can be purchased for approximately $80 (http://shop.sherston.com/furb-win-cdrm-1.html) with 21-day free approval. Students can agree on the parameters for a study, collect data individually, and use Furbles' bar and pie charts to sort and graph for them.

At the secondary level, students can conduct surveys or collect data from science experiments. Middle and high school students should be able to use digital spreadsheets, although they may have limited experience with graphing.

Of critical importance for teaching graphing skills is the conversation afterward about what the information shown by graphs means. Weather data provide excellent opportunities to examine differences among cities and countries. In one class, students used a spreadsheet template with the local average monthly temperatures already entered. Each student visited **Weatherbase** (www.weatherbase.com) to collect data on a city in another country and created line graphs that compared date from their own city to data from the other city. Students set the y-axis range of their graphs to span the coldest and hottest temperatures in the class so all graphs used the same range and could be compared. The best learning took place when students compared all the graphs. Temperature patterns revealed the global positions of the cities and the surprising fact that equatorial cities, which maintained consistent temperatures year-round, were colder than cities outside the equator during some months. Data about precipitation help students predict habitats in various parts of the world.

A new companion site to Weatherbase is **Geoba.se** (www.geoba.se), which contains facts about more than 8 million locations worldwide, including population and growth statistics, postal codes, local webcams, and Wikipedia articles.

A fifth grade teacher, aware of her students' fears about the transition to middle school, asked them to create a survey for middle school students, conduct the surveys, collect data, and graph the responses. When they saw that sixth graders had not been shut in their lockers and, in fact, liked middle school, the fifth graders' fears were allayed.

Students may generate other topics for which they create and administer surveys. For elementary students, surveys typically must be printed because online survey sites do not permit students under age 13 to generate or respond to questionnaires at their sites. Secondary students have access to online survey applications, such as SurveyMonkey (www.surveymonkey.com) and Zoho Survey (https://www.zoho.com/survey). The advantage of an online survey is its time-saving feature that tabulates results automatically. Teachers and students can concentrate on discussing what the results mean.

Several online tools can be used for graphing data as a whole class or for generating graphs for students' projects. The following tools are worth exploring.

Create a Graph (http://nces.ed.gov/nceskids/createagraph) is a government site where data can be entered and represented in different graph forms. The website also offers graphing examples based on government data and a tutorial on how to create a graph.

Using **Chartle** (www.chartle.net), students can make simple graphs and charts, interactive charts, and unusual graphic representations of data online. No registration is required.

ChartGo (www.chartgo.com), a graph maker tool, is designed for older students. Students set the parameters and choose chart or graph types. The charts and graphs can then be embedded on a blog or wiki.

Maps

Scribble Maps (www.scribblemaps.com) combines Google Maps' images with the tools to scribble, draw, add text, insert place markers, and embed pictures on the map. As a whole class activity, students could track Flat Stanley (www.flatstanley.com) or other literacy and traveling projects, identify the locations of Skype partners, or follow the Iditarod trail. Individual students might re-create the journey of an historic figure, locate U.S. presidents' birthplaces, or identify landmarks in a country under study. Marked maps can be saved as images.

Another mapping tool, provided by National Geographic, is **MapMaker Interactive** (http://mapmaker.education.nationalgeographic.com). World and national maps can be marked to trace a journey, as in the books *Letter from Rifka* by Karen Hesse or *Around the World in 80 Days* by Jules Verne. Maps can be saved as editable files, so that the class members can continue to refine their maps as they progress through the books. In history classes, students can map migration paths or explorers' trails.

Cartoons

Creating cartoons causes students to narrow an event to its essential parts, which requires high levels of thinking. Good cartoons tell as much through pictures or drawings as through the words. One fourth grade teacher has her students use clip art, photos, and shapes in slideshow software to create their own comics. Resources to demonstrate how to use slides for comics can be found in the Google Apps User Group discussion board under "Creating Comic Strips with Google Slides" (www.appsusergroup.org/presentations/comic-strips-with-google-presentations).

Cartoons need not be funny; often comics carry weighty messages using irony or satire. Students can use comics to express viewpoints, explain concepts, review books, tell (or retell) stories, present facts, outline processes, or sequence events. Cartoons can be integrated into science or any other content area through explicit teaching about puns and other wordplay. A good source for ideas for science cartoons can be found at www.eric.ed.gov. Enter the search term "ed501244" to find "Humorous Cartoons Made by Preservice Teachers for Teaching Science Concepts to Elementary Students: Process and Product," an article by Rule, Sallis, and Donaldson (2008), including an appendix with 24 slides of humorous science comics made by preservice teachers. There are two comics per slide with the science explanation beneath each slide. The article is free and may encourage students to think creatively about what they could do on other topics. This may be one time when clip-art is an effective media for conveying a message.

Elementary teachers have fewer online resources for comic building than secondary teachers. Some of the most popular cartoon generators prohibit children under the age of 13 from using the sites. **Bitstrips** (http://bitstrips.com/create/comic) and **Pixton** (www.pixton.com) have free areas where they do not allow children under age 13. Instead, elementary teachers must use the subscription-based versions: Bitstrips for Schools (www.bitstripsforschools.com) and Pixton for Schools (www.pixton.com/schools/overview).

MakeBeliefsComix (www.makebeliefscomix.com) is free and geared toward children. A limited cast of characters and palette make this an easy-to-master tool. (Users need a Flash Player 10 or above.) The printables and lesson plans on this site are incredibly helpful for elementary teachers. Finished cartoons can be printed or emailed, but not saved. Students may write talk balloons in English, Spanish, French, German, Italian, Portuguese, or Latin. The site has a Special Needs section with ideas and tips from those who work with special needs students.

Creaza Cartoonist (www.creazaeducation.com/cartoonist) states that, in compliance with child privacy laws, anyone 15 years old or younger needs parental permission to work on the site. As parents are likely to give teachers permission to use the site at school, this may span elementary through secondary programs. The site has additional tools that could be worthwhile to explore as well. Watch the short video on the registration page to see how to use the tools.

Marvel Comics (http://marvel.com/games/play/34/create_your_own_comic) offers Create Your Own Comic. The site requires registration. Children have access to Marvel action heroes, backgrounds, and dialog boxes to create superhero comics, either as a strip or a whole comic book. Consider letting students write mysteries or superhero tales in cartoon strips. The end products can be printed.

Primary Access (www.primaryaccess.org) is a free digital movie, rebus, storyboard, and cartoon making tool. Teachers can register for an account and manage a class list.

Graphic Novels or Short Stories

Increasingly, teachers are becoming aware of how graphic novels intrigue visual learners as reading materials. Graphic novels also benefit students who are learning English because the pictures carry so much of the story line. Consider the level of inference students must use to "read" the pictures in a graphic novel!

Graphic novels can be engaging and challenging for students to write as well. For students who struggle with words, graphic novels can help them express their own complex ideas, including various characters' emotions, motivations, and shades of meaning, that these students are not equipped to express using words alone.

I use the words "graphic novels" loosely when discussing student products. A true graphic novel would require more time and expertise than could be expected at the elementary or even secondary level among most students. Instead of full-length novels, students can produce short graphic stories, like simple comic books, that tell fictional stories, retell stories they've read, or review historical events.

As with cartooning, students need a plan prior to commencing their graphic stories, but unlike cartooning, creating graphic stories requires entire storylines. Ideally, students use storyboards to plan their ideas for graphic novels, so that they can review their stories with peers to identify any aspects that may be missing or confusing. Illustrations can be hand drawn or computer based. Depending on prior experiences, students could stage props to photograph for their novels.

Advanced students might combine photographic backgrounds with clip art and hand drawing in a drawing program. Fourth and fifth grade students at my previous school often pasted background photos and clip art into the Paint graphics program; then they used the drawing tools to add details. They would save the mashedup pictures and import them into presentations slides. In the slides, they used shapes to make speech bubbles and added text. This was not something teachers taught—students discovered Paint themselves and taught one another. Secondary students could easily replicate this.

Graphic novels or short stories can be produced in several venues mentioned throughout this book: slideshows, programs such as Photo Story 3 and iMovie, online book creation sites, or word processing programs. Use the tools that are comfortable for your students. Ideas for graphic books or stories should not be limited to fiction. Think about graphic nonfiction articles that explain concepts in content areas or make local history accessible to younger students. These could be bound (or converted to ebooks) to be part of the school library's collection.

 VOICES OF EXPERIENCE

Sally Brown, associate professor of literacy
Georgia Southern University, Statesboro, Georgia
SallyBrown@GeorgiaSouthern.edu

Graphic novels can serve as important scaffolds in reading comprehension for English language learners due to their visual nature. I decided to engage a diverse group of second graders in a nine-week inquiry centered on graphic novels. The inquiry began by immersing students in reading and listening to read-alouds of graphic novels, like *Babymouse: Queen of the World!* (Holm & Holm, 2005). At the beginning of the experience, I started a class blog to document student learning. Each child created a fake name to use on the blog to protect student identity. I used Edublogs (http://edublogs.org) because of all of the security features of the site. I met with excited students in small groups as they devoured these captivating books. Lessons were planned to guide students' exploration of text features, like panels and speech bubbles. As students learned the basics, they started experimenting with characters' voices as they read books in the same series. Other students investigated a multitude of books to help them get a sense

Continued

of story elements, such as setting, problem, and solution. In all cases, students concentrated on the visual elements of graphic novels to gain an understanding of the storyline.

After four weeks of reading, I moved the focus to writing. Each student wrote a graphic novel. Students were buzzing with ideas for their stories. Some of their ideas came from the graphic novels they had read, and others were from cartoons or personal experiences. To begin the process, the students brainstormed on paper about characters, settings, problems, and solutions. In addition, they drew draft images of their characters. Once they had a working idea, the students began drawing their graphic novels. They could choose from several blank papers with frames in varying configurations. The pencil drawing occurred before the writing to aid with construction of a meaningful storyline. When students were finished illustrating the entire sheet, they wrote their draft texts on small Post-it notes and placed the notes in the appropriate speech bubbles. In one-on-one conferences, the students and I edited their writing on the Post-it notes for spelling, grammar, and punctuation. After the entire page was ready, students traced their images and wrote their words with a fine tipped black marker. Students continued creating their novels over the course of about three weeks. The last step in the writing process was coloring the images with colored pencils.

Upon completion of the paper copy of the graphic novel, students moved toward the digital version, using Microsoft's Photo Story 3. This software was chosen because it is free and very easy to use. I scanned each student's graphic novel and loaded their files onto one of the three classroom computers. The students took over from there. They easily learned how to upload their images, add titles, record their voices, and embed music in their videos. I taught the first student the process, and then that student taught the next student. The project culminated with an authors' celebration: Each digital graphic novel was played for the class, and students wrote comments about each other's stories. To see the journey and final graphic novel projects, go to http://exploringgraphicnovels.edublogs.org.

Animations

Although most teachers will consider animations too difficult for whole class instruction and exploration, I've included this topic for teachers who work with students who love to challenge themselves with technology. Animation can be exceedingly engaging and fun. I've tried to present the simple version that students could explore if they finish work early or are in a club or after-school setting. Some online tools make it easy to use animation. I limited the list of sites to easier formats. Secondary teachers should explore the simple sites first and then do an online search for more advanced versions.

Children are fascinated with the potential of animations, but the task of making effective animations requires patience and knowledge of how animations work. Some free programming software packages, such as **Squeak** and **Scratch**, can be used to program animations, but few teachers have the skills, or the interest in building the skills, or the time to teach programming code successfully. Instead, I suggest that teachers direct students to online animation sites, which provide the tools to play drawings at high speed to simulate changes. When drawing images for animation, students learn that changes happen slowly over several frames. Before trying animation sites, students need to know the four ways images can change:

Size. An image can be made progressively larger or smaller.

Shape. The shape of an image can be progressively altered until it becomes something else.

Position. The location of an image can be changed to create the illusion of movement.

Addition/Subtraction. On each page, adding or subtracting part of an image creates the illusion that an invisible hand is drawing or erasing the image.

Students need several opportunities to try out animation tools before they begin to master the skills. Their first experiences will probably result in poorly executed animations, but they will learn through their failures. The technical and art aspects of animation require a lot of cognitive skill, so before they begin, students should have a simple plan for their projects in mind, perhaps including a storyboard. They could illustrate a (very!) short story, simulate a chemical reaction, or show an electrical current lighting a bulb. Consider demonstrating the water cycle or life cycle of a plant or how simple machines work. The animation tools students use will determine the complexity of their animations.

The resources available for student-generated animations range from sites where students direct the animation but do not need to understand the technical aspects to tools where students do all the work of creating the sense of motion. At first, students need to explore a few tools to learn how they work.

Fluxtime Studio (www.fluxtime.com/animate.php) combines personal drawings with movement and can be used to tell a simple story. Be sure to access the Quick Start Guide—reading it will save exploration time. This site is a blend between the professionalism of Go Animate and the technical art of animation. The site does not require registration, and the finished product can be emailed.

Flipbook (www.benettonplay.com/toys/flipbookdeluxe/guest.php) has simple, intuitive drawing tools. Students need to know that they are creating each slide of the animation. Since the slides flip quickly, changing something in every slide actually makes the animation jumpy, rather than smooth. Students should insert two or three identical slides before they make any slight change to the next slide. This simple rule will improve the animations significantly. Guests are allowed to create flipbooks of up to 100 frames without registering; flipbooks made by registered users are shown in a gallery on the site. If you need examples, you can print out a flip book sample at **Cosmic Kanga** (www.zuzu.org/printout.html) or see advertising flip books at **Flippies** (www.flippies.com/flipbooks-gallery).

ABCya is recommended for students in grades 3–5 and would be a great platform for the sequenced drawings mentioned above. In ABCya's first animation interface, **Make an Animation: Classic Version** (www.abcya.com/animate_classic.htm), students draw a background first, and then begin to make up to 40 slides of animations. A checkbox enables the animator to see the previous slide in an underlay, so that the elements of the previous panel can be redrawn with slight variations. It's also possible to copy a slide. The preview lets students know how the animation looks. Animations work best if slides are copied one or two times before any change is introduced because the slides move so fast. Saving the animation sends it to the computer so it can be saved to a student's file, the school server, or the desktop. The classic version is still available on the site, as well as an updated version recommended for grades 3-5 called Make an Animation (http://www.abcya.com/animate.htm). In the updated version, students can upload their own pictures for the background, adjust the frame rate, and make up to 100 frames. ABCya! is a great site for teaching students the fine art of animation. The tutorial on the site introduces the tools and potential of animation. Creating animations represents Bloom's taxonomy at its highest level.

PowToon (www.powtoon.com/edu-home) has an educator site that allows secondary students and teachers to create accounts. Many of the services are free, although the final products are watermarked and not downloadable. Student and teacher accounts are very affordable. With a teacher subscription, this site could be used with elementary students. Take a look at the Tutorials page to see what the site offers for your students.

The use of technology tools for visual learners balances the auditory/verbal activities that normally predominate in the classroom environment. When teachers increase the visual stimuli they allow students to use in the classroom, they notice an increase in student engagement, particularly for students who struggle to complete text-based tasks. Additionally, all students, no matter what their learning preferences, benefit from projects and ideas that encourage the use of visual skills.

Fifteen Fabulous Visual Projects

Drawings. Draw a family portrait or a glyph.

Show what you know. Draw and label a content concept.

Build an avatar. Design a portrait for an online profile.

Graphic organizer. Create a visual organizer from scratch.

Event timeline. Sequence an event with pictures and captions.

Illustration. Illustrate a writing project.

Sequence slideshow. Draw the steps to a sequence in a slideshow.

Visual dictionary. Illustrate vocabulary words.

Story cartoon. Draw a multiframe cartoon of a story or historic event.

Map a route. Trace the westward movement or the settlement of your state.

Graph it. Collect and display data.

Cards. Design cover art for thank-you or seasonal cards.

Idiom illustration cards. Illustrate idioms to post in the classroom.

Historical dialog. Import historical photos and add dialog boxes.

Book it. Create a wordless picture book.

CHAPTER 9

Leveraging Technology for Auditory Learning

AUDITORY/VERBAL LEARNERS prefer to learn through both sound and speech. Some people believe that auditory/verbal learners dislike writing; others believe that writing is a form of speech, and auditory learners mentally say the words they are writing. In the VARK learning preferences model, writing is considered part of the *read/write* learning preference. For the purposes of this book, auditory/verbal learning preferences will be treated as speech, sound, and writing. Students with a strong inclination for auditory learning represent less than one-third of students in a classroom, yet the majority of elementary instruction is delivered in an auditory/verbal mode. Use of digital technologies generally decreases the percentage of time given to the auditory/verbal mode, primarily because it increases the prevalence of visual stimuli.

Interestingly, most technology tools and uses either do not access auditory stimuli or combine it with visual stimuli in multimedia work.

However, students can use auditory and verbal tools to demonstrate their understanding of content materials. The following examples capitalize on students' auditory/verbal strengths, although some may combine the auditory/verbal mode with other learning preference modes.

Listening

In the U. S., students spend about 50% of every class period listening (Beall et.al., 2008, International Journal of Listening). It's no wonder that listening is a critical literacy skill addressed in educational standards. Good listening leads to academic success. The listening activities listed here can help students practice listening skills.

Online Listening. The Exploratorium (www.exploratorium.edu/listen/lg_intro.php) has listening activities as well as listening guides, which are videos of ways and reasons people listen to their environments. The videos introduce a naturalist who listens to the sounds of nature, a blind man who navigates by sound, a musician who creates instruments, an auto mechanic who listens to solve problems, and a deaf man who uses a cochlear implant for listening so that he can hear and communicate.

Primary Student Listening Interactives. The Utah Education Network (UEN) lists 10 listening activities for K-2 students on its Listening Page (http://www. uen.org/k-2interactives/listening.shtml). These activities are useful for classroom centers. Most require Flash.

Interactive Listening Activities. MED-EL, a cochlear implant company, has Interactive Listening Games (http://www.medel.com/resources-for-success-sound-scape/) designed to help implanted patients of all ages practice their listening skills. Teachers can access these activities as well. For instance, in Telling Tales (ages 10 and up), children listen to 13 different tales in three difficulty levels and answer questions after each story.

Audio Stories

Auditory learners enjoy input from audio stories and books. In fact, many class-rooms have listening centers with books on tape. The computer station can become a listening center as well. Audio stories are available on many sites, and some, but not all, are downloadable to MP3 devices. Some need to be streamed live. Unlike animated video books, streamed audio takes relatively little bandwidth, so streaming the stories does not slow down the network.

For elementary students, treat online audio similar to listening centers in the classroom. Minimize the story screen and open a drawing program so students can draw a scene from the story as they listen. Or, students can write responses to the story in a word processing or blog window. Pairing students to listen and then discuss the stories also has value. Sometimes the goal is simply to encourage students to enjoy stories!

Online audio books listed here are mainly for elementary students; many stories are available through digital apps for Apple products. Secondary students can access online listening through **The Internet Archive** (https://archive.org/details/audio_bookspoetry) or their public library's collection.

The Story Home (http://thestoryhome.com) offers many fairy tales, classics, fables, and original pieces as audio stories narrated by Alan Scofield, the site's creator. These can be downloaded through iTunes, accessed through an iPad app, or streamed online.

Storynory (http://storynory.com) also hosts many fairy tales, fables, classics, and original audio stories narrated by professional actors. These can be downloaded through iTunes, accessed through an iPad app, or streamed online.

Online Audio Stories (www.onlineaudiostories.com/category/all_stories/audio_stories) has stories and their texts for listening and reading. Many poems are housed on this site. Auditory learners particularly enjoy the rhythms of poetry.

Light Up Your Brain! (http://audiostories.lightupyourbrain.com) audio stories can be downloaded as zip files to put onto an MP3 device or can be listened to online. The texts for the stories are also on the site, so readers can follow along.

Lit2Go (http://etc.usf.edu/lit2go), sponsored by Florida's Educational Technology Clearinghouse, is a free collection of stories and poems sorted by K–12 grade levels. Each piece of literature has a citation, abstract, word count, and playing time listed. Files may be downloaded as MP3s or played online, with or without texts. Most stories and poems are tied to a reading strategy as well.

Writing

Students' writing springs from their imaginations, based on original thinking or on what they have observed, heard, or read, which makes writing an excellent assessment of how students understand concepts. Teachers can find bookshelves of texts about teaching writing, so, even though I earned my doctorate with research on student writing, I will not cover the topic exhaustively here. A couple of topics bear mentioning, if only because they reflect the most common questions I am asked at seminars and workshops.

To Keyboard or Not

At the primary level, typing a simple sentence can take a child thirty minutes or more, so how can teachers balance the benefits of word processing with the barrier of typing? In some classrooms, students spend hours learning proper keyboarding. For me, this unnecessarily wastes instructional time. Yes, students need to be familiar with letter placement on keyboards. Yes, they will be able to type faster—eventually—if they learn touch typing. On the other hand, no one can tell from the final typed piece whether it was typed with ten fingers or two.

Helpful Keyboarding Hints

In an undergraduate writing course I taught, most students did not use formal touch typing, and some had very strange typing practices. They adopted techniques that worked for them; primarily they learned to type by typing—emails, texts, and papers. With the increase of touch pads and small (phone) keypads, adult typing practices have changed. I've observed that many people use two-finger touch (one finger of each hand) to type on pad computers, thumbs to type on phone keyboards, and one finger on phone touchpads. Keyboarding skills may no longer be relevant in real life.

Still, students need to get their texts onto computers so that they can read for sense and revise. The following tips may be helpful:

- Unless a student's handwriting is too irregular for even the student to read, require that students handwrite rough drafts. Composing at the keyboard requires students to split their cognitive power between finding the keys and maintaining the sense of the text. The focus on the keys will drain their ability to write clearly until they become competent typists.

- If you choose to teach keyboarding, have students practice in short bursts at a center in the classroom or as a prelude to a different lab activity. Many students, particularly young children, cannot maintain a focus on typing for longer than ten minutes.

- Try an intense but very short typing course with authentic reasons to type.

- Encourage a "type fast, fix later" mentality. Turn off monitors if needed to keep students from constantly fixing typos. Editing can come later.

- Require students to use default fonts until all the words have been typed. As a reward for typing, let students make texts prettier by changing font types, colors, or sizes.

- Turn off spelling and grammar checks until students have finished their typing. The red and green underlines distract most students. (Sometimes they will develop creative solutions to rid themselves of red underlines. For instance, one second grader clicked on "Add to dictionary" every time he got a red underline, which rendered the computer's dictionary useless.) After the typing is done, reactivate the spell checker. The grammar checker is rarely worth using—it makes as many errors as the students do.

- Use older student buddies to type. Intermediate students, or even middle or high school volunteers, can help the slowest typists.

- At the lowest grade levels where texts are short, consider having students record stories or paragraphs to be transcribed by a volunteer.

- Ask parents to support students' typing skills at home by requiring students to practice for 5–10 minutes to earn television or computer game time. Students can use free online typing programs.

- If students have access to word processors at home, assign typing practice as homework.

VOICES OF EXPERIENCE

Lauren Brannan, former technology support teacher
J. E. Turner Elementary School, Wilmer, Alabama

We are planning to have a typing camp this year for our third graders to address the standards for keyboarding. I have found that students' lack of keyboarding skills hinders many lessons that include word processing.

This year we will set aside three hours in the afternoon for one week to have typing camp. We will have three stations in order to include an entire grade level. We will have the computer lab, where we will use the Almena Method program to teach keyboarding skills. We will also include collaborative stories and blogging in this station.

The second station is for using the mobile keyboarding equipment designed to help students learn to type, furnished by our local middle school. This system has built-in keyboarding practice and assessments, as well as the capacity to word process and print.

The final station is our campground, where students will keep a scrapbook about their camping experiences, sing songs, and enjoy camping snacks. After this week, our third graders will be typing their hearts out!

Free Online Keyboarding Sites

Give students a list of free keyboarding sites and a plan for their practice. To earn TV or video game time, they need to spend 5–10 minutes on a typing site. Offer an incentive if they track their improvement in a spreadsheet each time they use a site. After tracking progress for 20–30 sessions, they can graph the data (math reinforcement) and earn a reward. Rewards do not have to be big—students' names and pictures on a "Typing Titan" poster; a 15-minute, after-school computer break; or something else adapted to the school's practices. Although many other free online keyboarding sites exist, the following list provides sufficient choices for any school.

Find the Letter (www.freewebs.com/weddell/findtheletter.html) is a 30-second key recognition game. Students try to type as many letters as possible in 30 seconds; letters appear one at a time on their monitors. This is one short test students can take to track their keyboarding improvement.

Dance Mat Typing (www.bbc.co.uk/guides/z3c6tfr) looks more like a game than other sites, which makes it attractive to kids. Four levels of play teach keyboarding. The site begins with instructions, followed by the four learning sequences, information on healthy ergonomics when typing, and additional information on computing.

Sense-Lang (http://games.sense-lang.org) contains many attractive typing games that will engage students. Although tutorials are also available, students will prefer the games.

Super Hyper Spider Typer (www.hoodamath.com/games/superhyperspidertyper.html) also makes typing a game rather than serious business. And it's such a tongue twister, too!

 Learn2Type for Schools (www.learn2type.com/schools/whatis.cfm) provides classroom management accounts so that teachers can track students' time and improvement. This site is for serious keyboarding practice.

Introducing Word Processing

As the purpose of word processors is to process words, intuitively one would think that students should use word processors for inputting text. Reconsider. Word processors handle text well but can frustrate novice users if they want to add illustrations or captions. For instance, pictures sometimes import as text and sometimes as independent objects. As independent objects, the pictures can jump to different locations on the page or land on top of text. Textboxes can also exasperate novice users.

Presentation software (e.g., PowerPoint, Impress, Keynote) accomplishes the same tasks as word processors but with much less angst because the features work in more predictable ways. Teach young students to work in presentation software first. Students can write in text boxes and adjust the placement of words and pictures on the page to their satisfaction. No one can tell which program students used once their products are printed or turned into PDF documents.

Whether students use word processors or other programs that handle text, writing on computers does have a place in the elementary classroom. In fact, computers have revolutionized writing in some classrooms. Students with handwriting issues find typing easier and appreciate the professional look of the final product. Those who struggle with spelling, punctuation, and capitalization benefit from the automatic correction features. Most important, revisions are easier to accomplish on a computer than by hand.

Ideas for Writing

The following ideas emphasize word processing as a skill, not the use of a particular word processing program. The suggestions discuss writing only. Additions of graphic elements or integration of the text into a more visual mode may supplement the writing, but these options are not discussed here. Feel free to experiment with equipment and programs—and with online word processing applications.

Individual Text

Students regularly produce texts in all content areas in the elementary classroom, and any writing can be typed. Students should type from rough or corrected drafts. Ideally, teachers will ask students to revise once the text is typed. For the final draft, students may add visual elements and font effects to make the presentation more pleasing.

Classroom Peer Interactive Text

Inviting other students to read and respond to text pushes writing up a level in complexity. Giving and accepting writing support does not come easily or naturally to students. Typically, peers give feedback about editing rather than suggesting revisions, and many writers resist suggestions for improving their own texts.

We need to understand that writing, more than any other academic task, ties into the emotional sense of self. Hearing criticism of our writing feels like criticism of who we are. Teachers and students should talk frankly about this pitfall so that students can begin to disengage from emotional responses.

Also, students need to understand the differences between writers and readers. The writer's intent may be clear to the writer, but the reader does not always pick it up. This is true for all writers (professional and amateur) everywhere. As a published author who submits her work to a writing critique group, I have never conveyed my intent perfectly on the first draft! With any peer response, the reader's feedback—pointing out places where the reader is not sure about the writer's intent—should dominate. That is, students need to learn to accept and act upon feedback so they can improve their writing skills.

Saying only, "This is really good" cheats the writer. The text may have excellent sections, and writers need to hear about those specifically. But saying only, "This is really good" neither identifies the good parts nor gives the writer room to grow. Even young children can learn to say, "As a reader, I wanted to know more about …" or "As a reader, I was confused when. …" Using "as a reader" to introduce suggestions may help writers recognize that what is clear in their heads isn't always conveyed clearly to readers.

Until a piece of writing's content and structure have been revised to satisfy readers, students should not waste time on editing. After all, why edit something that might change completely in a revision?

Global Peer Revision

Sometimes, after students begin to value the viewpoints of readers, teachers can expand the peer revision opportunities to global partners. This approach can be as structured as two teachers in distant schools assigning revision partners between their classes or as loosely as inserting text in a global student-only space, such as **ePals** (www.epals.com/join.php) and then opening it to public comment. Writing for an authentic audience will motivate students to do their best writing, so aim to get students' writing out to a broader audience than just classmates. Before embarking on a wide network, though, be certain your students know about netiquette and online safety.

Writing for Audience Comment

Students may write to solicit feedback about their ideas. Solicited feedback generally has the purpose of furthering the conversation about content and not necessarily improving a student's writing skills. A common form of audience comment would be a blog. Teachers can use **Class Blogmeister** (http://class-blogmeister.com) or other student-only sites for hosting student blogs within a teacher's account. Students publish their projects or writings for comment. Blogs may also be useful for discussing books, reporting on class activities, and offering opinions on teacher-generated questions.

A site to explore to see samples of students' blogs and peers' comments is **Comments4Kids: Bringing Authenticity to Blogging** (http://comments4kids. blogspot.com). Participants list their class blogs and invite students to comment to student authors about what is posted. It's an excellent plan for connecting student bloggers. After you and your students study this site, you may decide to invite comments on your students' blogs.

Teaching Students to Blog

Teachers are often frustrated when students' blogs lack substance. Sometimes the problem is that students are asked to blog about something about which they have nothing to say, but more often the problem is that blogging skills have not been explicitly taught, *even though blogging is a specific genre of writing.* By this, I'm not referring to netiquette, although using proper manners online is important.

Blogging should be taught as a genre with specific characteristics. The essence of blogging is writing thoughtfully about topics on which the blogger offers personal insights, opinions, arguments, and new ideas. A blog is an individual's ongoing, chronological website of his or her own informed opinions and reflections. If a person's blog post on a particular day does not give readers something to think and talk about, then it will not start a conversation—triggering a conversation (i.e., comments from readers) is the goal of blogging. Because blogging attempts to initiate conversations, responses to a blog post should have the same characteristics as the original post: Responses must add pieces of new information—in the forms of questions, reactions, insights, experiences, or challenges—that give subsequent readers more reasons to respond. Research on online communities indicates that when responses simply praise or agree, the conversation stops. Learning to write good blog responses/comments will have beneficial effects on oral class discussions because the same techniques apply.

Collaborative Writing

Often in business, colleagues collaborate on writing projects. Students can also collaborate as writers. Teachers handle the collaborative process in different ways, depending on the goals of the project, design of the collaborative space, and access to technology tools. For instance, many school districts have created district-specific domains through Google Apps for Education, so that each student has an account and email within the confines of the district's filtering system. Because Google Docs permits multiple authors on one document, students can work in groups on a single text. Be aware that students may not wait for permission to collaborate. One third grade teacher discovered that her students were sharing their documents and soliciting feedback and collaboration weeks before she had planned to introduce the collaborative features of Google Docs. A fourth grade teacher talked about how her students carried their laptops to peers' desks so that they could ask for feedback on their writing. She eventually migrated their writing to Google Docs to make the collaborations easier.

Edmodo (www.edmodo.com) and **Schoology** (www.schoology.com/K-12.php) are learning management systems discussed in detail in Chapter 14, "Teacher Resources." Using these platforms, teachers can create groups of students, give each group different questions for their blog or collaborative space, and keep track of all students' work. Through these networks, teachers can communicate with other teachers worldwide and discover new resources.

Wikis also offer the option of collaboration on texts. Some people email the document from writer to writer to build a final piece. Whatever collaborative tool is used, the team needs to agree on a rough outline of the document and a method of working together.

Most writing requires high levels of thinking, particularly if students are writing for audiences other than the teacher. When students' writing goes global, even reluctant writers are eager to participate.

Writing Poetry

Auditory/verbal students love to listen to the rhythms of poetry, compose their own poems, and share by reading them to others. After listening to children's poems online (see Poetry for Listening below), students can access **Instant Poetry Forms** (http://ettcweb.lr.k12.nj.us/forms/newpoem.htm), a website that provides frames for writing poems. Students can choose the form of the poem from a list on the left side of the page. There are fill-in boxes for each line of the poem, and students are directed on how to fill them in with their ideas. A sample poem is included for each frame. Press the Create button, and the finished poem will appear. Copy the poem to a word processing program to touch up the fonts or add illustrations. As poetry forms vary in size, primary students can create poems as successfully as older students.

VOICES OF EXPERIENCE

Sheri Edwards, teacher and technology director
Nespelem School, Nespelem, Washington

Have you ever wanted to apply a technology tool in your classroom but hesitated because of a lack of knowledge? After participating in a free TeachersFirst OK2Ask (http://teachersfirst.com/OK2Ask.cfm) webinar on Google Apps Collaboration, I immediately applied the strategy in my classroom.

I could do this because the session allowed time for me to explore the strategy, discuss it with others and the presenters, and consider the application in my own classroom—all within an hour session!

My middle school students collaborated on a Google presentation as a thank-you to the people who provided them with an outdoor education day. Students logged into the document and added slides to include "who" and "what" text. The next day, as a class, we chose pictures from our iPhoto library to upload into the presentation and edited the text to correct our errors. It worked beautifully: we were able to be specific about the value of the day by explaining what we did and learned.

Two students from each class delivered a downloaded and printed color copy, now with student signatures and spiral bound by the librarian, to the Colville Tribal Council to share their learning. By writing about the slides themselves, students clearly stated with confidence their learning and appreciation for the outdoor day. The Council appreciated our "Thank-you." Google Apps has helped our students write and collaborate on projects that extend beyond our classroom.

Poetry for Listening

Young students can listen to poems written and recorded for children. Auditory learners are likely to understand poetry more easily if they hear it. Secondary teachers who teach literature have a wide array of poems for students to enjoy. Many online resources for listening to poetry are available, including poems read by the poets themselves, actors, and winners of recitation contests.

Poetry Archive (www.poetryarchive.org) features poets reading their own poetry. Young students can go to the students' page or the children's archive to hear poets. Older students may prefer the search feature to find particular poets or poems. When a poem title is clicked, the poem comes up as an audio file and as text.

Poetry Out Loud (www.poetryoutloud.org) is the website of the National Recitation Contest. In addition to hearing poems, students can learn recitation tips and listen to contest winners.

Open Culture (www.openculture.com/audio_books_poetry) has mostly classical and some contemporary poetry to stream or download.

Lit2Go (http://etc.usf.edu/lit2go/search/?q=poetry), mentioned earlier in this chapter, can be accessed for audio clips of poetry.

Library of Congress Web Guide for Poetry Audio Recordings: A Guide to Online Resources (www.loc.gov/rr/program/bib/poetryaudio) is an aggregator of audio poetry sources, more than can be listed here. Well worth a visit!

Songwriting

Although songwriting is another form of writing, in the same way that poetry and graphic novels are, not many students have chances to write and perform songs. In a fourth grade class, students read a plantation song that was presented in their text as a poem. The plantation song represented two viewpoints in different stanzas, one stanza from the master's point of view and the other from the slave's point of view, with a chorus that could be interpreted differently if it were sung by the master or the slave.

Students emulated the plantation song when they wrote two-stanza songs from the viewpoints of a teacher and a student, with a chorus that either teacher or student could sing. They then recorded the songs to share with classmates. Analyzing the characteristics of the original song, developing their songs to convey their conceptions of a teacher's and a student's viewpoints, and then writing a chorus that could be sung by either teacher or student required students to work at the highest level of Bloom's taxonomy. They considered it fun.

Authoring Books

One of the first writing purposes I saw in schools was writing books. Students revised and illustrated something they had written—fiction or nonfiction—and then went to the publishing lab to have the book compiled and laminated. Volunteers spent hours putting the students' books together back then.

With technology tools, students can combine their texts and illustrations to create books without the intervention of volunteers. Options vary. Students can arrange their texts and illustrations on slides in presentation software (oriented either as portrait or landscape), can print two-sided pages, and can bind the pages together. Or, they can use desktop publishing software, if it's available. Desktop publishing programs work differently, so teachers need to be familiar with the software's functions. Some online book publishers provide tools for assembling books online for generating ebooks or hard copies of books. These publishers operate on a fee for services basis.

The number of resources for creating online books feels overwhelming because so many target adults who write for children rather than student writers. Many of these sites could be used with secondary students; however, with elementary students, the goal is to find resources that have child-friendly tools and are easily navigated. The following resources suit different needs. Explore them to find the one that works best for your classroom.

PagePlus Starter Edition (www.serif.com/desktop-publishing-software) is a free, downloadable software package (for Windows only) that has book publishing capability, particularly if you have duplex printing available or can figure out how to print pages on two sides. The tools look similar to those in word processors. The features that come only in the pro version have red lines through them on the menu bar. I was able to save and print a short book.

RealeWriter (http://realewriter.com) is downloadable software for Mac or PC. The designers are giving away the Pro version of the software for free. However, the software is no longer being developed or supported. I used the original free version with students and liked the program. This software is worth experimenting with now that the Pro version is free.

my StoryMaker (www.carnegielibrary.org/kids/storymaker) is housed within the Carnegie Library website. The site is designed for primary students and language learners. It provides limited characters, scenery, and objects and helps students when they seem stuck. The final story can be published as a PDF to share with others. Students get a story number to access their story online. However, stories are deleted after one month, so students should also save a PDF version to print or share.

StoryJumper (www.storyjumper.com/main/classroom) has a classroom edition for enabling students to write and illustrate books. Teachers sign up their classes under a teacher account and set a time limit for each use. Parents can sign up for a free home interface with the school version. Parents can see students' work, and the final books can be uploaded or purchased at a special education rate (minimum of 15 books total). The StoryStarter workbook offers seven excellent steps for teaching students how to create interesting, detailed stories, which is a helpful teaching tool in itself.

Bookemon for Educators (www.bookemon.com/edcenter-home) provides private space for K–12 and college members (teachers, administrators, and staff members) to add students' accounts to their own accounts for monitoring students' work. To preview a book, you can download a PDF version of the book to a computer, but the PDF will not be printable from your computer. Once the books are edited and sent to be published, they cannot be changed. Publication is online (you can set privacy levels) with options to purchase printed copies.

ePubBud (www.epubbud.com) was created by a couple who had just experienced the loss of a newborn and wanted to tell their story. As the free site does require registration, for children under age 13, teachers have to create accounts and ask for parents' permission before using the site. Students can create books online, upload documents to be converted to e-publications, or digitize books for use on the iPad or other e-readers. The only cost is $19 for an ISBN number, which is needed if you wish to sell the book through Apple's iBookstore. The easiest way to use this site is for students to create their books first in slideshow format, save the book as a PDF, and upload it to the site for conversion.

Studentreasures (www.studentreasures.com) has online or handwritten options for publishing students' books. Students in all grades can publish class books, and students in grades 4 and above can publish individual books. This process works best if the books are written and illustrations finished before starting the online process. Details about publishing options can be found in the FAQs (http://www.studenttreasures.com/teacherslounge/free-resources/faqs).

Read, Write, Think (www.readwritethink.org/files/resources/interactives/flipbook) has a flipbook generator. Flipbooks are multipage books that are folded at the top. If you make one yourself first, teaching students how it works should go smoothly. These books cannot be saved, so they must be printed when completed. Drawing tools are available on this interactive tool. To save time, have students type their texts in a word processor so they can copy and paste them into the flipbook. Users must know in advance exactly how many pages they want to create.

Writing for Publication

Audiences for students' writing should be more than the classroom teacher. When the work is posted online, students can direct family members and friends to view their work, even when the students' names are not used. Writing for an audience motivates students to take extra care. Students can also submit their work for publication online. Sometimes students' work needs to be targeted to a particular topic or style, and at other times they can submit their best work on any topic in any style.

Online writing is generally more suited for students in late elementary through secondary school than for those in the primary grades. Each of the following sites indicates the age or grade ranges of the student authors targeted for publication.

Writer's Area (www.writersarea.com/kids/kids.html) accepts short stories, poems, articles, and other writings from students up to age 17 in the children's area. Not all submissions are published, so students should submit their best writing. Parents must give consent; to protect children, only the first letters of the writers' last names are published.

MY HERO (http://myhero.com) invites people of all ages to write, share art, or make movies about their heroes and submit them to the website. Registration is required by teachers or parents.

Cyberkids (www.cyberkids.com/he/html/submit.html) publishes work for and by kids ages 7–12. Creative works that include illustrations are more likely to be chosen than non-illustrated works.

Stone Soup (www.stonesoup.com/stone-soup-contributor-guideline) publishes fiction, nonfiction, poetry, and art from children ages 8–13 in its printed magazine. This link goes to submission guidelines. Stone Soup's editors prefer short short stories and poems in free verse. To read past issues of the magazine, which is published six times a year, go to the archive (www.stonesoup.com/archive).

Amazing Kids! (http://mag.amazing-kids.org/get-involved/write-for-us), an online magazine for kids by kids, invites manuscripts from students ages 5–18. Even if students do not write for this magazine, they may enjoy reading what others have written. This magazine accepts fiction; nonfiction, including tech, adventure, and cultural articles and kid-friendly recipes; poetry; jokes and riddles; art/photography; reviews; and videos.

Launch Pad (www.launchpadmag.com/write) encourages writers and illustrators ages 6–14 to submit materials via email for possible publication in its online magazine. Before submitting work, students need to check out the site's guidelines plus writing and art tips.

Magic Dragon (www.magicdragonmagazine.com) is a full-color, quarterly print magazine that publishes stories, poetry, and artwork from elementary school students. The site also contains Write It! Activities and How to! Activities.

Audio Recorders

Digital recorders enable students to talk and listen. Teachers can use any of the following equipment for acquiring audio files: digital recorders, MP3 players, and computers. Each has strengths and weaknesses.

Digital recorders cost $40 and more, are highly portable, and have the fewest buttons to master. Today's recorders hold 15–20 hours of sound files, which can be transferred quickly to a computer via a USB connection. Because of their ease of use, digital recorders may be the best equipment for capturing interviews, nature sounds, or other sound files that require leaving the classroom. Unlike other digital recording tools, recorders work exclusively with sound, so they are single-purpose tools. Students can record and listen to what they record. Place the recorders on surfaces when recording, or they will pick up noises from being handled. Many digital recorders accommodate an external microphone, and all have headphone jacks for private listening. MP3 players range from inexpensive audio-only devices to high-priced multimedia devices, such as the iPod touch. Some 2G and 4G players handle multimedia (sound, video, music, and audio-books) and still cost under $50. A distinct advantage of multimedia MP3 players is the ability to load video and music as well as audio books and live sounds. Devices may use buttons, wheels, rollers, or touch screens as controls, so learning how to run a particular MP3 player takes time. For this reason, teachers often seek grant monies to buy several of the same type at once. Students do not seem to struggle with the variety among MP3 players as much as adults do.

Generally, microphones are built-in, and MP3 players come with ear buds. However, some of the more expensive MP3 players require the purchase of a separate recording device. If you plan to use the MP3 player for audiobooks, realize that not all MP3 players handle books in the same way. Some will remember where an audio book was stopped; others start the book from the beginning every time. Be sure to research any player you consider buying so you get the best product for the uses you intend. The MP3 player I purchased most recently does not handle any files with digital rights management (such as the books I borrow from the public library), but nothing on the package alerted me to this limitation.

Some computers come with built-in microphones and cameras. In that case, students can record themselves directly at the computer. In a classroom where many students record at once, teachers should invest in headsets that include earphones and microphones. When using headsets, students need to experiment with positioning the microphone for the best sound. Sensitive microphones catch every breath; others sound muffled or exaggerate sibilants if they are too close to the person.

Headset costs range widely. Pay attention to whether you need the dual 3.5 mm plugs or a USB connection for the headsets because the connection type affects the price. USB headsets cost more. If a microphone is built into the computer, software to handle the audio input will also be built in; if you add a headset, you may need to download audio recording and editing software. The most commonly used free software is **Audacity** (http://audacity.sourceforge.net/download), which has versions for Windows, Mac, and Linux. A manual for Audacity is on its site, and an Audacity tutorial for teachers is available on YouTube (www.youtube.com/watch?v=9hUNR0gygEI).

Audio File Management

Not all digital recording devices create identical file types, and programs that import audio files sometimes accept only certain file extensions. This is particularly true if you try to switch between Windows and Apple platforms or if you use commercial programs. Only a few audio file extensions are commonly used by nonprofessionals, though hundreds exist. Programs from which students want to import sound may not accept all common audio file extensions. Audio files can be converted from one standard to another with conversion software. File conversion does not typically take long, and it will save the teacher time if two or three students become classroom experts on converting files.

Understanding Audio File Extensions

Most of the time, programs manage audio files in ways that don't require any intervention by the teacher or student. However, sometimes a file will not work in a particular program or transfer well between computer platforms. The error message may mention codecs (short for code-decode). Codecs are programs that encode and decode digital streams, such as audio, by compressing data for faster transmission. Knowing common audio file extensions and their uses can be helpful. File extensions are the letters that come after the period in a file name (such as .wav or .MP3). Here are some of the most common types of audio files:

.aiff or .wav—This format is used for Macs and Windows computers, respectively, for storing uncompressed, CD-quality sound files. These files are often quite large, about 10 MBs (megabytes) per minute of sound.

.flac—An acronym for free lossless audio codec, this file extension indicates that the compression of the file to save space does not reduce the quality of the file. This lossless compression format can be compared to using zip files to compress documents. FLAC coding formats are used most often for broadcasts and professional recordings.

.mp3—The most popular format for digitally storing sound files, MP3 files are compressed to about 10% of their original size by eliminating sounds that are essentially inaudible or unnecessary. Called a lossy compression format, MP3 is recommended for music files but not for voice. (And that's how MP3 players got their names—they were designed to play music files.)

.wma—Windows Media Audio format, owned by Microsoft, is used for Windows computers. Windows Media Audio format competes with iTunes software to be the default audio player for music and voices. Audio books borrowed from the library often download as WMA files and are transferable to MP3 players. Many library downloads can now be imported into iTunes to transfer to iPods as well.

.voc—Although not a common file extension, I include this as an example of a file extension that may appear on files from digital audio recorders. File extensions that seem unfamiliar generally reflect either the particular piece of equipment used or the default of an audio management file loaded on the computer. Sometimes files with such extensions import into programs easily, and sometimes they need to be converted.

Audio File Conversions

Occasionally, audio files have to be converted from one format to another. Many free conversion software packages can be found online and downloaded to computers easily. I have used the following two free conversion software packages.

Switch Audio File Converter Software (www.nch.com.au/switch), free for noncommercial use and usable on Windows and Apple platforms, is an audio converter only and very easy to use. The program gives the option to save the converted file in the same place as the original. With the suite comes a free audio mixer, which can mix sounds from more than one source, and a CD ripper, which copies music from one CD to another.

Format Factory (http://formatoz.com) operates on Windows only and converts audio, video, and picture files, so it is quite versatile as a converter. Unless directed otherwise, Format Factory saves converted files into a Format Factory folder on the computer's hard drive. The software is available for commercial and noncommercial uses.

Student Uses for Audio Recorders

In Chapter 4, "Instructional Use of Technology," digital audio recorders were mentioned as a tool for engaging students in listening to stories and recording reading assessments, and in Chapter 8, "Leveraging Technology for Visual Learning," several multimedia projects also included recording students' voices.

Students can also use digital recorders to generate other audio projects, such as these:

Story Reading

Enlisting students to record stories or books for younger students builds the older students' confidence and gives them practice reading aloud. Reading stories for younger students particularly helps striving readers or students learning English to build their reading and fluency skills. A good recording requires the reader to practice so that he or she can read fluently without stumbling. The teachers of younger students can store these audio files on a computer to transfer to MP3 players, so that their students can listen at home or at listening centers.

Storytelling

Reluctant writers may profit from talking through their stories before they attempt to write them. With digital recorders, they can record themselves as they tell their stories, listen critically, and then either re-record or begin to write.

For primary students, teachers can ask students to record their stories as a prewriting or writing activity. If the recording is used as a prewriting tool, students can record their stories, listen critically to determine whether they want to add details, and then write. Students who are not yet writing can still "write" stories by recording themselves. Their stories can be typed by volunteers and illustrated by the students. The beauty of having digital recordings is that the volunteer does not have to be present; the audio file can be emailed to the volunteer for transcription, which allows working parents to get involved with volunteerism. As primary students' stories are typically short, transcribing does not require much time.

Listening for Revision

Another way to avoid the editing-only feedback from other students while helping writers pay attention to their texts is to have writers record their stories for peer responses. For writers, reading stories aloud sometimes reveals flaws in logic, sentence structure, or content. Based on my dissertation study, having writers listen to their own read-alouds increases the likelihood that they will catch errors in logic or omissions. When peers listen to audio files of stories for critique, they are not distracted by mechanical errors and can focus on where stories become confusing or lack details. If you plan to ask peers to listen for critique purposes, provide a critique page with sentence stems: As a reader, I was interested when....

As a reader, I was confused when…. As a reader, I had questions about…. As a reader, I suggest….

Interviewing

Students can interview family members or community residents about local history, national historic events, childhood memories, or traditions. If residents have traveled, they may talk about places they've seen and traditions they experienced. Elected officials can talk about local issues, or individuals can talk about their careers or hobbies. When audio clips are combined with photographs, students can create stories that require less expertise than videos. The creativity required for this project extends it to the highest level of Bloom's taxonomy.

Podcasts

Podcasts are simply published audio files. The word comes from audio files ("casts" as in broadcasts) made for the MP3 player, the most popular of which is the iPod. Podcasts can inform parents about the week's activities in a classroom, teach concepts, capture students' opinions, deliver creative writing, share songs or raps, or resemble radio shows. Some student teams create podcasts that imitate broadcasts from their school and include interviews, grade level news, student-created jingles, and reminders about activities at the school. Good podcasts require writing a script and practicing before recording. Podcasts can be hosted on a school or district website or uploaded to iTunes.

Even though classrooms are typically heavy with auditory stimuli, the auditory input supported by technology is important to all learners. Teachers should provide opportunities for all students to write on computers and word processors. In fact, some schools consider language arts the most effective entry point for students using computers in classrooms. Audio recorders will interest auditory/verbal learners and probably also appeal to kinesthetic/tactile learners, so investing in one or more recorders can benefit many students in the classroom. Audio books, stories, and poetry can engage students who struggle to read grade level materials and may help auditory learners' reading comprehension.

Fifteen Fabulous Auditory Projects

Listen to a book. Listen to a text as you read along.

Write. Produce stories, poetry, scripts, and nonfiction works.

Practice fluency. Record yourself reading; listen to how you did.

Podcast. Podcast class news for parents.

Model reading skills. Create audio book files for younger students.

Interview. Listen to what community members know.

Skype an author. Hear an author discuss his or her writing.

Blog. Write your own or comment on someone else's blog.

Revel in poetry. Listen to a poem or record one of your own.

Self-critique. Listen to your own text for revision ideas.

Write a song. Perform it as you make a podcast.

Storytelling. Listen to storytellers or record your own story.

Peer critique. Review a peer's recorded text to suggest how the person can improve it.

Speak up. Add audio features to a slideshow.

Skype a partner. Engage with global partners through Skype.

CHAPTER 10

Leveraging Technology for Kinesthetic/Tactile Learning

KINESTHETIC/TACTILE LEARNERS prefer being active in the classroom. They want to experience and touch what they are learning about. Experts disagree about how many students have strong kinesthetic/tactile learning preferences. Some speculate that the majority of students in the early grades prefer activity and hands-on experiences, but the percentage decreases as individuals mature, until fewer than 10% of adult learners claim this preference.

Teachers will often recognize that some students need kinesthetic/tactile learning because of their restlessness. Other signs of kinesthetic/tactile learners are their penchant to explore everything physically and to excel in movement activities, such as dance, athletics, drama, and field trips. Sometimes these students are considered behavior problems because of their need to move.

Technology-based projects that appeal to other learning styles will likely appeal to kinesthetic/tactile learners as well because the projects require active participation. When working with technology, students talk and combine thinking with movement. If technology tools are mobile, such as laptops, digital recorders, e-readers, and cameras, kinesthetic/tactile learners can move around naturally. Even with desktop computers, students can adjust their workspaces to meet the need for movement. One second grader used to stand when he worked at a desktop computer; he was short enough to manage the computer without stooping, and standing let him move his body.

Both digital still and video cameras, covered in other chapters of the book, appeal to kinesthetic/tactile learners. Auditory tools, such as digital recorders and MP3 players, fascinate students with kinesthetic/tactile learning preferences. Fortunately, many active learners are also satisfied with computer-based experiences that require interactions with on-screen stimuli. Virtual experiences give users a sense of action.

In this chapter, the ideas will not focus on student-generated projects, even though those projects can energize kinesthetic/tactile learners. Instead, this chapter will highlight technology-related roles for students, virtual experiences, and the use of digital tools that invite hands-on, minds-on activity. Some digital tools in this chapter are even less common in classrooms than cameras or recorders. Obtaining them will require outside funding or a re-prioritization of technology funds in schools.

Roles in the Classroom

Often students with kinesthetic/tactile learning preferences feel unsuccessful in school because their need to move can interrupt peers' concentration. Create reasons for students with this learning preference to get out of their seats by assigning them active roles in the classroom. These students can serve as timekeepers, equipment managers, class photographers, and directors for video projects. Leadership roles in the classroom build self-esteem for all students, and these learners may have been squelched by previous teachers.

One third grade teacher gave a kinesthetic learner the role of technical support person when she used the document camera, streaming video, or the whiteboard. He switched the projector cords between the document camera and the computer. He also pulled the screen down or let it up based on what the teacher needed. This role kept him alert to her tech needs and gave him an excuse to move around the room.

A fourth grade teacher expects her kinesthetic students to attend to the cameras in her classroom: downloading and storing the picture files, charging the cameras, and storing them securely.

In another school, fifth grade kinesthetic learners managed the laptop carts and printers for the building. They noted when a laptop wasn't working well, tried simple troubleshooting, and let the technical support team know when problems required more expertise. They also charged the laptops between uses, moved the carts between classrooms, cleared paper jams, replaced empty ink cartridges on printers, and provided technical support to teachers in primary classrooms.

Hands-On Inquiry

Most students have never taken the cover off a computer and are curious about how the insides work. Older desktop computers can engage students in inquiry lessons that satisfy their curiosity while teaching them about the "guts" of computers. As a center in the classroom, provide an old computer chassis, some screwdrivers, and small containers for collecting screws. Students who participate in the deconstruction of the computer (and it may be necessary to have teams working on several computers) can also research the parts and their purposes through internet resources.

GCFLearnFree's (www.gcflearnfree.org/computerbasics/7) "Inside a Desktop Computer" video, as well as printable explanations on the site, titled "A look inside a computer," provide basic information.

At **Computer Hope** (www.computerhope.com/issues/ch000997.htm), a clearly labeled photograph titled "What does the inside of a computer look like?" can be found.

An excellent, detailed set of photos for older students titled "What's inside my computer?" together with explanations can be found at **How Stuff Works** (http://computer.howstuffworks.com/inside-computer.htm). A simple video, "Computer Tour" (http://computer.howstuffworks.com/23-computer-tour-video.htm), by How Stuff Works, shows the seven main components of a PC.

Student teams can develop presentations for their peers or other grade levels with pictures of the parts of a computer, labels describing their purposes, and other information that may interest specific audiences.

Caution: Remove power cords from old computers before handing them over to students, so that computers cannot accidentally be turned on. Also, warn students about the sharp edges inside a computer case. It's easy to pull hard on a part and end up cutting yourself. Wiggling parts is usually better than yanking when trying to remove them.

Physical Simulations of Virtual Worlds

At **Computer Science Unplugged** (http://csunplugged.com/activities), students learn about computers—while they are unplugged from computers! This site offers a large selection of physical activities students can do to simulate how computers work. Though the lessons are geared to students ages 5–12, they can be adapted for older age groups with only a few modifications. Students can learn about binary code, sorting algorithms, routing, and many behind-the-scenes tasks that non-computer scientists don't know about. The complexity—and mystery—of computers is revealed through the 25 activities with instructions and worksheets available on the website as PDFs. Volunteers created the activities with the help of elementary and secondary teachers. The site is licensed under Creative Commons. Videos and pictures are available for some activities. Although few teachers will complete all 25 activities with students in a school year, this might be a wonderful resource for a gifted/talented pullout, a technology club, or an after-school or summer program.

Touch Screen Devices

The advance of touch screen technologies gives kinesthetic/tactile learners another way to use digital power. Touch screens actually come in two versions: computer-connected devices and mobile technologies. They need to be considered separately as well.

Computer-connected touch screens are touch monitors and interactive whiteboards. These have limited uses, partly because of their expense and immobility. Touch monitors are usually treated as assistive devices to help students whose physical or cognitive disabilities make using a mouse or joystick difficult. With touch technologies, these students can participate in the same computer-based activities as their peers.

Interactive whiteboards are being used in many classrooms with varied results. In computer lab settings, where students may not be able to spot the cursor moving across a screen during demonstrations, interactive whiteboards enable the instructor to exaggerate motions to direct students to the correct places on the screen. Nonreaders, particularly, have difficulty knowing how to navigate anything with words like menu bars or program names. Interactive whiteboards can be a boon for demonstration situations, especially for students who do not read well or for whom English is a new language.

In classrooms, finding ways to use an interactive whiteboard *without simply animating traditional worksheet instruction* seems more challenging. Teachers can find collections of interactive whiteboard lessons online, and many classroom teachers wax enthusiastically about interactive whiteboards in their rooms. Most often, I've seen teachers use them as teacher tools where the interactivity is limited to teachers' lecture-like instruction. Or, students stand in line for a one-person-at-a-time chance to move text on a worksheet. Using the interactive whiteboard for active learning—where students are creating and manipulating and publishing their ideas and understanding—seems less common and certainly more difficult to plan.

Touchscreens on mobile devices combine two of kinesthetic/tactile learners' preferences: the use of touch and portability. Using a finger to swipe a screen or draw a circle or turn a digitized page keeps students' bodies in motion. Mobility means students can move around with the technology or work shoulder-to-shoulder with a pal. Many touch screens use bright icons rather than words so nonreaders can infer what programs will do.

Mobile touch screen technologies include tablets, slates, pads, iPod Touch and similar Wi-Fi touch devices, e-readers, and kid-specific pads. Price points range from under $100 to around $800. Interactivity among devices varies as well. Some, such as e-readers, are designed for consumer activities, such as reading, but allow some interactivity through bookmarking, making notes, and, more currently, recording a student's reading of a text. Others, such as tablets, slates, and pads, are fully functioning computers. All can be used with the touch of fingers or stylus, and some have handwriting recognition.

After working with my own mobile touch screen devices—four tablets, an e-reader, a touch-screen phone, and multiple nonphone touch screen devices, including iPod touch and iPad—I find myself using each device for different purposes. When I think about choosing touch screen devices for the classroom, I use a list of criteria that helps narrow the field.

Price matters more than "coolness" factors. In order to get tools into the hands of as many students as possible, budgeted monies have to stretch. A few touch screen devices may suffice for the students who need such support. This is especially true if the goal is to provide accessibility for children with physical and cognitive challenges. Or, a few handhelds could be mixed in with the other technologies in the classroom.

Fit matters, too. The cheapest device is not always the best for the situation. With e-reader software now downloadable on many devices, reading books does not have to happen on an e-reader. But students will read with an e-reader longer than they'll read on a desktop machine. If a device meets a particular need, the device may be worth the cost.

Peripherals add to cost. Buying apps, wireless keyboards, stylus devices, cases, or protective covers increases total costs substantially. For iPads, for instance, thousands of apps are available, and many cost from $.99 to $9.99 each. Some free apps are also offered, but many of the apps for programs that come as standard equipment on Macs are not free. Something as simple as productivity software (word processing, spreadsheets, drawing, and presentations) has to be added to an iPad. Costs mount quickly on a device that already is costly.

Durability matters. Parents' reviews of the inexpensive digital pads designed for preschoolers indicate that the glass front might not be durable. Technologies in schools are used a lot and must be designed to handle the wear.

Discernment about choosing apps is critical. Start by reading reviews of apps by education bloggers. My daughter saw a free app that claimed to teach algebra by having students drag parts of the equation to the other side of the = sign. "Hey, that's cool," she said. Then she looked again and said, "But there's nothing that helps the student know *why* the equation changes. I guess that's not so cool after all." If my daughter, who is not a teacher, catches the weakness of an algebra app, teacher bloggers will show even more perception and find apps that are definitely worth the expense, whether for Android, iPad, or other devices. The Texas Computing Educators Association (TCEA) reviews iPad/iPod resources and maintains lists of recommended apps on its website (www.tcea.org/learn/ipadipod-resources). Apps are categorized into 46 subject areas and 14 personal use areas.

Choose the right tool for the right task. A colleague told me about her 4-year-old grandson exploring reading by listening to audio books on an iPad and touching words to hear them again. A website like Starfall (www.starfall.com) would be easy for primary students to control with touch screens. A Web 2.0 tool like Blabberize (http://blabberize.com) would be much harder to handle via touch.

Touch screen technologies can be a boon or bust, depending on the planning and thoughtfulness that go into their acquisition. For tactile learners, in particular, touch screens can make a difference in engagement, but no single tool solves all needs all the time.

Virtual Experiences

Virtual fieldtrips and simulations can give students the sense of "being there." For kinesthetic/tactile learners, virtual experiences make content memorable, even though virtual experiences are more passive than onsite experiences. Consider that on field trips and even during hands-on experiences in the classroom, students have little control over what they see, how they explore, or the pace of the event. On field trips, adult leaders or tour guides generally direct student groups along predictable routes and present preplanned spiels. During hands-on experiences, teachers keep students working at a common pace for classroom management reasons. In the virtual world, students control the order and pace of their explorations and may take different routes from one another. Students can also revisit the virtual site on their own later if they wish. How often are they able to revisit the site of a field trip or repeat a hands-on classroom experience?

Virtual Field Trips

On virtual field trips, students need to experience activities that replicate being at locations. Before using a virtual field trip with students, review the site to ensure it will engage students in looking at, hearing about, or doing something related to the subject matter and not just reading text. Text-heavy field trips abound online, but few students have the patience or skills to wade through large amounts of text in order to learn about a location. A preview of a virtual field trip will also reveal whether the site has been maintained; links that go nowhere disrupt a planned event and frustrate students.

Consider the most appropriate ways to use virtual field trips. Because students should be encouraged to explore on their own or with a partner, these field trips may be best used in a lab or as a classroom center. Students who want a longer experience with a field trip can access the websites at home, in a library, or during free time.

I used the following criteria to narrow my selection of virtual field trips:

- Students must control the exploration in some way.
- Field trips must have more visuals and audio than text.
- Field trips must appear stable—supported by an organization that will likely continue to maintain the site.

Narrowing the selection meant more field trips failed to make the list than succeeded. Unfortunately, narrow selection criteria also resulted in field trips more suitable for upper elementary and secondary students than primary students, although teachers could use some of the sites for paired or whole group explorations.

Even with the criteria I set, the field trips presented here are not of equal value. Most require teachers to name purposes for using the site, and some are almost purely visual without animation. Only a few truly replicate visits to sites where students learn through others' experiences. These drawbacks indicate how difficult it is to find a good virtual fieldtrip.

Smithsonian Museum of Natural History (www.mnh.si.edu/panoramas) has a virtual panoramic tour of the entire museum for students. Although the signage for many exhibits is not magnified to be readable online, the virtual tour has zoom capability, and visitors can move from room to room or experience a virtual panoramic tour of a specific area. This is my least favorite of the field trips because it requires teachers to set a purpose for viewing. Also, almost all information is visual and, without background knowledge, students may not know what they are seeing.

Moon in Google Earth (www.google.com/earth/explore/showcase/moon.html), created in cooperation with NASA as part of Google Earth 5, lets students explore the US moon landings through video, audio, and 3D models of spacecraft. The site has beginner tutorials, which can be helpful for younger students. The advantage of this site is that students can explore independently; the disadvantage is that the site may require a lot of bandwidth if a whole class of students uses it simultaneously. Because bandwidth varies among locations, teachers and students might need to experiment to determine how many students can access the site at one time. Teachers should set a purpose with students for touring the moon.

Rocky Mountain Scenery.com (http://rockymountainscenery.com) shows the mountains and canyons of the American West (and a few panoramic pictures from other U.S. locales) as QuickTime videos. As someone who grew up in the East, I could not imagine the vistas of the American West. Now that I live in the West, I realize how much I could have benefited as a child from seeing pictures of other U.S. regions. Teachers need to set a purpose for viewing the pictures, as the only interaction is zooming or moving right or left in the pictures. Students may find pictures that would be good backgrounds for drawings or stories.

The Tenement Museum (www.tenement.org/immigrate) helps students understand immigration at the turn of the nineteenth century and particularly the experience of tenement living. I visited The Tenement Museum in New York, and the online experience parallels the live experience very well because of the videos and panoramic views of the museum. The site is audio-supported and actively involves students throughout, but the site controls the order of the tour.

The Secret Annex Online (www.annefrank.org/en/Subsites/Home), like the online experience at The Tenement Museum, makes history come alive for students. The Secret Annex was the hiding place for Anne Frank and her family. As a supplement to reading *The Diary of Anne Frank*, this site is unbeatable. Get to know the annex, as well as the people who lived there, through the video, primary documents, and a virtual tour. The site controls the order of the tour; occasionally, I needed to go back because I had missed something or had clicked in the wrong place.

Let's Take A Dip (http://fergusonfoundation.org/hbf-kids-zone/lets-take-a-dip) contains more writing than I would wish, but its concept is so compelling that I decided to include it. In this field trip, students learn about wetlands. They go on a virtual hike and visit a creek, swamp, marsh, and river and dip a virtual net into the water. Using a frequency table printed from the site, students record what they caught and where. The beauty of this site is that each visitor may end up with different numbers, just as in real life. I dipped ten times in the creek on two occasions and came up with different sets of data. When students finish dipping in all four waterways, they compare data and draw conclusions. This would be an excellent time to aggregate class data and graph them for each water type. The site has additional watershed interactives for students through grade 12.

Virtual Simulations

Far easier to find than virtual field trips are virtual simulations that engage students in using virtual learning objects. Virtual simulations allow students to conduct explorations they may never have opportunities to experience otherwise. Lack of funding for equipment, tight daily schedules, complexity of hands-on activities, or fears for student safety act as barriers to hands-on explorations of curricular concepts. Virtual simulations rarely present the same drawbacks. Also, virtual simulations can be used with a few students at a time, which can be easier to manage than full-class explorations.

Virtual simulations also replicate authentic hands-on experiences to introduce, reinforce, or assess concepts. For instance, before third grade students dissected owl pellets in class, they used the virtual owl pellet dissections at **KidWings** (http://kidwings.com/nests-of-knowledge/virtual-pellet) to build background knowledge. The virtual experience prepared students to be successful with the hands-on experience. Math and science teachers may choose to precede or reinforce real experiences with virtual manipulatives. Some teachers use virtual experiences to assess what students understand; others value virtual simulations because they can be used to correct students' misconceptions and reteach concepts.

Virtual simulations can serve as invaluable tools to help teachers differentiate among students. Sometimes only a few students will need to use an activity; at other times, all students will benefit. Some simulations have built-in levels of difficulty. Teachers can assess the difficulty of a simulation and pair students who can learn from each other. Simulations can also be assigned as homework if students have access to computers at home.

Atlantis Remixed Simulation

One simulation seems so unusual that it deserves special consideration. The **Atlantis Remixed** site (http://atlantisremixed.org) is a funded research project designed for students ages 9–16. An international learning and teaching project, Atlantis Remixed (ARX) incorporates material from its predecessor, Quest Atlantis. Students become immersed in the simulations' 3D environments as they accomplish educational tasks. Strategies used in commercial games that enhance students' motivation are combined with content to achieve meaningful learning.

The program is available only for use by teachers in schools or in after-school activities. Teachers must submit an inquiry form; upon receipt of confirmation as new users, teachers must attend a professional development workshop or complete online training. As the grant provides most of the project's funding, fees for receiving training and for using the program are reasonable, according to information on the site.

When students participate in the simulations, they are engaged in transformational play, that is, making difficult, real-life decisions. As students can view the potential results of their decisions ten years into the future, they are given options to reconsider and replay their actions. Some units lean heavily toward social action. This site seems worthy of exploration for the constructivist learning environment it supports.

Online Simulation Sites

Online simulations are so abundant that the following list provides only a smattering of ideas. By searching for additional simulations that explicitly tie in with your curricular units, you are likely to find at least one activity. Some sites, such as the National Library of Virtual Manipulatives, aggregate multiple simulations in one location. Most virtual simulation sites have lesson plans and how-to-use guides.

National Library of Virtual Manipulatives (NLVM) (http://nlvm.usu.edu) is an extensive compilation of interactive math explorations in all math strands for PK–12 students. Virtual manipulatives on this site give students instant feedback to make them aware of mistakes or misconceptions and to reinforce correct actions. They have opportunities to solve many kinds of problems. The fraction explorations, for example, may provide richer experiences for students than in-class explorations because feedback is immediate and students solve as many problems as they need to master the concepts. This site makes differentiation for math learning easy.

Interactivate (www.shodor.org/interactivate/activities/byAudience) provides virtual math manipulatives to support classroom learning for students from grade 3 through college undergraduates. While not as robust as the National Library of Virtual Manipulatives, activities on Interactivate complement the manipulatives on the NLVM site.

PhET (http://phet.colorado.edu), offers 48 math and science simulations for elementary students and many more for middle and high school students. These interactive modules engage students in trial and error as they learn concepts. Many science and math curricular concepts can be introduced or reinforced at this site.

Learning Science (http://learningscience.org) aggregates interactive science websites on the internet in one place by science topic and under each topic by grade level bands (K-4, 5–8, and 9–12). These interactive sites allow students to do hands-on science experiments that teachers may not be able to manage in the classroom. Annotations indicate grade level and length of activity.

Game for Science (www.gameforscience.com) is a free site with virtual science laboratory experiences. Designed for students ages 8 through 21, the site asks visitors to indicate whether they are under 13. Students 12 and younger may use the site as tourists to explore science experiments, but their work will not be saved when time runs out. Students 13 and older may register, experiment, and save their progress. With parental permission and a student's and teacher's or parent's email, children ages 12 and younger may register and use the site as members. Tutorials that explain how to use the site are useful. This may be most suitable for secondary students.

Investigating the First Thanksgiving (www.plimoth.org/media/olc/intro.html) is geared to elementary students and requires reading and listening skills. For primary students, this exploration may work better as a whole group guided experience, where the teacher selects what is appropriate for the students. Intermediate students may explore the website in pairs to play the female and male roles and answer essential questions they select or those posed by the teacher.

Edheads (www.edheads.org) describes itself as a nonprofit that provides unique web experiences for students in grades 2–12+. Activities designed for elementary students are Simple Machines, The Compound Machine, Weather, and Design a Cell Phone. Third graders in my school used the Simple Machines activity to build background knowledge or to reinforce classroom work. Activities for secondary students center on health topics and critical thinking.

iCivics (www.icivics.org) simulates government operations, such as elections and county management. The following curriculum units are offered as simulations, including teachers' guides for each game: the Constitution, the legislative branch, the judicial branch, state and local government, citizenship and participation, politics and public policy, government and the market, and persuasive writing.

CSI Web Adventure (http://forensics.rice.edu) has three levels of simulations that teach the methodology supporting what forensic scientists do. Given the popularity of CSI as a television series, the appealing, well-designed site is appropriate for secondary students.

Coolmath-Games' **Lemonade Stand** (www.coolmath-games.com/lemonade) and **Coffee Shop** (www.coolmath-games.com/0-coffee-shop) simulate running a business, with practical applications of numbers, strategy, and logic. Students need to pay attention to the weather, the balance of ingredients in the beverage recipe, quality control, purchasing supplies, inventory control, and flexible pricing. Entrepreneurs must also learn to satisfy customers and adapt their plans and actions accordingly.

Online Science Games for Kids (www.learn4good.com/games/scienceforkids.htm) lists sixteen science-based games for students in grades 3–12. They involve engineering, physics, biology, and chemistry; students have fun while using logic and problem-solving skills.

Fantastic Contraption (http://fantasticcontraption.com) teaches engineering and physics concepts through games that can be filtered by difficulty level. Students can register to save their games. Although children need an email address when they register, if they indicate they are under the age of 13, their email address is deleted from the database, and they are not permitted to post in the forum. As this site has many other features, parents should be made aware when teachers choose to use the site in school so that the parents can monitor its use at home.

NASA sponsors **Design A Planet** (http://astroventure.arc.nasa.gov/DAP), where students in grades 5–8 apply what they know about human needs to design a habitable planet different from Earth. A vocabulary list is supplied in English and Spanish. This simulation has audio support in the tutorial. Resources for teachers and supporting activities for students are coordinated with the simulations.

Historical Scene Investigation (http://web.wm.edu/hsi) is text-based, so it requires good reading skills. This site worthy of inclusion as a resource because primary source documents are referenced. At the elementary level, this site may be most appropriate for high achieving readers; secondary history teachers can use these investigations to enhance instruction.

Exploratorium Music Explorations (www.exploratorium.edu/music/exhibits) are six activities that allow elementary students to explore rhythms and music in unusual ways. Other music explorations can be found at the **San Francisco Symphony** (www.sfskids.org) and the **New York Philharmonic** (www.nyphilkids.org).

At Your Command (www.thetech.org/exhibits/online/robotics), an interactive robotics module at the Tech Museum of Innovation, features a remotely controlled vehicle that students can drive on Earth and on the moon. This activity seems appropriate for late elementary and early middle school students if it is connected to your curriculum.

Magnification

Once students make discoveries about the details in a couple of magnified, everyday objects, they'll think about the world differently. So much detail is hidden from the naked eye—and students do not understand this until they see the legs of a fly or the underside of a leaf under a magnifying lens. Students can use standard magnifying glasses to enlarge objects, but such tools work only for one student at a time. Teachers now have access to magnification tools that work with their computers and/or projectors to let all students see simultaneously. Additionally, teachers can put these tools into the hands of students to let them photograph and share what they see. Kinesthetic/tactile learners will gravitate toward magnifying devices.

CameraScope Digital Visualization Tool

A parallel software tool to enhance science and math lessons is CameraScope (www.teacherlink.org/tools), a digital visualization tool offered by the Center for Technology and Teacher Education at the University of Virginia. This open source software is free; the downloadable application supports a wide range of digital imaging devices, such as digital microscopes, some digital cameras, and common webcams. The software turns high-quality still images, digital movies, and time-lapse movies into observation tools, enabling students to see events too small, too fast, or too slow for normal observation. Volunteers upgrade the software to interface with new digital technologies.

Students can use the photos they take of magnified objects to create slideshows or digital photo albums; they write text captions or audio explanations for each object. The photos can also be used for comparing and contrasting objects before magnification (prediction) and during magnification (discovery). This activity also involves finding the most accurate descriptive language for each object and for making comparisons of multiple levels of magnification.

Did a student find an insect or earthworm on the playground? Put it in a petri dish and look at it more closely! Are our fingerprints really different? Take pictures of several students' index fingers; then magnify and compare them. Wondering about how colors mix? Grab a colorful advertisement from the newspaper or magazine and check out the pixilation.

Elementary schools rarely invest in digital magnifiers, probably because teachers don't realize their potential and relatively low cost. Digital microscopes can cost less than $50 (or more than $1,500), and many document cameras have magnification capability built in with the zoom feature.

Document Cameras

Most document cameras have the essential features that make them good tools for magnification. They can show 3D objects, zoom for magnified views, and capture still photos that can be transferred to a computer. Some makes of document cameras also capture video. While not as powerful as digital microscopes, document cameras at least give all students equal chances to see objects closely. When document cameras have zoom and optical magnification as well, they are even more powerful. If you use a document camera in your classroom, check its magnification capabilities.

Digital Microscopes

Digital microscopes suitable for elementary classrooms cost between $40 and $160, a good price range for small science and/or math grants. Price is not the only factor purchasers should consider, though. Other desirable features are the following:

- The capacity to take photos and/or video clips

- The ability to use the microscope as a handheld device

- A stand to hold the microscope steady at high magnification

- Compatibility with your computer's operating system

- Lighting from above and below

- Levels of magnification (aim for about 10x, 50x, and 200x)

- The supplies included in the package—slides and other materials for magnification and manuals

Three highly rated handheld USB digital microscopes to consider would be the Celestron Handheld, the Veho VMS USB-powered, and the MicroXplore PC200 Handheld. This market is changing, though, so use these digital microscopes as a baseline for comparison with new products.

Online Microscopes

Scientists upload digital photos captured through electron microscopes, so students can look at ordinary objects that have been scanned; many have been colorized to clarify their details. Students may enjoy touring the websites and even downloading some photos with citations for use in their projects.

Teachers also can obtain access for their classes to an electron microscope for an hour. **Bugscope** (http://bugscope.beckman.uiuc.edu) provides free internet access to an electron microscope at the University of Illinois Champaign-Urbana for scheduled one-hour live sessions that include chatting with scientists. Teachers must apply for sessions and send students' insect collections in advance of using Bugscope. Kinesthetic/tactile learners will enjoy collecting insects and then looking at them under magnification. Each year during their insect unit, students in one first grade class collect bugs and examine them with a document camera. If their teacher would schedule a Bugscope session via this site, they could see their bugs under an electron microscope and chat with a scientist! To help students get a sense of what they will see, have them try **Discovery Education's Electron Microscope** interactive (http://school.discoveryeducation.com/lessonplans/interact/vemwindow.html). Some specimens in this interactive were supplied by Bugscope.

Online Digital Microscopy Photos

When students express excitement about seeing objects magnified and press for higher magnification than the digital microscope can handle, consider letting them tour digital microscopy online at the following websites:

A great collection of digital microscopy can be found at **Dr. Dennis Kunkel's** site (www.denniskunkel.com). Pictures have been magnified more than a classroom digital microscope can handle; check out the eyelash! Dr. Kunkel sells his digital photos, but teachers can download pictures for educational purposes if they contact him as directed on the site. If students use photos from this website for educational purposes, they must cite the source.

MicroAngela (www5.pbrc.hawaii.edu/microangela/) has colorized photos of insects, cells, and other organisms. This site allows teachers and students to use the photos for educational purposes. If students use photos from this website for educational purposes, they must cite the source.

The Museum of Science in Boston has a small **Scanning Electron Microscope photo gallery** (http://legacy.mos.org/sln/SEM/sem.html), which shows ordinary objects magnified.

Robotics

Robots enthrall nearly all students, so teachers can be certain any form of robotics will engage the kinesthetic/tactile learners. Robotics also can introduce basic engineering and programming concepts.

Fully functioning robots have four characteristics:

1. **Robots have energy to self-propel.** Energy may come from electricity, batteries, or solar cells.

2. **Robots move.** Movement may consist of rolling, vibrating, walking on legs, or thrusting a part, such as an arm.

3. **Robots sense their environment.** Sensors replicate human senses: sight (eyes), touch (skin and nerves), smell (nose), hearing (ears), and taste (tongue). A robot may have one "sense" or a combination of simulated senses.

4. **Robots have intelligence.** Intelligence actually comes from the programmer who develops code to tell the robot how to respond. Robots need ways to "listen" to the computer programmer.

Not all robots have all four of the above characteristics, and building a functioning robot represents a complex, time-intensive project. For such projects, students have to learn many new skills, from building the robot to programming it, based on its sensor(s). At the elementary level, students are still learning how to follow multi-step directions. For them, the task of following directions to build a simple robot may stretch their skills sufficiently. Secondary students are able to explore more complex robotics. Costs increase with the complexity of the robot.

Teachers with little to no experience with robots may dread introducing robotics to students. That was my concern the first time I worked with robots and third graders. What I learned through that experience and since then may help you avoid some mistakes.

Lesson 1: Use kits for in-school robotic experiences. The third graders with whom I worked built robots from scratch. Although the instructions called the project easy, assembling the bare-bones electronic parts required more dexterity than the third graders possessed, although middle-schoolers would have loved it. Kits range from simple to complex. At the simple end are single-function robot kits. These have pieces that snap together, an energy source, and, ideally but not always, at least one simple sensor that detects light or a line on the floor. With single-function robot kits, students don't have as steep a learning curve as with more complex robots, and they can experience how sensors work. At the next level, the kits include multiple sensors and remote controls that respond to joysticks or buttons. Fully functioning robot kits, of which LEGO Mindstorms are the most common, have intelligence because students control them through programming. Note: A useful resource for teachers considering incorporating robotics into their instruction is Mark Gura's *Getting Started with LEGO Robotics: A Guide for K–12 Educators* (2011, ISTE).

Lesson 2: Have students work in pairs or small groups. Many students have limited patience and creativity for solving problems when they work solo. In teams, they are more self-sufficient, particularly if they need to read and follow directions. Team members bring different strengths (i.e., math, reading, and mechanical skills) to the group, which contribute to better problem-solving, as well as learning from each other and learning how to function in a group.

Lesson 3: Robots do not go home with anyone. With a kit, you should be able to deconstruct finished robots so that parts can be reused for the next project. This justifies the initial cost and is a selling point if you are requesting grant monies, because the program is then sustainable. Letting the robots go home with students, even for one night with dire consequences for nonreturn, puts them at risk for breakage or disappearance. Besides, then *everybody* wants a robot to take home. Students can make videos to illustrate building the robots, testing them, and showing how final versions function.

When students advance to creating programmable robots, they often get excited about competitions. Most robotic competitions are geared to secondary and college students, but NASA puts out challenges for Early Robotics competitions (www. earlyrobotics.org) geared to students in grades 3 through 8. Students may use four LEGO Simple and Motorized Mechanisms Kits for each team in the challenge. NASA recommends organizing neighborhood contests for fun. One elementary school with a robotics program invites other schools for a robotics competition day in the spring. To eliminate home team advantage and ensure that guest teams feel supported, the elementary students in the audience are assigned teams to cheer. Students thoroughly enjoy these competitions.

When teachers plan technology use with kinesthetic/tactile learners in mind, the activities do not always result in printable projects. Kinesthetic/tactile methods satisfy students' needs to be actively involved in learning. Learners with this preference may gravitate toward different skill sets, so while one student may find magnification devices a thrill, another may dive into robotics with abandon. As is true with ideas in the previous chapters, most students have a blend of learning preferences, so these ideas are fitting for the entire class.

Fifteen Fabulous Kinesthetic/Tactile Ideas

Deconstruct. Take apart nonfunctioning technology equipment.

Simulate. Participate in an online simulation.

Draw. Use touch screens or drawing programs.

Document. Model thinking with the document camera.

Manage equipment. Organize and maintain equipment.

Troubleshoot. Become expert in technical problem-solving.

Direct. Run the camera, direct the action, and record background music.

Consult. Coach others on the use of equipment.

Support. Provide equipment support for another classroom.

Assess. Test new sites or simulations.

Build. Use a robotics kit to build and run a robot.

Participate. Enroll in a virtual field trip.

Skype. Assist with equipment during sessions.

Design. Create backdrops for videos.

Compose. Create music and record it.

CHAPTER 11

Leveraging Technology for Multilingual Learners

ABOUT 25% OF CHILDREN in U.S. schools speak a language other than English at home and represent a dramatically increasingly diverse student population (U.S. Census, 2013). The majority of PK–12 teachers in this country are monolingual in English, and most have not been trained to meet the needs of multilingual students in their classrooms (Lucas, 2011).

When students with different levels of English language proficiency are placed in regular classes with native speakers, most teachers do not know how to adapt their instruction. English language learners (ELLs) and multilingual students are expected to progress in content knowledge and simultaneously develop their knowledge of spoken and written English. When teachers do not plan instruction that is appropriate for students' language development levels, multilingual students must work twice as hard to learn the subject matter and English on their own.

Many of the digital tools referenced in other chapters are excellent for involving multilingual students in learning content and demonstrating their knowledge. Visuals, graphic organizers, manipulatives, hands-on experiences, and multimodal presentations give multilingual students supports for understanding new concepts while they are still building the language knowledge to express these new ideas. Leveraging students' first languages and their parents' life experiences can promote home-school connections that honor diversity in cultures and make learning personal. The following ideas are intended to supplement information in other chapters to highlight digital tools that specifically benefit students developing literacy and fluency in English as a new language.

Visual Supports

One of the most important instructional changes teachers can make to support multilingual students is to use many visuals. The best visuals are *realia,* actual physical objects, such as light bulbs, gavels, magnets, plus any items students need to learn to name. For cumbersome realia that are difficult to find or bring into the classroom, photographs work. Photos usually include contextual clues in the background, so students can remember words for items based on their contexts. Drawings are acceptable, although cartoonish drawings may distort viewers' understandings. After all, if students are unfamiliar with "bat" as a mammal and a cartoonish drawing features fangs, students may make the assumption that all bats have prominent fangs. Such a misconception is not easily discovered and corrected.

Monolingual teachers may not always realize which terms need to be supported with pictures. A fourth grade teacher used realia, a picture-based glossary, and many hands-on experiences to teach the concepts of electricity along with appropriate vocabulary. When a multilingual student failed the standard assessment on electricity concepts, the teacher administered an alternative, oral assessment to find out what this student had learned.

The teacher was surprised when the student described a circuit correctly but referred to "those yellow bendy things" instead of saying "wire." It had never occurred to the teacher that a student might not have the word "wire" in her everyday vocabulary. On reflection, the teacher realized that when "wire" is spoken, rather than written, multilingual students may think they are hearing "why're."

The words students need to learn are often different from the words set in boldface type in content-specific texts. Although "evaporation" may be an important word for expressing a science concept, the word rarely appears in everyday school life when compared to a word such as "analyze," which does not appear in bold. And yet, most content areas require students to analyze data, making the word essential for studying in English. As teachers, we need to build our consciousness of words that have high usage in school to be sure to teach them so that multilingual students' abilities to comprehend texts or express their thinking are not blocked needlessly. (See the sidebar titled Recognizing Language Demand.)

After analyzing the language demands of a lesson, collect realia or find images online to supplement instructional use of the words or sentence structures you've identified. One useful online resource for pictures is the **ESOL Online Picture Dictionary** (www.esolhelp.com/online-picture-dictionary.html), which is free to use for educational purposes, and, of course, an image search on any search engine will provide many options. Look for everyday items in **LanguageGuide.org** (www.languageguide.org), which includes common words in 24 languages. Rolling the cursor over a picture will bring up the word and pronunciation in the selected language. The audio is built in, so pronunciations are instantaneous.

The **Culturally Authentic Pictorial Lexicon** (http://capl.washjeff.edu) or CAPL, has authentic photographs representing many languages. Each photo is specific to a language group or location to demonstrate a dictionary word without the necessity of a caption. Pictures are published under Creative Commons and can be downloaded and manipulated for educational purposes. These photos may provide context for students to write about experiences in their home cultures or differences between cultures. The images may also be used to illustrate vocabulary, give students writing support, and make accommodations on assessments.

Videos and video clips are tremendously useful visual resources. Use video clips to help students build background knowledge before they read new material. When you preview videos, try to evaluate their appropriateness through the eyes and ears of a multilingual learner. For example, some ELL students who watched a BrainPOP video clip mentioned that the vocabulary was too sophisticated, the video too fast, and the demand for inferences, especially in the conversations between Tim and Moby, way too difficult for them. You may need to provide graphic organizers and pause videos often to answer students' questions. Turning on closed captioning may help as well.

Recognizing Language Demand

Teachers should examine lessons in advance to identify the language demand placed on multilingual students. Teachers who have not received linguistic training may find that recognizing troublesome or difficult language in their course materials is difficult, particularly because the subject matter is so familiar to them. The following list provides starting places for thinking about language.

Tier Two words. These are words that are not commonly used for social interactions and have school-specific meanings across content areas, such as "compare," " fortunate," "justify," " industrious," and "classify." An online search for Tier Two word lists brings up many examples, but there is no definitive list.

Polysemous words. These are words that have multiple meanings and can lead to confusion. When students hear the word "table," they generally visualize an image of furniture, but academically the word refers to organized data. Think about the multiple meanings of "foot," "bank," "power," "trunk," and "stable."

Homophones. Some words sound alike but have very different meanings: wire and why're, waste and waist, rays and raise, sum and some. A word's context usually signals its meaning, but for students who know only one of the words, context is not helpful.

Idioms. Idioms are particularly difficult to discern from context—and your speech may be peppered with them ("peppered," of course, is idiomatic). "We're running behind on the schedule" is confusing if you interpret "running behind" as chasing and "on" as on top of.

Functional sentence structures. Sentences have specific structures in each language, and these structures need to be explicitly taught. Cause and effect use an "if-then" structure, and comparisons are expressed as "_____ and _____ are similar because _____ ." An excellent collection of sentence frames can be found on **Miss Hultenius's website** (http://teachersites.schoolworld.com/webpages/hultenius/sentence.cfm).

Modal verbs. Modal verbs (e.g., could, will, might) behave differently in sentences from normal verbs and must be explicitly taught when teachers expect students to understand and use them correctly. Because these structures are adopted unconsciously for native speakers, teachers may not realize the rules governing modals. An excellent tutorial is available at **English Page** (www.englishpage.com/modals/modalintro.html).

Language Detectives

Encourage multilingual students to become language detectives to help you. They can use digital cameras to take photos of objects and places for which they lack words. Had that been common practice in the fourth grade class studying electricity, the student could have taken a picture of the wire and submitted it to the teacher. The whole class can discuss students' pictures, or the teacher can simply incorporate the picture, word, and definition into the next day's lesson.

Students can also use audio recorders to record phrases or situations that confuse them. This has to be done in a safe and sensitive way. If students fear others will laugh at them, they will not use the recorders and will be unwilling to raise their hands to ask for clarification or repetition. However, if this is treated like a game of detecting words and phrases that are unclear, monolingual students are likely to get involved as well. It's surprising how often children, both monolingual and ESL, have never heard idiomatic expressions and do not feel comfortable asking about them.

Native Language Use

Multilingual students are fluent, but not always literate, in their first languages. Remember that while students speak their first language at home, they may never have learned to read or write it. When teachers can tie school language to students' native languages, research confirms that multilingual students learn second languages faster. Encourage students to read and write in their native languages at home with their families and, when appropriate, at school. During instruction, try to connect the academic terms in English with words in students' home languages. *Do not expect that the multilingual students will know these academic terms in their home languages.* Academic language is taught in schools. Nevertheless, if students can see the words in their native languages, they can use the words to talk with their parents about concepts from school.

How can teachers communicate clearly with multilingual students when teachers are not fluent in the students' languages? Use multilanguage dictionaries. One of the best online dictionaries is **WordReference** (www.wordreference.com), which translates words among fifteen languages. The power of WordReference is that each definition lists a part of speech, a comparable word in a second language, and sample sentences in both languages. Each page also lists related words and their definitions. WordReference can be downloaded as a phone app.

Another useful tool for teachers and students is **Forvo** (www.forvo.com), an online pronunciation dictionary with audio clips of words pronounced in more than 200 languages. Contributors are adding words regularly, so the database of audio files is growing. Warning: Swear words may be included because the goal is to include the pronunciation of all words in reputable dictionaries.

The Cultural Orientation Resource Center has downloadable and printable **Phrasebooks** (www.culturalorientation.net/index.php/resources-for-refugees/phrasebooks) in 14 languages. Each phrase book contains about 140 pages of common, conversational phrases useful for communicating about everyday life.

Website Translations

Lingro (http://lingro.com) is a dictionary interface for websites. Type a website address into Lingro's search field, and Lingro will ensure that all the words on the webpage may be translated into the language you select. Click on any word on the page, and a translation in the target language will appear. Lingro offers translations for eleven languages. If students use Firefox, Lingro can be downloaded as an extension, so that instant translations will be available on every webpage visited without typing the URL into Lingro.

Another resource for supporting multilingual students' learning is **2lingual** (www.2lingual.com), a Google search engine that returns two columns of search results, each column in a different language. Users can choose from 36 languages. This tool should help students build background knowledge about a topic in their home languages as well as in English.

Reading in Dual Languages

Students can access virtual books and story videos from around the world on **MisCositas** (www.miscositas.com). Books are available in four languages. Other resources for teaching multicultural students are also available on the site.

Dual Language Projects

Students can create books in dual languages—their home language and English. Examples are available at **Dual Language Showcase** (www.thornwoodps.ca/dual), a project at Thornwood Public School in Toronto, Ontario. Students created books and audio files in their home languages, often with the help of family members. Older students or community volunteers translated the books and audio files into English. Texts in both languages are printed side by side in books. Families may borrow the dual language books and tapes.

Learning About Folktales

The folktales at **American Folklore** (http://americanfolklore.net/folklore/esl-reading) come from North and Latin America. While these can give glimpses of cultural groups, be aware that the stories are often written in the vernacular, so their vocabulary and figurative language will be difficult for many multilingual students. Pairing multilingual students with native speakers for reading and discussing the tales will promote conversations about language and culture.

Assisted Writing

Students can annotate pictures or write simple poetry at **PicLits** (http://piclits.com/compose_dragdrop.aspx), a website that features pictures and words. Select a picture from the gallery, drag and drop words from the vocabulary list, or write your own words. The final pictures can be saved or shared. Registration is required, so elementary teachers need parental permission for students to use the site. For multilingual students, this site is particularly rich because pictures and pertinent word banks are provided.

Resources

Two annotated collections of resources for English Language Learning are available online in **LiveBinders**. Jennifer Gibson has compiled **English Learner Technology Resources** (www.livebinders.com/play/play_or_edit?id=81858), and Jennie O'Dell has compiled **LiveBinder of ESL Apps** (www.livebinders.com/play/play_or_edit?id=378216). Undoubtedly, many additional lists of resources can be found online, so treat these as a starting point.

If your students are bilingual in Spanish and English, **Casa Notes** (http://casanotes.4teachers.org) provides a way for you to customize templates for twelve standard letters or forms to communicate with parents. Templates range from field trip permission slips and medication forms to congratulatory notes and progress reports.

Working with multilingual students requires teachers to be mindful about promoting students' growth in content knowledge together with language development. Technology can be a strong motivator and instructional support.

CHAPTER 12

Web 2.0 Tools

EDUCATORS DO NOT AGREE on whether the word "web," as in websites on the internet, should have numeric designations as Web 1.0, Web 2.0, or Web 3.0. I use the term Web 2.0 to convey a simple concept: Web 2.0 tools enable individuals to contribute content to the web and to interact with others about content on particular websites. Web 2.0 tools—the tools discussed in this chapter—are different from the interactive websites listed in Chapter 5.

Many websites fall between the read-only Web 1.0 (the earliest types of websites) and the read-write (two-way communication) of Web 2.0 websites. In other words, many Web 2.0 websites have a primary purpose of providing information for site visitors (like Web 1.0 sites), but Web 2.0 websites are designed to do much more: they also invite visitors to interact with the sites' content, their authors, and others who visit the sites by writing comments and by tagging keywords and topics on these websites. On some Web 1.0 sites, visitors interact with the material (like the sites described in Chapter 5), but they do not contribute their own content. In contrast, the Web 2.0 tools we discuss in this chapter invite students to read what others have created and to write their original ideas (i.e., contribute content) on the Web 2.0 websites.

Generic Tools

Email

Because adults use email regularly, teachers may underestimate how much training young students need before they can be unleashed with email accounts, even in protected settings where they are emailing only one another within the classroom. I have, on multiple occasions, introduced email accounts to students. Never has the training been sufficient to keep everyone out of trouble! You can teach netiquette and web protocols, but students choose whether to follow the guidelines. For that reason, even at the high school level, teachers must monitor students as they work in Web 2.0 environments.

The PBS Kids site featuring the characters from **Arthur** has a page that shows the parts and purposes of email (http://pbskids.org/arthur/games/letterwriter/email.html). This may be a way to introduce the necessity of putting something in the subject line, a task new email users often forget. Arthur also treats the email as a more formal document than children might have experienced if they've been emailing already. Still, this webpage can make the style of emails more familiar to novices.

Before students use email, even among their classmates, teach them about tone. The joking comments they say to close friends in person sound far different when reduced to text. Readers cannot tell whether writers are joking or serious, ironic or direct. Discuss with students what the consequences of email nastiness or bullying will be—and then follow through. Because written words appear without the voice and facial cues that accompany spoken language, even emoticons may be misunderstood if the words themselves sound mean or sarcastic. This is particularly true when the two individuals using email have never met and email is their only conversational tool. Consider how often adults misunderstand one another when speaking, as well as in written text. Elementary students have similar troubles, and for some, communicating clearly in writing can be a persistent problem. Have students brainstorm guidelines for email etiquette, and post the guidelines where students can consult them. Email services via school accounts usually allow teachers to review messages before they are sent. Stress to students that emailing on a school account is a privilege, not a right.

Email Services

Email services for elementary students need to be safe environments, where teachers can monitor the messages students send and receive, incoming emails are limited to approved email addresses, and students may connect globally. In the past, finding a free email service for elementary students was fairly easy, but now the number of services has dwindled. The following represent the two most common free email services for elementary schools.

ePals (www.epals.com) offers free, teacher-monitored email accounts for students. Free email is available for individual teachers (with 30 student accounts), schools, or districts. Once registered, teachers can participate in a Global Community where they can develop collaborative partnerships with other ePals members from around the world. ePals addresses safety through language and content filters and staff moderation of site-wide galleries, blogs, and forums.

Google Apps for Education (www.google.com/enterprise/apps/education/products. html) provides free student and teacher email service through Gmail but with district-controlled inbound and outbound filtering. Districts decide whether students can send or receive email outside the schools. As the Google Apps service is free, many districts are cutting costs by subscribing.

Email Games

Email games can give young students practice with emailing and generate high levels of thinking. Conducting an email game may not replicate everyday use of email, but students can learn the parts of email messages and practice writing them in a low-risk setting. Additionally, teachers can choose curricular topics for email games.

Half-Life. Half-Life is an email activity that teaches students to write concisely. Teachers propose a question, and students write responses that are exactly 32 words long. This may require modeling in advance of the assignment so that students know they can write longer answers and then edit their answers to fit the 32-word requirement. Consider questions about interpersonal relationships, such as, What is a friend? How do you handle a bully? or How should students behave on the playground? Essential questions with many possible answers could relate to content units, such as, Is life better in an urban, suburban, or rural area? or Which invention is the most important to humans today? The idea of this game is to ask questions on a topic, issue, or concept that all students will not answer in the same way.

To play the game, the teacher asks the question in a mass email to all students, and they email their 32-word answers to the teacher. The teacher pastes all answers in a document and emails the list to the students for their enjoyment. Students then trim their 32-word responses to 16 words to convey the same message (although the words may change, the message should not) and email their second responses to the teacher. Once again, the class reviews all the 16-word responses. Then students trim their responses to 8 words and email those. Most students will struggle to get down to 8 words, but if they are successful and want a bigger challenge, cut the responses in half again. This may seem like an unusual activity, but students will be doing the work of journalists, who often have to trim their articles to specific word counts. Additionally, students learn to pick out the essential information, and emailing the messages back and forth gives students practical experience.

Tolerance. Choose a topic about which students have strong and opposite opinions. At the elementary level, it's best not to get into politics or family values, so a school issue may work better, provided you have one. The goal is to force students to express an opinion. You could present a scenario: If one class had to be eliminated at school, how would you feel about cutting physical education? (or art or music; choose based on your school programs). Each student emails a number from a 1–10 scale with 1 being very unhappy, 5 neutral, and 10 very happy, as well as a reason why. The teacher averages the numbers and, in a response email, invites students to guess the average response. Students need to guess a number to two decimal places, such as 6.07, because the average is unlikely to be a whole number.

Students email their guesses, and the teacher responds with information about who was closest. Then the teacher randomly assigns half the students to take a very unhappy stance and half to take a very happy response and come up with reasons. Students email their reasons (one per student) to the teacher, who compiles them into a list. By randomly assigning stances, the teacher forces students to consider viewpoints that may not match their own. Students then receive the list via email, think about it, and send in their number score on the topic (1–10) again. The class can average the scores as a class project to see whether the exercise swayed anyone.

This project lends itself to graphing responses, as well, so that students can practice interpreting the data on graphs. The goal is not to find consensus, but to expose the variety of opinions that people might have on issues. Teaching students to consider other opinions will have long-term benefits for them as adult citizens when they need to practice tolerance about political and social issues.

Blogs

Though blogs may seem like a secondary education tool, elementary students can benefit from becoming bloggers once they understand the purpose and process of blogging. The point of blogging is to produce enough content so that others can comment and, in ideal situations, enter into conversations about interesting topics. Also, bloggers generally write on a regular schedule so that the people who follow the blog have reasons to visit often. Teachers need to remind students that like email messages, blogs cover appropriate topics only, and when they comment on others' blogs, their comments should be thoughtful and polite. Hold a discussion on how important it is to disagree with others' opinions in a kind way. Remind them to follow basic safety guidelines about protecting their identities as well.

As elementary students tend to write short sentences and paragraphs, teachers need to encourage them to use lots of details and examples in their blogs. When students are learning to blog, allow plenty of class time because typing a blog post can take primary students a l-o-n-g time. Before typing, students can write on paper a few key words about their main ideas and examples. As they type, more ideas will come to mind and can be added. After they type the blog posts, they can add a few more details to make it more convincing.

Blogs do not need to be perfect. Expect students to write at their current levels. This means some students may misspell words, make mechanical mistakes, or write incomplete sentences. If teachers insist on correcting every error, students will resist writing in blogs, and teachers will go crazy managing the load. Encourage enough revision so that the content is readable and enough editing so that gross errors can be cleaned up. Students can edit each other's blogs for these basic types of errors. Not all students will enjoy blogging at first, but after they receive comments from other students on their blogs, they will become more enthusiastic.

Student blogs should be set up so that each student has a blog page in a class blog site. Students maintain their own pages. Teachers can decide how directive they will be about the blogs. In some schools, students write their posts on word processors during center times, have posts approved by their teachers, and then copy and paste them into their blogs. In other classrooms, students write their blog posts in response to writing prompts or as reading responses. Some teachers rotate students through classroom computers to post blogs; others pull in laptops or use lab time for the posts. One teacher asks students write their blogs as though they were writing diaries.

Stress that the goal of blogging is to generate comments and to keep conversations going back and forth. A blog post should pose a question or state an opinion on a controversial topic. When students comment on peers' blog posts, their responses need to add new information, connect the original blog to a personal experience, pose a question, or present a different viewpoint. If comments on blog posts are simply praise, agreement, or disagreement without reasons, the conversation and discussion of the concept stops.

Although for adults commenting on blogs is optional, on elementary blogging sites, comments need to be mandatory. Require students to respond to two other blogs as goodwill measures. Everyone likes audience response, so reading comments on their work will delight students. Additionally, learning to make meaningful comments conditions students to think about their peers and themselves as writers. It's easy to practice commenting as a whole class, especially if you access blogs of students in other classrooms and write responses to their posts. Students are tempted to write something nice but empty, like "Cool!" When they talk about various comments as a class, students quickly see that a message that responds to the content of the blog post, such as "It's interesting that..." or "I wonder..." or "A question I had was..." opens a conversation with the blogger. Some bloggers respond to responses, and others do not. A blogger is not obligated to respond to every comment.

VOICES OF EXPERIENCE

Kathy Cassidy, first grade teacher (kathy@kathycassidy.com)
Westmount School, Moose Jaw, Saskatchewan, Canada
Class blog: http://mscassidysclass.edublogs.org

My six-year-old students each have their own blog.

We blog for many reasons. The blogs showcase what is happening in our classroom for the parents of my students. It allows the parents to see their child's artifacts and writing at any time of the day, whether the parents are at home or their workplace. It gives students an authentic, global audience, allowing us to connect with others around the world. And it helps students begin to understand how to create great digital footprints for themselves, something that they will surely need in our ever more digital world. Our blog is not an "add-on." It is a vital part of demonstrating our learning.

Students use their blogs as online portfolios of their learning from the first week of school until the last. Although they come to me as prewriters, I ask novice bloggers to just type in any sounds that they hear in the words they want to use. Then, I ask students to read me what they have written, and I put an editor's note in brackets at the end, detailing what students *wanted* their writing to say. I continue to do this through the year. Gradually, as their writing becomes readable to the general population, I stop using the brackets. The students, their parents, and anyone else who goes to our blog can see the progression in the children's writing through their first grade year.

Their blogs are not just for writing, but for reflecting their learning in reading, math, science, and social studies as well. We post drawings, podcasts of our reading fluency, student-created videos of their learning in various subject areas, and use embeddable tools, such as Storybird, to showcase what we have done.

Students post something on their blogs about once a week through the fall and more often in the spring, as they become more proficient at blogging. At first, we blog together in our computer lab; as the students become more independent, they begin to blog on their own during literacy times in the classroom.

Continued

No matter when the students write an article, whether at home or at school, nothing is ever posted until I approve it first. I approve all comments before they are posted as well. Nothing goes online until I have seen it.

Blogging isn't an option in my classroom. It's what we do. All districts have different policies with regard to posting students' images, names, and work online. Fortunately, our district has always been forward thinking and allows all of these with parents' permission. My personal policy is that I post images of students and first names, but I never match the two. You could know that I have a student named Dusty but would never know which of the pictures were of him. If a parent had difficulty with this, I would have the child blog under a pseudonym or not include pictures of him or her.

Our blog is embedded into our classroom life. Group reading revolves around reading comments. We learn to write by responding. We learn about the world outside our city by reading the blogs of others. We invite that world into our classroom by posting ourselves. I can no longer imagine my classroom without a blog.

Blogging Resources

As with all Web 2.0 tools, elementary teachers have fewer options for blogging than secondary teachers. The following services are geared to elementary students and provide the necessary controls for the teacher to monitor students' work. Before introducing blogging, teachers should check with the IT department to learn whether blogging is considered acceptable use for the elementary school and whether the district has its own blogging tool. For instance, some districts with Google Apps for Education may have included Blogger as an app for elementary use. If not, the following might work well for elementary teachers.

Edublogs (http://edublogs.org) hosts only education blogs. Students do not need email to sign up and can have one free blog. Teachers often use their Edublog accounts as a class website. For a small monthly fee, teachers can have a class account for up to fifty student blogs. The site design is clean and attractive.

ClassBlogmeister (http://classblogmeister.com) does not look fancy, but it is free, designed for elementary students, and popular around the world. Teachers can create an account and include student blog pages within the account. Explore the site to see how teachers and students are using blogs.

KidBlog (http://kidblog.org), a free service designed for elementary students, has a kid-friendly interface. In KidBlog, students do not need passwords because they log in using a class registration code and choose their names from class lists. Blogs are private by default and can be semi-private (visible only to parents).

KidzBlog (http://kidzblog.en.softonic.com) is free, downloadable blogging software geared for early elementary students. Children can draw in the blog as well as type. The software can be hosted on a school server and kept private.

Wikis

Wikis (adapted from the Hawaiian phrase "wiki-wiki," meaning "quick-quick") are one of my favorite tools. Unlike blogs, where the organization is one contributor and multiple commenters, on a wiki, members work collaboratively to create shared content that reflects the work of all contributors.

Teachers have two options for wikis: a teacher/school wiki, which is generally a communication tool for parents, or a class wiki on which every child has a page for his or her work. I encourage both in every classroom.

Teacher/School Wikis

A fifth grade level team created an informational wiki for parents and students. Each homeroom class had its own wiki page, where students and parents could find the daily homework assignments. Because the fifth grade teachers mixed their students for content instruction, being able to access all homework assignments for all teachers in all content areas helped parents stay informed about expectations. On a general page, the fifth grade teachers posted details about class events, copies of permission slips, and requests for volunteers.

Similarly, a first grade teacher created a teacher wiki resource to answer common questions from parents of first graders. This wiki had individual pages devoted to academic topics (e.g., supporting your child as a reader and writer), parenting topics (e.g., advice about bedtimes, television, and computer use at home) and social topics (e.g., advice for students' problems, such as bullying, not wanting to come to school, and not understanding assignments).

A school office and the parent-teacher organization combined to maintain an informational wiki for school families. All school forms, policies, newsletters, requests for volunteers, announcements, and celebrations were uploaded to cut down on the amount of paper sent home with students. The wiki was set up so that selected members of the school staff and parent community could edit the information as needed.

Class Wikis

A class wiki can serve both teachers and students. Some pages can be designated teacher-only for communicating with parents. Additionally, each student or team (for collaborative work) can have an individual page for posting works in progress, completed projects, links to a blog, or other materials the students want to access outside school. Students' pages can be kept private to only classmates or made public to invite comments and collaboration outside the classroom walls.

Wikis can be edited easily, can use track changes so that the owner can revert to a previous version, and can be worked on by several students at once, as long as they are working on different pages. The tracking feature is particularly helpful for a class wiki. Students, especially at fourth grade and up, sometimes consider it a prank to delete another student's work or to write inappropriate comments on a peer's page. The history tab identifies who made the change and when. Students should be held accountable for their actions as part of netiquette. After inappropriate comments are deleted, pages are restored to their original status. One student removed all the web links her teacher had assigned for homework. The teacher was able to restore the links quickly and then show the student and her parents the evidence of the disruptive behavior. Another student embedded swear words in an essay on a classmate's wiki . The teacher caught the change, restored the page to its original content, and implemented consequences for the misbehaving student, all before anyone else knew about it.

Free Wikis for Teachers

Creating a wiki remains one of the best free options for teachers. Several wiki hosts reverse the strategy of other education domains: wiki hosts offer free wikis to educators and charge the business world and general public. So, although a teacher can *choose* to pay for expanded wiki services, subscriptions are unnecessary for most wiki users. I have created educational wikis for over ten years and have experienced no problems with any of them.

PBworks Basic Edition for Education (www.pbworks.com/education.html) encourages teachers to create a workspace and add up to one hundred students and parents to work within the space. Free accounts have 2 GB of upload storage and limited protection for pages or folders. Teachers can pay to upgrade for more features.

Wikispaces (www.wikispaces.com/content/for/teachers) has free, ad-free, wiki accounts for K–12 educators with unlimited pages and an easy method for adding students as members of the wiki. Recently, Wikispaces launched Wikispaces Classroom, still free and ad free, as a platform with even more flexibility for teachers. Wikispaces Classroom offers a social newsfeed, new options for mobile devices (including an iPad app), and a more education-focused feature set. Wikispaces employees are responsive to online requests for help; I've generally had answers to questions within one to two days and sometimes within hours.

Uses for Wikis

Setting up a wiki is just the first step. Teachers need to think about how wikis might be integrated into their classrooms for collaborative or individual projects.

Collaborative Projects

Students can write books in wikis about curricular topics. For example, elementary students in primary classrooms often are supposed to learn local history, but local history materials are written at too high a reading level. Older students can create ABC wiki books to teach local history. Each page of the wiki could be an alphabet letter, and students can contribute their ideas, or students could combine all the alphabet letters on one page of a wiki. The wiki would not be printed but accessed online. Wiki books can cover any content area. Consider habitat guides with pictures of animals and plants within a habitat and other notable information. Other book topics could be outer space, the Civil War, math in everyday life, or reading guides to novels. Students could make glossaries of content terms, contribute to building background knowledge in a new unit, or build a list of the top 100 books for reading at their grade level. Whatever the topic for a collaborative wiki, students need to organize the materials they collect so that the wiki is usable, which places such a project high on Bloom's taxonomy.

A collaborative wiki your class might like to join is **Classroom Booktalks,** (http://classroombooktalk.wikispaces.com), which invites students around the world to create book talks about their favorites and upload them. Book talks can be done as slideshows or with several Web 2.0 tools listed in this chapter.

Individual Work

Students can upload works in progress to invite comments and suggestions for improvement. They can also showcase their finished work. Students who want to share their passion for a sport or skill may create original materials that others can read and view. Students could each choose a hero and dedicate a page to information, photos, and direct quotations. Students' wikis can serve many different purposes: as a note catcher, an area for test review, or space for expressing creativity. With any online web presence, unless the content changes often, parents and students will not be inclined to visit.

Websites

Creating websites used to require knowledge of html code, but today's tools make website construction and updating a cinch. The lines that separate blogs, wikis, and websites are now blurred; in essence, wikis and blogs are types of websites. The tools listed here offer website design with the options of including blogs and discussion groups. I recommend these sites for teachers who want a little of everything in one place.

Website Design Resources

Weebly for Education (http://education.weebly.com) allows students and teachers to build classroom and individual websites. It offers free teacher accounts and permits children under 13 to use teacher accounts with parental permission. The site has easy drag and drop features for creating the website and includes embedded blogs as an option.

SchoolRack (www.schoolrack.com) offers a free website and blogging service for teachers, their students, and students' parents. The service includes a portal where teachers can store grades, communicate through email with parents, and hold online discussions. Teachers can make groups for parents only, students and parents, or students only and use different passwords for each group. This feature allows discussions to be private if needed. The discussion groups make a fine option for online book studies among students or between students and their parents.

Google Sites is similar to Weebly and is part of Google Apps for Education (www.google.com/enterprise/apps/education/products.html), available to teachers whose schools or districts use this free service. Students can build their own sites, and many templates are available. Tutorials for using Google Sites are easy to find on YouTube.

Provider-Specific Tools

While for the previously mentioned tools, teachers can make choices based on their preferences or needs, the following tools have carved out niches that no one else seems inclined to fill. These also seem to be specialty tools that teachers may use only on occasion. That does not detract from the powerful effects they can have on students.

Voki

Voki (www.voki.com) enables students to make talking avatars or personalized robots. Students create avatars and type in text for the avatar to speak. Voki avatars are quick to create and are limited to 60- (free) or 90- (subscription) second audio messages. On the site is a video about using Voki for oral tests—students type answers for their avatars to read aloud to teachers when they grade the tests.

Teachers can create free sites and share with students who have parental permission. Children under 13 are not forbidden to use the site, but the free accounts require an active email account belonging to a parent or teacher (these have ads). Voki's terms and conditions indicate that parents need to supervise children under the age of 13 if they are on the site. Or, teachers can subscribe to Voki Classroom accounts, where students can work under the teacher's supervision; these have a low subscription fee of $30/year.

Blabberize

In Voki, students create avatars that speak typed text, but in **Blabberize** (http://blabberize.com), students' voices are animated with pictures. For blabbers, students import pictures, generally of an animal or person, use online tools to outline the lower part of the mouth, and record themselves as though the objects in the picture were talking. Pictures may be photographs or drawings, so it would be possible to add a mouth to a drawing of a tree or sun or mountain and animate it. Recordings can be private or public and can be exported to other websites.

Students will find the tool intuitive and fun. Caution them that they might prefer to use drawings rather than photos of real people; having real people blabber sometimes looks freaky. Also, students should know that they cannot use copyrighted photos on a public forum such as Blabberize.

The tool can be an excellent way for students to show what they've learned about animals, famous people, or other objects of study. They can upload a picture of their study subject and let the character talk. The site has several drawbacks. The terms of service indicate that children under the age of 13 need permission to use the site, although no log-in is necessary. When a blabber is finished, an embed code allows embedding, but the blabber has to be converted to video. The greatest drawback, though, is that students will be able to access and watch any public blabbers on the site, and the content may not always be appropriate.

VoiceThread

VoiceThread (www.voicethread.com) has created a unique tool for collaboration. Before you consider it, though, realize that VoiceThread has undergone changes that require users to subscribe. Educator licenses start at about $80/year. At that price, teachers need to know they will use this tool often.

The heart of a VoiceThread is a collection of pictures (drawings or photographs) on a theme that are uploaded into a thread. Each picture can then be discussed or commented on by individuals. Commenting happens in any of five ways: typing, recording into the computer, uploading a voice file, phoning a comment, or uploading video. Users also have access to the Doodler, which is a colored pen that can draw on the pictures. The Doodles stay visible on the page only as long as the contributor is talking about the doodle.

Account holders control whether the thread accepts outside comments or is open to comments only from invited guests, such as the students in one class. Each commenter has an identity icon, and comments play in the order in which they were recorded.

Ideas for using VoiceThread (http://voicethread.com/about/library) help teachers see how others have used the tool. The tool is most powerful when multiple people comment on the same page or picture. This can be an excellent experience in using primary digital resources, such as historic photos, and having students comment on what they notice. It can also become a reflection after a unit. Teachers often create VoiceThreads during poetry units so that students can post and read original poems. Listeners then comment on feelings and thoughts evoked by the poems, the poems' imagery, and student poets' presentations. As with other tools that allow students to comment, teachers should set ground rules so that students comment and critique appropriately. When classes from different countries collaborate on projects, students can contribute to and post comments on VoiceThreads.

Skype

Skype in the Classroom (http://education.skype.com) makes it easy for teachers around the globe to collaborate. Essentially, Skype is free teleconferencing for any computer platform, although subscription services are available. With free Skype accounts, teachers can connect their classrooms with other classrooms, authors, experts in content areas, families worldwide, and universities. Using built-in cameras or inexpensive webcams, both groups can see one another while they talk. On one-to-one (i.e., one person or group to another person or group) calls, callers can share their screens, so if an author has a slideshow, the students can see it. Free services also include sending files through Skype and the potential for group calls (recommended limit currently is five). A similar, but less known video conferencing service similar to Skype is Zoom (https://www.zoom.us/), which allows free 45-minute calls between two locations. If your district uses a Learning Management System, video conferencing may also be a tool embedded in the product.

Learning to use Skype is so easy. I was taught how to use Skype by a kindergarten student who called his grandfather in Hong Kong daily. This child was so adept at using Skype that he had the audacity to show his impatience with me as a learner!

Teachers use Skype in a multitude of ways. Often two classrooms from different parts of the world connect with Skype and can see one another in context. When students who have been sharing emails and projects finally see and speak directly with each other, their excitement is contagious.

Skype in the Classroom has a network of teachers and projects that teachers can explore to find perfect ideas that match their students' interests and curricular requirements, and there are additional resources for finding Skype partners. Teachers can also find Skype partners at **Around the World with 80 Schools** (http://aroundtheworldwith80schools.wikispaces.com) or through services such as ePals, mentioned earlier in the chapter.

VOICES OF EXPERIENCE

Jean Reidy

Jean Reidy is a children's author and two-time winner of the Colorado Book Award. Her books include *Too Purpley!, Too Pickley!, Too Princessy!, All Through My Town* (all published by Bloomsbury and Scholastic), *Light Up the Night* (Disney Hyperion and Scholastic) and *Time Out for Monsters!* (Disney Hyperion) with more on the way. You can visit her at http://jeanreidy.com.

Hi there. My name is Jean Reidy. And I'm a children's author.

Every year I do lots of virtual visits with schools, libraries and classrooms all over the world. It's a valuable experience and it's so, SO easy.

Author visits show kids that people who write and/or illustrate books are real people. A visit can get them excited about reading, writing, poetry, history, art – you name it. But with school and library budgets shrinking and curriculum demands filling the school day, in-person author visits are falling by the wayside.

Virtual visits allow authors to meet students, but with no travel time, no travel expense, minimal equipment and modest effort. Plus, at around 20–30 minutes per visit, each fits easily into a teacher's, librarian's or author's schedule.

But the surprising advantage of virtual visits is that they can actually be MORE personal. In-person author visits are usually assemblies, which makes customization and personalization nearly impossible. Virtual visits can be customized for an individual classroom or curriculum and can open doors to more personal interactions between students and an author.

Many authors, like myself, do virtual visits. I can't tell you what they all do in theirs, but I can tell you what I do in mine.

I treat my virtual visits with the same care and planning as I treat my in-person visits.

In advance, I link teachers and librarians to my visit package complete with posters, parent letters, book orders, teachers guides and—most importantly—a menu of suggested program ideas.

For my youngest audiences (PreK-1st grade), we often do a 25-minute interactive session– with readings, games, stories, costumes, movement, questions and noise. We learn to explore and discover picture books and learn about the important role illustrations play. We may even do some project sharing.

With older students, we usually talk about writing and I share with them my "Top Ten Super Secret Writing Tips." We may do a group writing exercise or, again, project sharing.

More on project sharing: Often in my virtual visits kids will share with me artwork, writing or other projects they've created in their classrooms. Many of these ideas are found in my Visit Idea Menu or my Curriculum Guides. For example, one preschool class made "Yukky" and "Yummy" plates based on my book *Too Pickley!* They shared their plates with me during our visit and we discussed sorting and favorite foods. An older class journaled, made "trioramas," and created a class "time in" corner based on my book *Time Out for Monsters!* They gave me a tour of their creations and read from their journals during our visit. It was inspiring.

When kids share their work, I offer each of them my 30-second "What I love most ..." critique. This is my favorite part of a virtual visit because it allows me to connect one-on-one with students and honor their creativity.

"Question and Answer" sessions make for great virtual visits and can be customized to a variety of curriculum points or time slots. I suggest that classrooms prepare questions in advance. Then, during the visit, each student will have an opportunity to come up to the camera to ask his or her question. I get to learn their names and answer them directly. And I usually ask them a question right back. It's exciting from both ends.

As I mentioned earlier, one of the great advantages to virtual visits is the ability to customize the visit to a classroom. For example, one class was learning about rhyming, so we did an activity with rhyming words. Another class wrote stories using *Too Pickley!* as a mentor text. As students read their stories to me during their visit, their excitement for writing beamed through.

I keep the technology simple. I read from hardcopy books and hold up hardcopy photos. Even features like Skype "screen share" can be slow and out of sync. So I let the connection be the only technology involved. Which is easier on everyone.

Continued

Finally, at the end of all my visits I mail autographed book stickers to the school for kids who have purchased my books.

So there you go! That's what I do.

It's easy to bring an author virtually into your classroom (or library). Here's how.

1. Find your author. The following websites list authors who are open to virtual visits.

    Skype in the Classroom https://education.skype.com

    Skype an Author Network http://skypeanauthor.wikifoundry.com

    Kate Messner http://www.katemessner.com/authors-who-skype-with-classes-book-clubs-for-free/

    Jean Reidy http://jeanreidy.com

2. Contact your author. Simply follow the method advised on the website.

3. Set your date and time. REMEMBER to coordinate time zones.

4. Coordinate your mode of connection. While Skype may be most popular, it isn't the only game in town. Google Hangouts, FaceTime, Facebook Video Chat and other sites offer options.

5. Decide on your visit program and prepare. Read some of the author's books. Brainstorm questions. Get the kids excited. Classrooms that prepare have the very best experience.

6. Keep the visit short—under 30 minutes, for a variety of reasons. Plus, connections often falter as time goes on.

7. Check with a tech friend or your tech support staff in advance to make sure that your internet speed is fast enough and band width broad enough to support the video connection.

8. Test your equipment and set up a few practice video calls *with people outside your building.*

9. Remember virtual visits go two ways. Make sure your students can see AND hear your author. Make sure your author can see AND hear your students. Remember, your venue doesn't have to be perfect. Just like my office, your classroom is not a production studio.

10. Expect technical problems. It's the nature of the internet. If you have a dropped or bad connection, simply "end" the call and try again. Kids are less nervous about problems if the teacher and author remain calm.

And, if possible, make sure each student has a way to individually participate in the virtual visit. That personal connection might be the spark setting off a renewed enthusiasm for reading, writing, artistic expression and learning.

Through **Skype an Author Network** (http://skypeanauthor.wikifoundry.com), teachers can find authors for 10–15 minute Meet an Author visits, typically free, as well as longer In-Depth Author Visits, which are not free. Meet an Author is an excellent way to audition authors for in-depth school visits or practice using Skype.

For Read Across America Day, consider reading a book to another classroom via Skype. Or, when students are absent from particularly important events, include the students via Skype. This happened in several classes I visited and was a powerful way to for the missing students to stay connected. If students or their parents are visiting a place that is part of the class's curriculum, ask them to Skype from the location and take the students on a virtual tour.

Teachers are typically thoughtful about preparing for Skype visits. Their students build background knowledge about the topic of the visit, brainstorm questions, and agree on roles during the call. The call itself motivates students to listen carefully and treat the guest or guests with respect. Remember to debrief students after the visit, not just to talk about how cool it was, but to discuss strategies that might have enhanced the visit. Was there a point where the students needed more information? Talk about how to plan to ask probing follow-up questions. What surprised students during the visit? What questions remain about the visitor or the topic? How can they find answers to these questions? How can students express their thanks and pleasure to the visitor?

Glogster

Glogster EDU (http://edu.glogster.com) has excited many teachers, yet I hesitate to include it. In Glogster, students create online multimedia posters with text, photos, videos, graphics, sounds, drawings, and data attachments. The tools on the site are drag and drop, and even young students can master them.

Why do I hesitate to recommend this site? I am concerned that some teachers are not thoughtful enough about the quality of their students' products and to what extent students' own creative processes are being engaged by using the site. Unless teachers provide focused guidelines, many students get distracted by the site's glitzy possibilities and forget the purpose of communicating content through a poster. They tend to clutter their posters with effects, animations, and wild colors. The quantity of backgrounds and elements on posters influences how long glogs take to load: more elements equal longer load times. I've visited educational wikis with several glogs embedded, which took minutes to load, only to note that the glogs had little to no meaningful content. On the other hand, I've seen glogs with powerful messages and eye-catching designs on the site, so glogs can be done well. Teachers who commit to using Glogster also need to commit to demanding high quality, content-filled work rather than lots of glitz.

I used to be concerned also about Glogster's cost, but the price of a single educator license with full access is about $40/year for 30 student accounts, which is in line with other educational products.

Collaboration Resources

Some Web 2.0 tools host lists of teachers seeking collaborations using the tools. This is certainly true of ePals and Skype for Educators, for instance. But teachers who want to join projects that are not necessarily tool-dependent have resources they can tap as well. Some internet sites focus on providing projects that teachers can join. The following list provides a sample of sites with free collaborative projects.

The Center for Innovation in Engineering and Science Education or **CIESE** (www.k12science.org/currichome.html) sponsors science, technology, engineering, and math projects for K–12 schools. Although most projects are geared to middle and high school students, some have been designed for elementary.

Journey North (www.learner.org/jnorth), **Global SchoolNet** (www.globalschoolnet. org), and **eLanguages** (http://elanguages.org) have similar structures. Teachers register free on each of these sites and join collaborative projects. The projects generally have specific timelines for joining and submitting projects. Because of the timelines and specific goals, the projects enable teachers to gauge how much time will be required. For instance, one project on Journey North engages students in planting tulip bulbs and tracking their growth. Journey North also tracks the migration of Monarch butterflies, among many other projects. Recent projects on Global SchoolNet have included Animals in our Landscape where students exchanged information about local animals and The Art of Gratitude where students create a Gratitude Art Box. eLanguages projects often focus on cultural exchanges such as Dance and Culture and Historical Monuments Across the Globe.

Projects by Jen (www.projectsbyjen.com) might be a great source for finding an online collaborative project your students can join. Projects can be joined by students in grades PK–6 and cost nothing except for supplies, with the cost kept below $10. Jen Wagner has been providing projects since 1999, and she welcomes ideas for additional projects from others. Created for teachers by a teacher, the object of the site is to bring fun for everyone back into teaching!

Web 2.0 tools excite students and give them a voice in the global world. These tools often mimic the tools that the adults around them use in business and in their personal lives. Students who practice working collaboratively in a global context gain skills that will help them become competent and confident adults who understand how technology can be used as a tool for working, communicating, and overcoming interpersonal and geographic boundaries.

Web 2.0 Tools Reviewed in this Chapter

TOOL	GRADE LEVEL	COST	COPPA COMPLIANT	COMMENT
Blabberize	3–12	Free	Parental permission	Student speaks for animated character
blog	All	Free	In sheltered environment	Needs explicit instruction about entries and comments
CIESE	K–12	Free	Yes	Science and engineering projects
eLanguages	K–12	Free	Yes	Global collaborative projects
email	3–12	Free	In sheltered environment	Requires preteaching about netiquette
Global SchoolNet	K–12	Free	Yes	Global collaborative projects
Glogster Subscription	3–12	$40/ year	Yes	Interactive posters; up to 30 student accounts
Journey North	K–12	Free	Yes	Global and regional science data collection and analysis; small supplies costs
Projects by Jen	PK–6	Free	Yes	Global collaborations, small supplies costs
Skype	K–12	Free	Yes	Internet video calls to anywhere
VoiceThread Subscription	K–12	$79/ year	Yes	Collaborative tool; unlimited Threads; class account
Voki Free	3–12	Free	Parental permission	Short (60-second) audio from typed text; some ads
Voki Subscription	3–12	$30/ year	Yes	Short (90-second) audio from typed text; no ads, teacher account for students
website design	3–12	Free	In sheltered environment	Can encompass blogs or wikis
wiki	All	Free	In sheltered environment	Define the purpose; add content often

CHAPTER 13

Advanced Multimedia

INCREASINGLY, EDUCATION EXPERTS recognize the value of multimedia tools as aspects of teachers' instruction and students' demonstrations or presentations using technology. Classes or lessons using multimedia appeal to several senses at once, increasing nearly all students' prospects for learning. When students create multimedia projects, they need to call on multiple skill sets—visual literacy, verbal skills, spatial concepts, and sound effects. Because few students are strong in all of these skill sets, production of multimedia projects is ideal for teamwork.

This chapter explores two types of multimedia work: making digital videos and computer programming. Of the two, the use of videos is the easier digital practice. Some teachers, particularly those who film videos at home, may find student videos easy to teach. Teachers less familiar with video cameras need to build their skills with digital stills and other technologies first.

Computer programming can be introduced through basic, easy tasks. However, it quickly escalates to highly technical work. Sometimes, though, programming appeals to teachers and students more than any other digital process. When schools sponsor robotics programs, for instance, students are introduced to basic programming, and many are eager to explore more advanced programming tools.

Teachers need to scaffold skills for students with advanced multimedia work so that students experience success. Generally, teachers should start with modeling or whole class experiences before releasing student teams to work independently. These activities represent constructivism at work; they will probably be messy, noisy, and energizing, and students will learn a lot!

Making Digital Videos

With the introduction of inexpensive, handheld video cameras, creating videos or movies became accessible for schools. Video cameras are now so small, inexpensive, sturdy, and easy to use that even young children can manage them. Additionally, some tablets and pad computers have built-in video ability. The intuitive movie-making applications bundled into Microsoft and Apple products, as well as the expanding capacity of computer memory, make creating digital movies a breeze. Online repositories, such as YouTube and TeacherTube, provide huge audiences for video footage and have convinced the general public that anyone can make a movie. Many students now create videos at home and would be eager to apply their movie-making abilities to school work, as well as to share their expertise with classmates.

For the purposes of this book, I will discuss creating videos at the simplest levels as encouragement for teachers to take first steps into using digital video with students. For more advanced discussions of making videos, I recommend consulting print materials or online resources such as the following.

The **Kids'Vid website** (http://kidsvid.4teachers.org) "offer[s] teachers and students assistance in enhancing learning through the power of digital media." In addition to a teacher lesson plan module that provides suggestions for introducing video making to students, the site provides a manual for four areas of production: scripting, making, editing, and show time. I recommend this as the first stop if you want to make a 2- to 5-minute scripted video with students.

EdTech Central's "Using Video Production to Improve Student Learning" page (http://powayusd.sdcoe.k12.ca.us/projects/edtechcentral/digitalstorytelling), by Poway Unified School District, California, is no longer being updated, but its resources are excellent. It offers links to how to use video in the classroom; storyboards; music, photos, and video clips; copyright guidelines; and video galleries. The page's Good Readers video produced by first graders won awards.

Class Movies (http://hil.troy.k12.mi.us/staff/bnewingham/myweb3/Movies Final. htm) is a webpage about the movies made by the Hill Elementary third graders in Troy, Michigan. This site has student-made movies, an explanation of the moviemaking process, and a "behind the scenes" look at a class movie to provide tips for improving movies.

Instructions on how to use **Windows Movie Maker** can be found on the Science Kids website (www.sciencekids.co.nz/lessonplans/technology/moviemaking.html).

Storyboard Pro (www.atomiclearning.com/storyboardpro) is free, downloadable software from Atomic Learning that students can use to plan their videos. At the site, you can view tutorials about creating a storyboard using the software. This incredibly helpful website guides students through all preparation work for filming a video.

Getting Started Making Videos

All video productions call for higher-order thinking skills because of the requirement that students choose a topic, plan the shots, shoot and edit the footage, and create a final product. Even when teachers direct whole class experiences, students will be involved in all aspects of the creation.

For a first foray into making videos, consider either a whole class project or short (30–60 second) videos done by groups of four to five students. These projects might be book reviews or retelling folktales. One teacher asked students to film their peers giving campaign speeches for student elections. At the simplest level, videos should be viewable without requiring editing or adding any features.

Adding a few features, such as titles, transitions, and credits, will enhance the video without pushing the difficulty level too high. Be prepared, though, for students to explore and add special effects that you may not have mastered. Because students have more time than teachers and are motivated to learn how to use cool tools, some students explore video software at home, ask older siblings or friends for help, or look for advanced features on the web. Celebrate their initiatives by asking them to teach you and their peers!

If you use learning centers in your classroom, making a video camera available for students to document what they are doing can be a powerful motivator. I once saw a kindergarten student grab a video camera to film her peers practicing the alphabet. The video was uploaded onto the class website so other students could watch it as often as they liked at school or at home. Any new skill can be treated that way: Students can have access to a video camera to film an impromptu lesson. Students often master academic skills efficiently and effectively when their peers teach them the skills.

The first videos that students produce may not meet teachers' high expectations, but as the process becomes more familiar, their videos should take on higher quality. Once students become comfortable with video cameras and editing software, teachers can release students to develop ideas for videos, plan the process, and edit the final products on their own. Be prepared, though, for students' passion for video to grow as they become more skilled. They may ask to turn every project into a video.

Peripheral Equipment

Even for a short video, certain peripheral equipment will make a difference. Tripods are almost mandatory for filming. It is difficult enough to hold a camera still, but to pan across a scene or zoom without a tripod requires far more agility than any student or teacher has. Tripods do not need to be expensive, and they are worth every cent of cost.

The other piece of equipment that will make a difference is an external or detachable microphone that feeds into the camera. The built-in microphones on handheld video cameras generally are too far away from the subjects to collect speech without also collecting environmental sounds. Investigate what will work best for your situation. A shotgun microphone might be the best basic microphone because it can pick up multiple people. A lapel microphone is generally small and can be hidden, but it works only with one person at a time. A handheld microphone will be visible in the film, but it works well for videos of news reports. Prices vary drastically, as does sound, so read online reviews to decide what will give you the best sound within your budget.

Preparing to Film

Before students start to film their videos, you will need to guide them through some preplanning activities including idea development and storyboarding.

Idea Development

Brainstorm ideas for short videos about a concept or event. Keep the ideas simple so that they can be covered in a 30-second video. Once you have zeroed in on a topic, consider four questions: 1) What is the main idea? 2) Who is the audience? 3) Where can we film this topic? 4) What gear will we need? For a first experience, students should use a simple concept, such as the Earth Day Three Rs, a book review, or a school event promotion for a 30-second clip.

Students will want to rush right away into filming, but the preplanning has just begun. Teachers may want to show video clips of other students' productions or of short, simple commercials, so that students can see how others have made videos. View the samples more than once to help students concentrate on one thing at a time, such as the background sounds, the script, and the number of shots. If possible, try to sketch out the parts of the clip to see how many "scenes" were filmed. This would be comparable to a rough storyboard.

Alternatively, the class could storyboard a picture book. Generally, picture books have one scene per page, and the text on that page fits with the illustration. Videos should have a similar feel—the script should fit with the shots. When students understand the concept of storyboarding, try to sketch out the class's idea for a 30-second video.

Storyboarding

Storyboards are videographers' best planning tools. Storyboards not only plan the shots and tie photo shots to scripts, but they keep the videographer on track. My class once tried making a video without a storyboard, and we learned, when we watched the resulting film, that we had forgotten to shoot one crucial scene that held the story together. It's true that with movie-making software, the scene can be reshot and edited in, but if the discovery is not made quickly, the logistics of pulling students together to shoot the scene may prove daunting. Asking students to duplicate their outfits and hair styles on a subsequent day to reshoot a scene seems simple until you try it!

You can print storyboards from **Xinsight** (http://xinsight.ca/tools/storyboard. html), develop your own template by setting parameters at **Incompetech** (http://incompetech.com/graphpaper/storyboard), or use the **Storyboard Pro** software (www.atomiclearning.com/storyboardpro) from Atomic Learning. If students already have experience with storyboards for digital storytelling or other sequenced activities, they will find storyboarding a video easier than if this is their first exposure. When the storyboard is done, it's time to film.

Saving and Converting Video Files

As with digital pictures, video files may be saved with different file extensions, but not all extensions play equally well on all systems. Understanding the basics of common file extensions will help teachers and students save or convert video files to work smoothly with their computer programs.

Common File Extensions

Video formats vary by quality, compression, and compatibility with players and platforms. This list indicates some best of uses of each format.

.avi (Audio Video Interleave) format was developed by Microsoft and is best viewed on Windows computers.

.divx files are high quality, compressed movie files, so the videos are clear, yet small in data size. Many programs can play movies made in this format. DivX (www.divx.com/en) offers a free, downloadable player and converter.

.flv or **.swf** extensions signify the Adobe Flash or Macromedia Shockwave formats, popular for online animations. A free, downloadable Flash plug-in is required for viewing animations in these formats in a web browser. These formats are popular on interactive websites for students, but they are not supported for Apple's iPad.

.mov refers to Apple's QuickTime movie format and is popular because it can be played on both Mac and Windows computers by the QuickTime Player, which is a free, downloadable component for Windows.

.mpg or **.mpeg** (Moving Pictures Expert Group) files have compressed audio and video data, are popular on the internet, and are cross-platform; that is, they can be played either on QuickTime Player or Windows Media Player.

.mp4 or **.mpeg-4** is the preferred extension for the internet. YouTube recommends .mp4 for uploads and converts all videos to .flv or .mp4 for distribution.

.rm or **.ram** (Real Media) files can be downloaded or streamed with low bandwidth. Because of the low bandwidth requirement, the quality of the videos is often reduced. Files are played on Real Player.

.wmv (Windows Media Video) format was developed by Microsoft and is played on the Windows Media Player that is standard on Windows computers. A free Windows Media Player component plug-in makes many, but not all, .wmv files playable on non-Windows computers.

Converting Video Files

When students use digital storytelling software, such as Microsoft Photo Story 3, or movie-making programs, such as Windows MovieMaker or iMovie, their final products may not be accessible on the devices at home. Movies might be uploaded to the internet to allow access, but often students want to take DVDs or USB drives home with their particular projects loaded. In that case, teachers should download a free video converter that will change the files to more compatible formats, accessible on home devices.

Format Factory (http://formatoz.com) is the free, downloadable, Windows-only video converter I use. The program can import most Windows or Mac files from flash drives and convert them to other formats. I have used this program to convert Photo Story 3 files, which are Windows-specific WMA files, to MP4 files that can be played on both Windows and Mac computers.

Free Studio (www.dvdvideosoft.com/free-dvd-video-software.htm), like Format Factory, is free, downloadable, and Windows-only. It also converts video to formats suitable for Windows, Macs, YouTube, phones, and Apple devices.

Freeware: Any Video Converter (www.any-video-converter.com/products/for_video_free) can be downloaded for either Windows or Mac computers. Not flashy, the site's software is sufficient to convert video files and the only free converter I have found for Macs.

Ideas for Student-Made Videos

There is no end to the types of videos students can create but the following activities have been proven to work well in the classroom.

Book Trailers

Librarians and teachers wish they could entice nonreaders to pick up books for pleasure reading. Student-created book trailers can act as peer-to-peer recommendations of books. Many samples (and the opportunity to add your own) can be found at Mark Geary's **Book Trailers—Movies for Literacy** site (www.homepages. dsu.edu/mgeary/booktrailers). Book trailers do not need to be long, and students synthesize what they read to determine the key points that would entice another reader.

Public Service Announcements

Asking teams of students to create public service announcements (PSAs) involves them in researching and thinking about messages they consider important—for themselves, their peers, and people everywhere. The PSAs may be tied into curriculum or left to students' choices. For example, one fifth grade class created PSAs related to their health unit on making healthy lifestyle choices. Another class created advocacy PSAs on self-selected topics, such as animal welfare, recycling, and dental health. In one middle school, students created passionate videos about global issues, such as child labor, endangered animals, natural disasters, and environmental issues. These projects often take a significant length of time, sometimes as long as two to three months, to complete because of the complexity of the issues to be researched and then figuring out how to write about them so that others will pay attention. The great benefits of this and similar projects are that students stay engaged and must use higher-levels of thinking throughout. When they take on global issues, as they learn more about how important these issues are to human beings everywhere, they become even more excited about conveying what they have discovered.

How-Tos

Students often learn best from other students, and videos allow the messages to be repeated as often as needed. For instance, math students could teach alternative algorithms to peers, and language arts students could present mnemonic devices for remembering how to spelling tricky words. A video can also explain how to play a game, pack for a trip, or participate in the school's recycling program.

Authentic Audiences

When students know that their videos will be seen by audiences outside the classroom's walls, they are motivated to refine their final products. The larger the potential audience, the more professional the videos need to appear. Consider the following ideas for opportunities to reach wider audiences:

- **Other classes in the school.** Students can create videos for younger students or their peers.

- **School lunchroom or lobby.** Videos can be shown on a loop in any high-traffic areas.

- **Parent-teacher association meetings.** When parents know that two to three short, student-generated videos will be shown at a meeting, attendance will increase.

- **School or other website.** Uploading students' videos to the internet makes them accessible to family members and friends.

- **Local cable station.** Some television stations will air the best representative samples of videos, particularly if the videos carry messages about local issues.

- **Contests.** Companies and websites advocating for student-generated videos will sometimes sponsor contests. One active organization is **Next Vista for Learning** (www.nextvista.org). On this site, students can learn about, for example, a Service via Video contest: "Tell the stories of those who make your community better and you could earn an eligible charity a $200 donation, along with helping them gather new support and volunteers!" Searching for student video contests in a search engine will bring up links to other contests.

Figurative Language

Like photos, videos frequently illustrate figurative language more effectively than additional language. A search on **SchoolTube** (www.schooltube.com) for "Chasing Metaphors" will bring up several examples of videos that illustrate students' metaphors. The concept is based on a lesson originally housed on the Apple Learning

Interchange site, which closed in 2010. Although the original video is no longer available, the lesson plan can be found through a simple web search.

Interviews

Students can use video cameras to record interviews with community residents. Ideas include town history; the use of math, reading, or writing in careers; safety tips; childhood memories; or town services. One teacher assigned local sites, such as historic buildings, cemeteries, sculptures, and museums, for students to research independently. Students created video clips that were used in teaching a curricular unit on local history. Secondary students and local residents in one community collected interviews and artifacts to document their town's railroad history.

Retellings

Students can act out stories, such as legends and fables. The process of translating a text into video and being selective about scenes because of time limits, heightens students' awareness of key elements in a story. Time restrictions also put boundaries on the amount of memory a video takes.

Demonstrations

Science experiments take on new meaning when students record their activities to share with others. In one classroom, students and parents used video to capture students' science experiments at home with simple machines. They then showed their movies in class. Appearing as experts bolstered the self-confidence of some otherwise quiet students.

Capture Events

Every class has special events that parents miss. Whether the events are field trips, oral presentations, or appearances by guest speakers, students can create a collection of video clips that summarize the activities. In such endeavors, it is probably better to have several videographers so that the editors have many options for footage. This would, of course, push video making into the advanced realm, so it should not be an introductory experience. At a simpler level, students could video the performances of any students whose parents were not able to attend the event, so that these students would have a record to share with their parents later.

Paying attention to preplanning will improve students' chances of successfully creating videos worth watching. Beware of comparing students' work with other videos found on the internet—it's impossible to tell how much or which parts of uploaded videos have been planned, edited, or controlled by adults. With practice, students develop great movie-making skills.

Even if your students' videos never reach award-winning quality, using video cameras in the classroom can inspire students to think about what aspects of their experiences are worth capturing on film for sharing. Some teachers put the students in charge of the cameras; their students' videos tend to be spur-of-the-moment highlights of everyday learning. Other teachers plan extravagant lessons with well-rehearsed student performances for video teams to film. Their students' videos tend to be finely crafted movies—useful for other students' learning. In some classrooms, using videos is a one-time event; for others, it's regular part of documenting classroom activities. Because teachers of elementary students have more leeway to plan the timing and structure of their lessons than middle and high school teachers, the elementary level may well be the ideal place to begin to teach video making.

At some middle schools, learning how to make videos is an optional lunch or after school activity for students who show interest. Secondary schools often offer video making as an elective. There's no one way to do it correctly. Any exposure students get to movie making will enable them to be more literate with visual media. As visual media surrounds students' lives, learning to be discriminating viewers is a lifelong skill all teachers have every reason to cultivate.

Programming

Learning a programming language requires more abstract skills than primary students typically have, so it's best to introduce programming at the third grade or higher levels. Do not expect all students to grasp the concepts quickly; some students will latch onto programming as an exciting tool, and some will find it too hard or tedious. Students who prefer kinesthetic/tactile learning approaches may enjoy learning programming because of the vicarious pleasure of making something move through typed commands. The good news is that teachers do not need to be programming experts, though they need to understand the basics of how it works. Online and software tools provide opportunities for students to discover how programming operates and write some simple programs. Additionally, if students have worked with robotics, as outlined in the chapter on kinesthetic/ tactile strategies, they will have already explored programming.

The purpose for learning and using programming language is generally embedded in the software or module. Typically, students are trying to make something virtual (or in robotics, an actual object) move, maneuver, and respond to commands. The skills students master in simple programming open the door to later explorations of designing games or even to careers in software development. When students have developed some proficiency, they can demonstrate their programs or take screen shots of what they mastered so that others will see their accomplishments. Learning programming languages can be differentiated as well. Some students will be content to master the virtual experiences from the **National Library of Virtual Manipulatives** (http://nlvm.usu.edu) by moving the turtle or hiding the ladybug. These games are found in the Geometry section. Others might want to use other instructional websites or programming software listed below. When students are learning and applying programming software, they are also using problem-solving and evaluative skills. Some programs will quickly move students from the concept of mastering a language to creating a game or animation of their own.

Another option is to use the **Hour of Code** page (http://code.org/learn) to plan an introductory lesson for beginners. Choose from the tutorials and set students up to learn (pairing is good!) about programming. The site has additional educator resources worth exploring. They provide a free K–8 Intro to Computer Science curriculum.

Teachers need to consider whether programming fits their students' needs and interests better as a whole class discovery or as a differentiated center in the classroom. It will not appeal to all students, but perhaps all students need at least one exposure to programming to determine whether they want to explore it further. Most programming resources do not distinguish between elementary students and other users. They typically do not gather data through registration, so they are suitable for any age. Prior to trying any of these, use online virtual manipulative activities to sensitize students to what they will be doing.

Programming Basics (www.programmingbasics.org) has basic lessons on writing Java scripts to control two robots. This is a great starting place for learning about programming languages because the lessons are child-friendly and the website requires no log-in, so even students under age 13 can use the site. While students will have to read instructions, the text is simple and encouraging. Teachers can download resources such as lessons, guides, and a simple code editor. The site also has links to additional programming ideas.

The Code Monster from Crunchzilla (www.crunchzilla.com/code-monster) teaches Java programming through 59 lessons; young people (and adults) are encouraged to try making changes to lines of code to discover what happens. Instructions on the screen indicate that Code Monster remembers where you stopped, as long as you return on the same browser on the same computer. Anyone who can read can use this online programming tool.

Pluralsights' Free Courses for Kids (https://www.pluralsight.com/kids) requires registration, so students under age 13 will need parental permission. The site offers courses covering programming basics, programming with Scratch (site listed below), building apps with MIT's App Inventor, programming with Kodu to learn how to create games, programming with Hopscotch to learn how to create an interactive game, and basic HTML publishing language. Even though the YouTube video on the site shows young children, these courses are suitable for students at all levels.

Light-Bots (http://armorgames.com/play/2205/light-bot) is an online programming game that gets progressively harder. Students learn to program and use repeat features through trial and error. I struggled with the game at first because I did not realize the goal was to have the robot stand on every blue square, not turn all squares blue as the opening lines stated. With trial and error, though, I learned, as students will.

Scratch (http://scratch.mit.edu) is a programming language, available as a free download offered through MIT. Scratch requires creativity because students must draw and program. The creators encourage Scratch designers to look at the code written by other designers, not only to see how the programming was done, but also to remix the original projects with ideas of their own to change, improve, and re-imagine the original idea. As open-ended as this software is, students can stretch themselves artistically and technically. Scratch can be downloaded for use on Windows, Macintosh, and Linux platforms.

Simple (www.simplecodeworks.com) is a free downloadable programming language for Windows computers. Although described as programming for kids, it is suitable for anyone who wants to learn programming in a Windows environment.

Fifteen Fabulous Advanced Video Project Ideas

Note: Although these projects primarily refer to video, they could be done with a combination of simpler technologies, such as digital cameras, voice recorders, slideshow software, or Web 2.0 tools.

Instructional film. Teach a concept or procedure.

Interviews. Interview experts about their areas of expertise.

Program experiment. Try a programming exercise online.

Book reviews. Film a book review and upload it for the school library.

Public Service Announcements. Create PSAs to reinforce values (caring, sharing, safety, and other positive guidelines for interacting with other people and the environment).

Analogies. Turn figurative language into visual representations.

Contest entries. Enter a film competition.

Family stories. Reminisce with family members.

Poetry slam. Capture students' performances and upload the best ones.

Memory collage. Capture events throughout the year.

Immigrant tales. Learn about an immigrant family's journey.

Reenactment. Film a reenactment of history or of a book.

School film. Describe the school for global partners.

Class presentations. Tape students' performances to send home.

Students' election speeches. Broadcast 1-minute campaign speeches.

CHAPTER 14

Teacher Resources

CAN YOU IMAGINE having a teaching partner or assistant who could generate exciting ideas for lessons, help deliver instruction, reinforce students' classroom experiences, engage students in higher-level thinking, assess students' thinking skills, and support your professional growth? Such a paragon would be welcome anywhere, right? Yet, an excellent teacher's helper capable of all this assistance often collects dust when it could ease your and every teacher's workload: an internet-connected computer.

In Chapters 5–12, the websites and activities have generally been targeted toward students. This chapter focuses on teachers' needs. Two types of resources are covered: aggregator sites, where many online resources for students are gathered and free professional development courses. Sometimes one site provides both.

A Beginning Place: TeachersFirst

TeachersFirst (http://teachersfirst.com) is a premier teacher resource site for professional development and interactive internet sites. The heart of TeachersFirst (TF) is its extensive database of lessons, units, and web resources used by teachers worldwide. Teachers can search the collection by keyword, grade level, curriculum topic, or content strand. Each entry in the collection is identified not only by grade level ranges, but also by icons that identify the resources at the site, detailed explanations of the site's features, and an "In the Classroom" write-up of how to use the site with students. As all the resources are sampled and reviewed by teachers, the realistic descriptions will help you decide whether particular resources will work well with your students.

If that were the only service provided by the TeachersFirst site, it would be a rich resource for teachers. However, the site offers much more. For instance, TF creates content. Blog Basics and Wiki Walkthrough help teachers learn how to use these tools. Globetracker's Mission is TF's response to a need for more elementary-appropriate geography materials. Throughout the year, students track international travelers, using Geo and Meri. Under the tab *TeachersFirst Exclusives,* you can find other TeachersFirst-created content to fit your needs. Check out the 50 States pages!

TeachersFirst also has resource collections for universal topics, such as 100th Day of School, Martin Luther King, Jr. Day, Earthquakes, Internet Safety, Presidents' Day, Measurement, and Elections. These collections pull together topic-specific resources to save you from searching for them.

On the professional development end, TeachersFirst offers OK2Ask sessions to encourage teachers in the integration of technology. These webinars are designed to build teachers' skills with technology and are moderated by teachers. If your district allows using outside resources for professional development hours, taking several OK2Ask sessions may qualify for in-service credit.

Even if you excel at finding good interactive websites for your students to use, a search in TeachersFirst will bring up sites you probably have not seen before. If you register on the site, you can receive an email every Sunday with tips, featured sites, and other goodies.

VOICES OF EXPERIENCE

Sheri Edwards, teacher and technology director
Nespelem School, Nespelem, Washington
sheri@nsdeagles.org

Is your school emerging into the journey of infusing technology into lessons? Does the process seem overwhelming? It did to our school district, but after attending an OK2Ask session on Schoolwide Literacy, I understood that our novice tech teachers (those not tech savvy) needed a slower approach.

As a Google Apps for Education school, our staff needed some introductory sessions on the tools they would use most. Because of the session, I choose only three tools to introduce (email, calendar, blogs) over six sessions, which would benefit teachers' communication with each other and with families.

In addition, the session model used by OK2Ask provided a template for each of the six hour-long sessions at our school: Expectations, Exploration, Explanation, Engagement with Explanations, and Expressions (reflect and assess).

In an OK2Ask session, the processes of expecting and exploring help participants feel comfortable and ask questions about the technology. A demonstration (explanation) provides the background for engaging with the tool. Finally, participants express what was learned and evaluate the tool, strategy, resources, or process for use in the classroom or school.

I was uncertain how to help my colleagues manage the changes that technology was bringing to our school. Taking a free webinar about using technology eased our journey and saved time, travel, and money. I learned a strategy for implementing technology tools throughout the school and a process for presenting the professional development to staff.

VOICES OF EXPERIENCE

Candy Shively, retired director of K–12 Initiatives, TeachersFirst
Source for Learning, Reston, Virgijnia

As a 27-year teaching veteran, my current teaching assignment is guiding the TeachersFirst team of Thinking Teachers. TeachersFirst is a free, ad-free service from a nonprofit, the Source for Learning. Everyone who writes for us is an experienced teacher. We feel very strongly about saving our colleagues time "finding the good stuff" on the internet and sharing ways to use free, web-based resources effectively in their classrooms. We know the theories, but we also know the realities of the classroom and the nitty-gritty of adhering to curriculum requirements. So when we explain what a wiki is and how to use it, we can put it in terms of what a third grade class might be studying or what a high school physics class might do for a project. You can search TeachersFirst by grade, subject, curriculum topic, or keyword to find just what you need.

When the Sunday night panic hits, and you realize that the 100th day of school is tomorrow, TeachersFirst has resources ready on our Classroom Planning Calendar—just in time for tomorrow's class. We know teachers appreciate topic and date-related collections, so we have them ready.

We also know that there is a wide range of technology expertise among teachers. We try to offer everything from the simplest websites that any tech novice can use to support students at a classroom learning center, to an interactive white-board, to creative ideas for using the latest web tools safely and within school policies. Technology is a rapidly moving target, so TeachersFirst makes a great effort to save teachers time while learning the latest tech tools for classroom use. We believe all teachers can grow and learn together with their students—whether they are using teacher-reviewed websites or launching a class wiki with guidance from the Wiki Walk-Through (www.teachersfirst.com/content/wiki).

Teachers tell us our professional content is inspiring, thorough, and practical. For those who prefer learning "live" and interacting with other teachers, TeachersFirst offers free, online professional development snack sessions we call OK2Ask.

Once teachers discover TeachersFirst, they never leave us. We are Thinking Teachers Teaching Thinkers.

Professional Development Sites

Inservice training and professional development offer two different types of experiences for teachers. When teachers attend required district- or school-level training to learn about new curriculum, standards, or tools, they are attending inservice training. The purpose of an inservice is to promote the institution's agenda. Inservice may provide information about the institution's approach to curriculum, but it often has little influence on teachers' professional practices.

Professional development happens when teachers pursue assistance to improve their professional practices. Because individuals have quite different needs from one another, rarely will a whole school or district engage in professional development. Instead, teachers seek out rich learning opportunities appropriate for their own professional growth. Because teachers pursue training that will advance their own teaching practices, professional development often prompts them to change their instructional strategies. In other words, inservice is generally imposed, and professional development is a teacher's choice. And professional development has the potential to trigger within teachers the desire to make changes to improve their modes of instruction.

Online learning can provide convenient, targeted professional development because the training can be individually accessed and managed. With online coursework, teachers can access just-in-time help, often provided in effective instructional modes. For instance, many online professional development courses include videos of teachers demonstrating best practices in their classrooms. Teachers rarely see other teachers teaching, so having access to videos of other teachers' classrooms has significant benefits. Online professional development also allows for individualized staff development; teachers can choose staff development in areas where they are currently trying to improve their practices. This makes online professional development, particularly when it is also free, a blessing for teachers and administrators.

Free, high-quality professional development is available from several online sources. Some may qualify for continuing education units (CEUs). In some districts, for example, teachers can write up independent or group studies to get credit for licensure and/or pay increases. Check to see whether your district and/or state will confer CEUs with evidence of completion of online modules. The chance to earn CEUs while you learn, at home in your jammies or in a study group, will keep you motivated! The following resources provide free professional development for teachers in specific content areas.

Annenberg Learner (www.learner.org) offers online professional development courses in all content areas for K–12 teachers. A list of courses can be accessed at this page of the website: www.learner.org/workshops/workshop_list.html. All materials, video and print, are free, and teachers can use them in three ways: for self-guided study, as a study group with a facilitator (guide available online), or as a graduate course through Colorado State University (fee required for credit). This high-quality professional development training would not be easy to find locally.

BioEd Online (http://bioedonline.org) hosts free online science workshops and short courses from the Baylor College of Medicine. Teachers, scientists, and science educators provide the courses' content. Teachers receive a certificate for contact hours upon completion of each workshop or short course.

Concept to Classroom (www.thirteen.org/edonline/concept2class) is a free series of self-paced, K–12 workshops on teaching and learning. Workshops include materials and videos. The site also provides documentation materials, including a letter for the superintendent, an extensive syllabus, and a post-course rubric for evaluation to assist teachers in requesting continuing education units from their districts.

Library of Congress Online Modules (www.loc.gov/teachers/professionaldevelopment/selfdirected) are free, one-hour, self-directed, online learning modules that focus on copyright law and using primary sources for K–12 teachers. At the conclusion of each module, teachers receive certificates of completion that may qualify for professional development hours.

Curriculum Associates Topics in Education section (www.ca101.com) offers free, self-paced training. The opening page shows the company's product training, but clicking on the Topics tab will take you to 60–90 minute modules on discipline, struggling readers, differentiated instruction, higher-order thinking skills, Response to Intervention (RTI), teaching the six traits of writing, the connection between home and school, test preparation strategies, motivating students, and vocabulary for English Language Learners. The modules include videos and handouts. Teachers have to register with Curriculum Associates to access the training. No indication appears on the site about professional development units.

Best Practices Weekly (http://bestpracticesweekly.com) has taken a clever approach to professional development. Recognizing that teachers rarely have time to read the latest research, this website team emails teachers a weekly research review that condenses current research on education. Past weeklies are archived on the site. Weeklies include a summary, short videocast, and supporting materials in Word or in a PDF. Teachers can use the strategies from weeklies immediately. Although the weeklies may not qualify for professional development hours, they certainly help teachers feel connected to good practices in education with an investment of about 10 minutes a week.

Teacher Resources Reviewed in this Chapter

SITE	FOCUS	FORMAT	CREDIT
Annenberg Learner	All subject areas	Online self-study courses, lengths vary	CEUs or graduate credit for a fee
Best Practices Weekly	Pedagogy	Weekly email	None
BioEd Online	Science	Online self-study courses, 3–6 contact hours	Certificate of participation
Concept to Classroom	Pedagogy	Online self-study courses, 30–35 hours	Provides materials to request CEUs from your administrator
Library of Congress Online	Copyright and Primary Sources	Online self-directed workshops, 1 hour	Certificate of participation
TeachersFirst	Technology integration	OK2Ask webinars, 75 minutes	Certificate of participation
Topics in Education	Pedagogy	Online self-paced workshops, 60–90 minutes	Unknown

Learning Management Systems

Learning management systems enable teachers to create classroom accounts, upload student accounts, and have one online place where students interact with one another, work collaboratively, take assessments, turn in assignments, and generally track their school lives. Rather than hosting a blog in one website, a wiki on another, and a discussion board on a third, many K–12 teachers are migrating to platforms where they can do it all in one space. Several K–12 learning management systems provide free teacher accounts or low-cost district or school accounts.

Edmodo (www.edmodo.com) has gained popularity among teachers, not only for the look and feel of social media, but also for the professional library and community it provides. Teachers can draw from a library of lessons and resources created by other members of the learning system. Teachers can also easily arrange for their students to interact with other classes in the system.

VOICES OF EXPERIENCE

Jennifer Bond, third grade teacher
Glengary Elementary, Commerce Township, Michigan
www.edmodo.com/jenniferbond

I was first introduced to Edmodo in March 2009, at Michigan's technology conference. Steve Dembo mentioned it quickly during one of his sessions, and I added it to my notes. A month later, I was preparing to share what I had learned at the conference for my colleagues, and I checked into Edmodo. I easily created a teacher account and created a group for my students on a Friday. I signed all of my students up and sent them home with their usernames and passwords. Many students logged in and participated in discussions over the weekend, but the discussions went more like this, "Hello! Hi! Anyone there? Is anyone on Edmodo? I am at my house." "Me too! Hi Mikayla!" I regularly checked the group, and I tried to get the kids to understand this was not a chat room through posts, as I envisioned students staying glued to their computer screens, waiting for someone to reply back. I was concerned what parents were thinking about this new platform. I realized that I had set my students free on this site without giving them the tools and expectations for using the site. On Monday when they returned, we created norms for using Edmodo, and I taught them the difference between a chat room and a social learning network.

This is my third year using Edmodo with my third graders, and our uses for Edmodo have come a long way. My students still like to share things about their lives outside of school, from links to fancy hairstyles for the Daddy/Daughter

Dance or their little sister swimming through a hula hoop in swim class, yet they are also uploading photos of festivals around Michigan or creating commercials to go along with our economics unit. I easily create quizzes that are automatically graded and put in the Edmodo grade book, as well as create assignments. When we go into the lab, I often use Edmodo to organize our lab tasks. For example, we did an activity where we had to go virtual shopping for a Thanksgiving meal. I linked sales ads from four stores to a post, and the students had to choose one where they would shop. Then they had to post a reply telling how much their dinner cost. I also have embedded Google Maps and asked the students to post what natural and human features they found. Often I add sites or videos that help reinforce concepts we have studied in class. Yes, I can post the same sites on my webpage, but my webpage does not allow the interaction. Each Edmodo group I create is a constantly evolving community that allows all people involved to contribute!

Speaking of contributions and community, Edmodo has also evolved through the years to be an amazing site for connecting with teachers from around the world! Teachers can join content communities, which allow people to post helpful websites, pose questions, add files, and so on. The best part of it is if someone posts a great resource, you can click "Library" and add it to your own library to be used at a later date or shared with others. There are so many talented teachers willing to share their ideas and build a global educational community!

I have called myself the EdTech Cheerleader, cheering others to technology integration, and Edmodo is the site I have cheered most about because of its ease and the fact that the folks from Edmodo (most of whom have education backgrounds) are always listening to teachers, offering strong support, and building Edmodo to be stronger each day! I recently talked to a middle school teacher who was introduced to Edmodo this year, and he said, "In the decade I have been a teacher, Edmodo is the single most dynamic thing that has impacted the way I have taught." Edmodo is dynamic at all levels of education, and I can only imagine it will make impacts on classrooms around the world more and more as the years go on!

Schoology (www.schoology.com) is similar to Edmodo, although each learning management system has its own personality. Schoology apparently has an excellent interface with iPads, which is a winning feature for some users. A comparison of the features between Edmodo and Schoology is available on this blog (www.teachinglikeits2999.com/2013/02/schoology-vs-edmodo-round-2.html).

Aggregate Sites for Content Areas

Some websites pull together resources from multiple sites in order to shortcut the searching teachers used to do. Called aggregators, these sites might focus on one or many content areas. Bookmarking one or two aggregators will cover the best interactive resources available in specific content areas, provided site managers keep the sites updated. When you are looking for just the right interactive website for kids, begin with TeachersFirst and then move to content-area aggregators. The following list represents the best of the aggregators. Preference is given to sites that are extensive, organize by content areas and grade levels, and primarily list interactive sites instead those that list lesson plans and worksheets.

Internet4Classrooms (www.internet4classrooms.com) organizes links to student activities by grade levels and content areas. Often within the content areas, the activity links are organized by standards. This site is extensive and concentrates on activities students can do to practice their learning. Some sites may only be skills drills.

Utah Education Network or UEN (www.uen.org/k12student/interactives.shtml) has a less extensive set of links than other sites but has an attractive and user-friendly interface. Links are organized by grade levels, K–2, 3–6, and 7–12, and then by content areas. Within each content area, the links are arranged with icons, and plug-in requirements, such as Flash or Shockwave, are noted.

Instructional Support Websites

For lack of a better place to list my favorite websites, the ones I believe teachers need to know and explore, this section will highlight websites that are particularly useful for teachers. Some may be mentioned elsewhere in the book. Instructional support websites are those that offer teachers knowledge and materials for teaching in content areas. Some may contain activities for students that teachers can access, but their primary role is to support teachers as they plan instruction. Of course, this list is not comprehensive.

Instructional Resources for Multiple Content Areas

PBS LearningMedia (www.pbslearningmedia.org) serves schools by providing digital resources for free. The site is a combination of PBS TeacherLine and Teachers' Domain. Many digital videos and materials can be downloaded after free registration. Some of the videos can also be mashed or put into a video editing program for teachers or students to manipulate. The PBS LearningMedia site is free for teachers and students, and a customizable, fee-based version is available for districts.

Instructional Resources for Language Arts

Mosaic Listserv (www.readinglady.com/mosaic/tools/tools.htm) has hundreds of resources for teachers who use reading comprehension strategies for elementary students. This listserv has been in existence for more than ten years; thus, it can legitimately be considered a community of practice for educators who teach reading.

Into the Book (http://reading.ecb.org) has a teacher side and a student side for working with the comprehension strategies. On the teacher side are videos of teachers teaching the strategies, lesson plans for extensions, and other teacher resources. On the student side, students explore each comprehension strategy through videos and activities. Although this is listed as a K–4 site, most of the student activities would be difficult for anyone younger than grade 4 without teacher intervention and could be used through early middle school.

Reading Strategies for Students All Ages (www.farr-integratingit.net/Theory/ReadingStrategies/) lists and annotates reading strategies alphabetically. Almost every reading theory is represented in the list, with excellent ideas for how strategies could be incorporated into classrooms.

Reading Rockets (www.readingrockets.org) takes teachers some time to explore, but if you teach young students how to read or you work with striving readers, this website needs to be on your radar. Any teacher would love the more than 100 podcasts of interviews with children's book authors as well.

A companion site to Reading Rockets is **¡Colorín Colorado!** (www.colorincolorado. org), an English/Spanish bilingual site for families and educators of English Language Learners. While the site is in English and Spanish only, the strategies are appropriate for working with all students learning English as a second or an additional language.

Read, Write, Think (www.readwritethink.org/classroom-resources/student-inter-actives), sponsored by the National Council of Teachers of English, provides more than 50 interactive tools for students. The site also offers lesson plans that include using the student interactive tools. While this site is built for student use, teachers will need to explore and find appropriate interactive tools for their students to meet instructional goals.

WritingFix (http://writingfix.com), the baby of the Northern Nevada Writing Project, has so many writing tools and supports for K–12 classroom teachers— many of which spill into teaching reading as well—that the site is almost overwhelming. You will find something useful on this site for every writing lesson you plan!

Recipes to Good Writing (http://farr-integratingit.net/Theory/RecipesForWriting) looks like a recipe box, but the "recipe cards" cover different types of writing genres. Each genre has a recipe, graphic organizer, and checklist—all of which can be downloaded and printed. Build your personal knowledge of the writing genres or use the recipes with students.

Instructional Resources for Math

Khan Academy (www.khanacademy.org) provides supplemental and differentiated video support for students' learning. Currently, the bulk of the videos and practice modules cover secondary topics, but the math section has been completed for K–12. Because the site requires registration, putting students on the site neces-sitates extra work. Teachers must obtain parental permission to ask students to register. If the school has a Google Apps for Education domain, then students may have Gmail addresses for registering themselves (with parental permission) and can associate themselves with teacher accounts. If the school lacks student email accounts, parents need to register their own students under age 13, but the registrations can then be linked to the teacher. Teacher/coach tools on the site are quite helpful for differentiating and tracking students' progress.

The important thing to know about this site is that it is always changing. The developer has made most videos himself and continues to add videos regularly. When students are struggling with math concepts, his method of explaining—a different voice, a different way of phrasing the information—may reach students who never seem to understand you. The videos often have practice exercises with new and different problems every time. When students cannot solve the problems, they can click to access step-by-step tutorials.

Instructional Resources for Science

At **Learning Science** (http://learningscience.org), teachers and students share links that will engage students in learning science. Click on a strand of science, then on the standard to see a table of science interactive tools with annotations about the activity, grade level, and length of activity. Other links on the home page go to Tools to Do Science, Google and Science Education, YouTube science channels, and Help Scientists Do Science. In the Help Scientists area, citizen scientists (including young people) can collect data to participate in real science projects. This site combines teachers' resources with students' links.

The GLOBE Project (http://classic.globe.gov) also encourages citizen scientists to participate in data collection and collaboration on environmental science topics. Teachers must be trained in the GLOBE science measurement protocols (a list of workshops is listed on the site, as well as hints for learning about training if no workshops appear in your area) before participating. GLOBE is an acronym for Global Learning and Observations to Benefit the Environment. The research is conducted hands-on; reporting is an online activity.

Scientific American's Citizen Science page (www.scientificamerican.com/citizen-science) and the **Cornell Lab of Ornithology Citizen Science Blog** (www.birds.cornell.edu/citsci/projects) list many citizen science opportunities that can integrate with curricular units or with teaching science. Not all projects are suitable for all students, but exploration of citizen science project lists will turn up several possibilities for any grade level. Several individual projects have good educator resources and can be done by classes or individuals. For instance, **Project BudBurst** (http://budburst.org) invites citizen scientists to observe and report information about how and when plants change. The site offers free resources and low-cost professional development to enable teachers to involve their students in scientific observation and reporting. While the activities are not entirely computer-based, the value of reporting data online for synthesis with what others observe makes the activities authentic. Other favorite citizen science projects are **Lost Ladybug Project** (www.lostladybug.org), **School of Ants** (http://schoolofants.org), and **Celebrate Urban Birds** (http://celebrateurbanbirds.org).

Teacher Link provides science lessons that integrate technology (www.teacherlink. org/content/science/instructional). Many lessons are detailed instructions for project ideas listed in earlier chapters of this book. Some use digital microscopes; although the units call for a particular microscope, the ideas can be adapted to the microscopes or magnifiers that teachers have in their classrooms.

ARKive Education (www.arkive.org/education) has free education resources for teaching about the natural sciences. Resources are organized by age group. Each file contains links to amazing wildlife photos and videos, as well as activities and teacher notes.

Instructional Resources for Social Studies

Bringing History Home (http://bringinghistoryhome.org) offers a curriculum for engaging K–5 students in the rigorous study of history. Because social studies is not usually tested at the state level, elementary students in some school districts have few opportunities to study history. The curriculum at this site supports good instruction in nonfiction reading, visual literacy, and writing.

Teacher Resources Highlighted in this Chapter

WEBSITE	RESOURCE TYPE	FOCUS
ARKive Education		Science units on natural sciences
Bringing History Home		Rigorous history curriculum
Citizen Science sites		Citizen science projects
¡Colorín Colorado!		English/Spanish bilingual reading
Edmodo	Learning management system	Involves a strong educator community
GLOBE Project		Citizen science projects
Internet4Classrooms	Aggregator	All content areas
Into the Book		Reading (Comprehension Strategies)
Khan Academy		Math video lectures
Learning Science	Aggregator	Science interactive sites
Mosaic Listserv		Reading (Mosaic of Thought)
PBS LearningMedia	Aggregator	Digital media resources for all content areas; highlights science
Read, Write, Think	NCTE	Interactive language arts tools
Reading Rockets		Reading resources and author podcasts
Reading Strategies for Students		Annotated reading strategies
Recipes for Good Writing		Writing genres
Schoology	Learning management system	A strong iPad interface
Teacher Link		Science lessons that integrate technology
Utah Education Network	Aggregator	All content areas
WritingFix	Northern Nevada Writing Project	Writing tools and supports

CHAPTER 15

COPPA, Internet Safety, and Copyright

AT THE ELEMENTARY LEVEL, technology integration requires more intentionality than at the secondary level. Secondary teachers work with students who have abstract thinking ability and can comprehend the consequences of their behavior, even if they choose not to heed them. Elementary students generally lack the maturity, experience, and abstract thinking ability to anticipate consequences of their behavior. Thinking about how their behavior on the internet today could harm them later exceeds their capacity. For that reason, elementary teachers bear responsibility as their students' protectors.

The world has changed dramatically for everyone—but perhaps most of all for young people—with the pervasive influences of the internet on American culture. Neither parents nor educators anticipated or prepared for these changes quickly enough. Elementary teachers, as well as teachers at every level, feel as though they are always running to catch up with technology. The intent of this chapter is to give teachers a deeper understanding of how they can build students' capacities to thrive in the digital world.

Children's Privacy Laws

Elementary teachers bear the responsibility to protect their students while they are too young to protect themselves. Pay close attention to the privacy policies of web tools. It does not matter that students may, at home, use sites geared to those over age 13. At school, teachers must 1) use wisdom in choosing Web 2.0 tools and 2) teach young students about safeguarding their personal information at school and at home. Many education bloggers recommend online tools without considering the special circumstances of elementary students, so elementary teachers must stay vigilant.

When teachers want to use websites and even apps for iPads or Android tablets, they must analyze whether the tools or sites comply with the Children's Online Privacy Protection Act (COPPA). Title XIII, the "Children's Online Privacy Protection Act of 1998" (COPPA), is a U.S. federal law located at 15 U.S.C. §§ 6501–6506 (Pub.L. 105–277, 112 Stat. 2681–728), enacted October 21, 1998 (www.gpo.gov/fdsys/pkg/PLAW-105publ277/html/PLAW-105publ277.htm). The act was designed to protect the privacy of children under the age of 13, and its requirements for websites and downloadable apps are stringent.

Basically, COPPA requires that all websites, online tools, and downloadable apps targeted to children under age 13 protect privacy by not collecting or saving any personal information about children. This means the site cannot request names, email addresses, school names, or geographic locations from children under age 13.

Note: All websites, online tools, and downloadable apps listed in this book have been checked for compliance with COPPA. Most do not require registration, although some tools do. When tools require teacher accounts and parental permission, these have been noted in the descriptions.

When you consider a website, online tool, or downloadable app for elementary children's use, ask the following questions.

Does the site require registration?

If a site does NOT require registration, young children may use it. If it DOES, closer examination of the site is required. This is not a concern for secondary teachers.

Does the registration ask for students' personal information?

Some sites with registration do not require personal information, although this is rare. For instance, **Into the Book** (http://reading.ecb.org), a reading comprehension site, asks students to give a first name (it could be an alias), and the site generates a password. This enables students to return to the site and resume work in progress.

On sites where teachers register and then create accounts for their students, no personal information about the children is required. An example would be **Wikispaces Classroom** (www.wikispaces.com), which provides free classroom wikis for K–12 teachers. Educational subscription sites also use this protocol. Such sites can be used without concern about violating privacy.

School districts that use Google Apps for Education provide protected emails for students under teachers' names and district domains, so children under age 13 can use the tools within Google Apps such as Blogger or Google Docs behind the protective walls of the district or school.

If the site registration requires a student's name, email address, school name, or location, one more question remains:

Does the resource comply with privacy laws?

On the home page of the site and on any page where a student must register or sign in, the site must prominently display a link to the privacy policies. Read the policies. Some sites ban children under the age of 13 from using their sites. Others have made provisions for young children to use the site provided parental permission has been acquired by following the procedures in the privacy policy. Any advertisements on the site or app must also display a link to their privacy policies.

Teachers can request parental permission for some sites and serve as surrogate parents. An excellent document to consult, *How to Protect Kids' Privacy Online:*

A Guide for Teachers (www.educationnewyork.com/files/teachersFTC.pdf), can be downloaded. Compliance with the law is mandatory for elementary teachers, even though it sometimes eliminates the use of some "cool tools" that elementary students would love.

Compliance with COPPA in elementary schools is an ethical issue and professional responsibility. Teachers may resist this restriction because it means tools that their students would love cannot be used during the elementary years, even when teachers feel their students would handle the sites responsibly. The law's concern is not what students do when they are under teachers' supervision, but rather how using the tools at school influences students outside of school. Even under tight supervision, some students find ways to circumvent teachers' expectations and get into trouble. Outside school, the same students are less cautious. At the elementary level, where teachers' decisions still have a strong influence on their students' behaviors and beliefs, teachers must choose to model ethical and responsible behavior.

Many teachers cannot afford the annual or monthly subscription fees for the education portals of Web 2.0 tools. Do not let that dissuade you from using other tools and noncomputer technology equipment. Recently, a colleague decided her video camera would be the responsibility of two students in the class. She's taking a risk with a noncomputer tool in a low-pressure way. The videos the students take do not have to be polished or uploaded, and she can get a sense of what students think needs to be filmed in her classroom. This small step has already changed the character of her class. Her action signals that the students have roles for deciding what happens in their classroom. COPPA certainly does not need to stop teachers from teaching students in constructivist ways; it should simply make teachers more aware of their responsibility to protect vulnerable youth.

Internet Safety

Teachers also have the responsibility of teaching students (and often their students' parents) how to be safe on the internet. Curriculum and internet activities are available on the web for teachers. Many sites found in a simple search will also provide information for parents. The hardest part may be zeroing in on what students need in any particular classroom.

I set the following guidelines with my students when we are using their materials online or when they are working collaboratively outside the classroom walls:

- For safety reasons, students will use pseudonyms or first names only.

- No photographs of individual students will appear on a website, including the school website. If students want certain items to go public, they cannot include pictures of themselves. Group photos are sometimes allowed, depending on the context and purpose, but students' names are not listed.

- Because the school location is typically listed on the website, students in group photos will not be identified by the teacher's name or grade level.

- Students' projects, even on their personal wiki pages, will not include last names. Monitoring this requires the teacher's vigilance.

- Students will not share personal or family information or nonschool emails with collaborative partners.

- Students will choose appropriate pseudonyms and avatars for school work. "Foxy Female" or "Studman" would not be appropriate.

Usually, I ask students to write the guidelines with me. They are far stricter than I might be and can think of situations I might miss. Inevitably, though, a few students will make mistakes online that I had not prepared for. Students know the goal is to keep them safe, so guidelines may need to be tightened up if a situation arises for which we did not plan.

Most teachers were past elementary age when the internet exploded into a resource fraught with pitfalls, so online safety was not part of their elementary education. As adults, teachers navigate the web with skepticism; children navigate with trust. While no one wants to frighten young people, teaching them some internet smarts helps to keep them safe.

Digital Literacy and Citizenship Classroom Curriculum (www.commonsensemedia. org/educators/curriculum) offers a free curriculum that covers many topics of internet safety. Free curriculum for internet safety is shrinking, and this one looks well-organized and documented.

iKeepSafe has teachers' lesson materials (www.ikeepsafe.org/educators) and short YouTube stick figure videos to use with students (www.ikeepsafe.org/videos). Teachers can choose the lessons their students need based on the topic.

Safety Land (www.att.com/Common/images/safety/game.html) by AT&T has a game with eight questions about safe behavior on the internet for elementary students. This might be a good whole class activity where students think about their responses and discuss them. This is one activity where students' response systems, also known as clickers, would give teachers valuable information about what children do and do not understand about internet safety.

Educational Games (http://mediasmarts.ca/digital-media-literacy/educational-games) by Media Smarts, Canada's Centre for Digital and Media Literacy, teaches digital literacy through games. Age and grade levels for each activity are listed on the site. Elementary games are supported by audio.

Bad Guy Patrol (www.badguypatrol.ca) is a question and answer site for students ages 5–7 and 8–10 that covers internet safety with audio support.

Copyright for K–12

Entire books have been written on copyright, and still the topic remains hazy. The current copyright law was passed in 1976, before personal computers proliferated and the internet permeated our lives. Thus, the law did not address the digital world our youth live in now. In the 1990s, a group wrote guidelines for fair use that dictate just how many lines or seconds of copyrighted materials constituted fair use, but these are not part of copyright law and are severely limiting. Teachers cannot draw definite guidelines from court rulings, because they often seem contradictory.

Fair use covers four essential considerations:

What are you using and how are you using it? In other words, is your work transforming the copyrighted material to another purpose than its original purpose? Often, mashups transform copyrighted materials to serve new, creatively different purposes. This is preferable to using copyrighted materials in their original forms.

What is the nature of the copyrighted work? If you are using nonfiction, for instance, you have more leeway to use long, direct quotations than when quoting from fiction. Or, if you use published works, you have more freedom than you do with unpublished works because authors of unpublished works are entitled to determine the first publication of their work.

How much of the work are you using? How substantial is the borrowing? This is not about numbers of lines or length of songs. Yes, using shorter direct quotations or paraphrasing fewer sentences may be better, but not if the short amount is the key or "heart" of the original. Sometimes a single measure of a song can be its heart. So, is what you are borrowing small enough both in amount and substantiality not to affect the value of the original?

What effect does your use have on the potential economic value of the original? Obviously, the less your use affects the value of the original, the more likely it is to fall under fair use.

Fair use is difficult to define and may not be treated in the same way by all judges. Students need to justify their use of copyrighted materials, such as an inability to find or create work that will satisfy the intent of a project as well as the copyrighted material will. But teachers should first consider whether students have exhausted the possibilities within the Creative Commons and copyright-free government sources first.

I use the following guidelines—neither laws nor legal advice—with students:

- Whenever possible, create original materials for projects—pictures, music, and video.

- When original work is not possible, look for materials that are in the public domain or are published under the Creative Commons license (and check the details of the license because Creative Commons has three levels).

- Any copyrighted work has to be justified by showing how it is transformed to a new purpose through the project.

- The sources of copyrighted materials must be cited, both verbatim and paraphrased materials.

- Most projects that use copyrighted materials will not be uploaded to the internet.

There are many resources for copyright information. The following list is not exhaustive. I have tried to find resources that represent different viewpoints, so teachers can consider where their practice might fall. The use of documentation to explain the reasoning for using copyrighted materials seems a wise move; at least documenting the intent of using copyrighted materials indicates thoughtful consideration before the fact. Some schools and districts may have written copyright guidelines, in which case, teachers should follow those. If your district's guidelines seem too restrictive, look out for yourself and your students by following the guidelines while you argue for change.

Code of Best Practices (http://mediaeducationlab.com/code-best-practices-fair-use-media-literacy-education-0) and the Teacher Case Study Video: Elementary (http://mediaeducationlab.com/teacher-case-study-video-elementary) present an updated look at what practices make sense at the elementary level. This information may be at odds with the Fair Use Guidelines on some points. When in doubt, make the more conservative choice.

Documenting the Fair Use Reasoning Practice (http://mediaeducationlab.com/document-fair-use-reasoning-process) helps students analyze whether their use of copyrighted materials meets the criteria of Fair Use.

Join the © Team Educator Resources (www.jointheteam.com/educators_resources.html) has curriculum, digital resources, and other materials for teachers to download and use in teaching copyright concepts.

Fair Use Checklist (http://copyright.columbia.edu/copyright/fair-use/fair-use-checklist) helps students review the four criteria of fair use. The link to a PDF version of the checklist is located near the bottom of the page. This is a succinct example of documenting fair use when teachers are using copyrighted materials in their classrooms.

This chapter only skims the surface of COPPA, internet safety, and copyright issues. The intent is to give teachers enough background to understand the responsibilities of protecting and guiding elementary students. Teachers can benefit from exploring the resources in more depth and/or discussing the issues with administrators in their schools or districts.

Final Thoughts

Try to choose a path to technology integration that will fit your teaching style and engage your students. Remember, even though you read about many great tech tools, implement one at a time, with a goal of three maximum in a school year. That's a lot more change than you can imagine before you begin.

Many thanks to the Voices of Experience contributors who shared their expertise throughout the book. Their experiences demonstrate how any path can lead to great outcomes for students. Let their models be your inspiration!

Remember to visit the book's wiki, http://bonihamilton.wikispaces.com/home, to access the following links, research, and updated information:

- Live links to website sorted by chapter
- Research to support the claims in many chapters
- Samples of projects when available
- Updated information about the chapters, links, and author

ISTE Standards

ISTE Standards for Students (ISTE Standards•S)

All K–12 students should be prepared to meet the following standards and performance indicators.

1. **Creativity and Innovation**

   Students demonstrate creative thinking, construct knowledge, and develop innovative products and processes using technology. Students:

   a. apply existing knowledge to generate new ideas, products, or processes

   b. create original works as a means of personal or group expression

   c. use models and simulations to explore complex systems and issues

   d. identify trends and forecast possibilities

2. **Communication and Collaboration**

   Students use digital media and environments to communicate and work collaboratively, including at a distance, to support individual learning and contribute to the learning of others. Students:

   a. interact, collaborate, and publish with peers, experts, or others employing a variety of digital environments and media

   b. communicate information and ideas effectively to multiple audiences using a variety of media and formats

   c. develop cultural understanding and global awareness by engaging with learners of other cultures

   d. contribute to project teams to produce original works or solve problems

3. **Research and Information Fluency**

Students apply digital tools to gather, evaluate, and use information. Students:

   a. plan strategies to guide inquiry

   b. locate, organize, analyze, evaluate, synthesize, and ethically use information from a variety of sources and media

   c. evaluate and select information sources and digital tools based on the appropriateness to specific tasks

   d. process data and report results

4. **Critical Thinking, Problem Solving, and Decision Making**

Students use critical-thinking skills to plan and conduct research, manage projects, solve problems, and make informed decisions using appropriate digital tools and resources. Students:

   a. identify and define authentic problems and significant questions for investigation

   b. plan and manage activities to develop a solution or complete a project

   c. collect and analyze data to identify solutions and make informed decisions

   d. use multiple processes and diverse perspectives to explore alternative solutions

5. **Digital Citizenship**

Students understand human, cultural, and societal issues related to technology and practice legal and ethical behavior. Students:

   a. advocate and practice the safe, legal, and responsible use of information and technology

   b. exhibit a positive attitude toward using technology that supports collaboration, learning, and productivity

   c. demonstrate personal responsibility for lifelong learning

   d. exhibit leadership for digital citizenship

6. Technology Operations and Concepts

Students demonstrate a sound understanding of technology concepts, systems, and operations. Students:

a. understand and use technology systems

b. select and use applications effectively and productively

c. troubleshoot systems and applications

d. transfer current knowledge to the learning of new technologies

ISTE Standards for Teachers (ISTE Standards•T)

All classroom teachers should be prepared to meet the following standards and performance indicators.

1. **Facilitate and Inspire Student Learning and Creativity**

   Teachers use their knowledge of subject matter, teaching and learning, and technology to facilitate experiences that advance student learning, creativity, and innovation in both face-to-face and virtual environments. Teachers:

   a. promote, support, and model creative and innovative thinking and inventiveness

   b. engage students in exploring real-world issues and solving authentic problems using digital tools and resources

   c. promote student reflection using collaborative tools to reveal and clarify students' conceptual understanding and thinking, planning, and creative processes

   d. model collaborative knowledge construction by engaging in learning with students, colleagues, and others in face-to-face and virtual environments

2. **Design and Develop Digital-Age Learning Experiences and Assessments**

   Teachers design, develop, and evaluate authentic learning experiences and assessments incorporating contemporary tools and resources to maximize content learning in context and to develop the knowledge, skills, and attitudes identified in the ISTE Standards for Students. Teachers:

   a. design or adapt relevant learning experiences that incorporate digital tools and resources to promote student learning and creativity

   b. develop technology-enriched learning environments that enable all students to pursue their individual curiosities and become active participants in setting their own educational goals, managing their own learning, and assessing their own progress

    c. customize and personalize learning activities to address students' diverse learning styles, working strategies, and abilities using digital tools and resources

    d. provide students with multiple and varied formative and summative assessments aligned with content and technology standards and use resulting data to inform learning and teaching

3. Model Digital-Age Work and Learning

Teachers exhibit knowledge, skills, and work processes representative of an innovative professional in a global and digital society. Teachers:

    a. demonstrate fluency in technology systems and the transfer of current knowledge to new technologies and situations

    b. collaborate with students, peers, parents, and community members using digital tools and resources to support student success and innovation

    c. communicate relevant information and ideas effectively to students, parents, and peers using a variety of digital-age media and formats

    d. model and facilitate effective use of current and emerging digital tools to locate, analyze, evaluate, and use information resources to support research and learning

4. Promote and Model Digital Citizenship and Responsibility

Teachers understand local and global societal issues and responsibilities in an evolving digital culture and exhibit legal and ethical behavior in their professional practices. Teachers:

    a. advocate, model, and teach safe, legal, and ethical use of digital information and technology, including respect for copyright, intellectual property, and the appropriate documentation of sources

    b. address the diverse needs of all learners by using learner-centered strategies and providing equitable access to appropriate digital tools and resources

    c. promote and model digital etiquette and responsible social interactions related to the use of technology and information

    d. develop and model cultural understanding and global awareness by engaging with colleagues and students of other cultures using digital-age communication and collaboration tools

5. Engage in Professional Growth and Leadership

Teachers continuously improve their professional practice, model lifelong learning, and exhibit leadership in their school and professional community by promoting and demonstrating the effective use of digital tools and resources. Teachers:

    a. participate in local and global learning communities to explore creative applications of technology to improve student learning

    b. exhibit leadership by demonstrating a vision of technology infusion, participating in shared decision making and community building, and developing the leadership and technology skills of others

    c. evaluate and reflect on current research and professional practice on a regular basis to make effective use of existing and emerging digital tools and resources in support of student learning

    d. contribute to the effectiveness, vitality, and self-renewal of the teaching profession and of their school and community

Index

Page numbers followed by "t" (such as 47t) indicate tables.